About the author
Ian Wishart is an award-winning investigative journalist with extensive experience in newspaper, magazine, radio and television journalism since 1982. He is the author of two previous number one bestsellers: *The Paradise Conspiracy* and *Lawyers, Guns & Money*.

For Heidi, with love

THE PARADISE CONSPIRACY II

Ian Wishart

Howling At The Moon Publishing Ltd

First edition published 1999
This edition published 2012
Howling At The Moon Publishing Ltd
PO Box 188
Kaukapakapa
Auckland 0843
New Zealand

Email: editorial@investigatemagazine.com

Copyright © Ian Wishart, 1999, 2012
Copyright © Howling At The Moon Publishing Ltd, 1999, 2012

The moral rights of the author have been asserted.

The Paradise Conspiracy II is copyright. Except for the purpose of fair reviewing, no part of this publication may be copied, reproduced or transmitted in any form or by any means, including via technology either already in existence or developed subsequent to publication, without the express written permission of the publisher and copyright holders.

All rights reserved.
ISBN 0-9582054-0-X

Typeset in Adobe Garamond Pro and Helvetica Neue
Cover concept by Heidi and Ian Wishart
Front cover photo by Michael Flippo
Cartoons used by permission © Tom Scott, © Laurence Clark
Book design and layout by Bozidar Jokanovic

Contents

Introduction & Warning	7
Prologue	8
Genesis	11
The Old Mongolian Yak Trick	20
Political Interference	37
Boomerang Chickens	47
Mayday! We're Going Down	59
The Peters Factor	69
Boagus Film Crews	90
Proceed At Your Own Peril	102
A Betrayal Of Trust	120
It's Worse Than That: He's Dead, Jim	137
Acquitted On A Technicality	144
Blind Justice	154
A Change In The Wind	163
The Real Inquiry	184
Criminal Intent	204
The Devil's Advocate	211
The Verdict	217
Methinks They Doth Protest Too Much	223
On The Wrong Side Of The Law	229
A Finding Of Corruption	238
Unfinished Business	249

Acknowledgements

There are always people to thank in any venture of this magnitude, but top of the list is the woman I love. In a two-person, one baby publishing company, the burden falls pretty heavily.

Thanks for the motivation, the inspiration, and keeping the production line moving while one of us pulled his hair out writing this book.

Howling At The Moon Publishing Ltd is a team effort. Small team, big effort!

Thanks also to legal advisor Tim Allan, and others in the legal profession who must remain nameless.

Introduction & Warning

In 1998, a Wellington man killed himself.

His problems had begun with an unpaid tax bill of $84. Over seven years of trying to make ends meet and failing to pay tax, his debts to the IRD had reached almost $90,000 in principal, interest and penalties. He was 35 years old when he took his own life.

Nine months later his grief-stricken 13-year-old son killed himself. Another victim of the way the Inland Revenue Department is prepared to hound small taxpayers and their families to the bitter end.

Brierley Investments failed to file tax returns for thirty subsidiaries for 10 years. No prosecutory action was taken.

European Pacific Investments and Fay Richwhite engineered tax deals that removed millions from the New Zealand revenue. No prosecutory action was taken.

Partners in lawfirm Russell McVeagh allegedly blackmailed the IRD into letting them off a fraud, and letting them pay less in tax than other participants in the same scheme.

There is one law for the rich and powerful, and another for the rest of New Zealand.

In regard to issues raised in this book, I make the following point in the strongest possible terms. I believe that crimes have been commited. In some cases this is an abstract look at a particular point of law, without looking at individual guilt or criminal intent.

While a law or laws may have been broken, to be a crime there must be an "intent". While in many cases I raise evidence that I believe points to criminal intent, the reader must remember that these are my own *opinions*. Often I am raising these points because other parties have suggested there is no evidence. I disagree and have looked for evidence to the contrary.

But ultimately, I am not in a position to judge whether there is *sufficient* evidence to prosecute any individual named in relation to these issues. This remains, as always, a question that only a court can answer. Readers familiar with my earlier books will have come to know my approach by now: please read this book in the same context.

Prologue

"Remember, democracy never lasts long. It soon wastes, exhausts, and murders itself. There never was a democracy yet that did not commit suicide."
John Adams (1735–1826), US President

The phone call from the private investigator was quick and dirty.

"You can forget about the Winebox Inquiry bud, the report is a complete whitewash."

Someone grabbed my innards and squeezed them like they were expressing the meat from a sausage. Whilst the moment had been anticipated, its arrival was nonetheless sickening.

"Whaddayamean it's a whitewash? The report isn't being delivered to the Governor-General for a couple of days yet."

"Sorry Wishart," the gruff voice on the other end responded, "but we've had word from Wellington. The report completely exonerates Fay Richwhite, European Pacific, the IRD and the SFO. Winston Peters, on the other hand, gets a bollocking."

I hesitated in silence momentarily, drinking in the implications. A secret report, whose contents allegedly weren't even being divulged to the Prime Minister before its release later in the week, had been leaked in advance. My contact indicated the source of the leak was a Government department.

"Bloody hell!"

And so it was with a well-honed sense of farce and theatre that I listened to the Paul Holmes breakfast show on Newstalk ZB two days later, as Prime Minister Jim Bolger earnestly informed an equally earnest Holmes that even *he* wasn't aware of the contents of the Winebox Inquiry report, which was being handed to the Governor-General later that morning.

"Yeah, well, ya miserable little scuzzbag, I *do* know!" I swore at the clock-radio.

So too did lawyers for the fading, but still vocal, Fay Richwhite merchant bank. They wore grins that would have put any self-respecting Cheshire Cat to shame as they picked up embargoed copies of Sir Ronald Davison's epic three-volume report.

"This'll be a bestseller that'll knock *Paradise Conspiracy* off the charts," chuckled Russell McVeagh partner Mark Gavin as he carried off an entire carton of the reports. He and his colleagues at the giant lawfirm had carried Fay Richwhite's torch throughout the inquiry, and for all I knew they were probably going to autograph the volumes and send them out as Christmas presents.

Hell, there was some obvious merit (and diversionary amusement) in the idea of Russell McVeagh taking literary credit for it. As one lawyer later boasted: "The report couldn't have been any better if I'd penned it myself."

Maybe he was there in spirit. Because, as you will discover in this book, the verdict delivered by Sir Ronald was a crock: a multi-million dollar joke at the expense of ordinary New Zealand taxpayers. It flew in the face of the evidence and, most importantly, it was completely in conflict with private statements Sir Ronald had earlier made to staff and others.

You will also read of the full extent of a news media coverup of the issues surrounding the winebox and related topics. This is hopefully the last of my books on the winebox. This time it is no holds barred. New Zealanders are about to find out just how corrupt I believe our country really is.

As a harbinger of the punch this book will pack, here's a scene you *didn't* see on the television news reports at the end of the inquiry:

> "I can't believe it," the lawyer choked. "This country is so bloody corrupt!"
>
> I watched as fury welled up in her eyes, teardrops boiling like molten lava, but never falling. She was too angry to cry. Sympathy? I had it by the bucketload. Fury? That too. For three years we had both endured the Winebox Inquiry, and 'endured' is definitely the right word.
>
> Three years of blatant lying, obfuscation and the kind of collective corporate amnesia that suggested to me that most of the executives and company directors involved in these so-called leading companies were unfit for their jobs and cheating their shareholders by the mere act of drawing a salary.
>
> Suzanne Clark's fists were clenching and unclenching – she knew something that the rest of us could only guess at. As 2nd Counsel Assisting the Commission, she had helped uncover the stunning evidence at the centre of New Zealand's longest running Commission of Inquiry.
>
> It was obvious that she now believed corruption had permeated the very Commission of Inquiry set up to investigate allegations of corruption. What

wasn't clear was why she believed this. The mere existence of such a belief, coming from one of the Commission's own lawyers, rocked me to my very core.

Clark and her colleague, senior Counsel Assisting, Colin Carruthers QC, had seen the Devil. One of perhaps only five people in the world who knew what lay at the centre of a giant web. She looked up at me and I could see it in her eyes: knowledge. Knowledge of the kind that haunts you forever. And right at that moment, I would have killed to know what she knew ...

As you proceed through this book, you will discover there is a big difference between what is really happening in New Zealand and what you are being told about, and that is perhaps the biggest scandal of all.

Chapter 1

Genesis

"The dominant and most deep-dyed trait of the journalist is his timourousness. Where the novelist fearlessly plunges into the water of self-exposure, the journalist stands trembling on the shore in his beach robe."
— *Janet Malcolm, author, The Journalist And The Murderer*

The lawyer gestured toward the windows. For a moment I wondered if he was inviting me to jump. It was nine stories to the ground, although admittedly an architectural protrusion on level two would alleviate the boredom on the trip down by providing a diversionary bounce.

Outside, a vista of palm trees and pohutukawa baked in Auckland city's early summer heat.

"Curtains," he said after a moment.

"Yes, very nice," I offered politely, wondering if he had personally chosen the appalling puce colour himself. Evidently Colin Carruthers QC could see I had absolutely no idea what he was on about.

"The curtains," he explained patiently with only a hint of frustration, "are security curtains."

This was reassuring. At least the Winebox Inquiry would be safe from Superman's prying eyes.

"We've had the Security Intelligence Service through here to check our security," he was continuing. I didn't have the heart to tell him that the SIS were the biggest bunch of burglars this side of the Black Stump. Given that the building right next door, which housed mega-lawfirm Russell McVeagh McKenzie Bartleet & Co, had totally coincidentally earnt the nickname "The Black Stump", this was not the brightest of omens.

There was in fact a delicious irony in the identity of the neighbours, as well as that of one of the previous tenants in the Commission's own building.

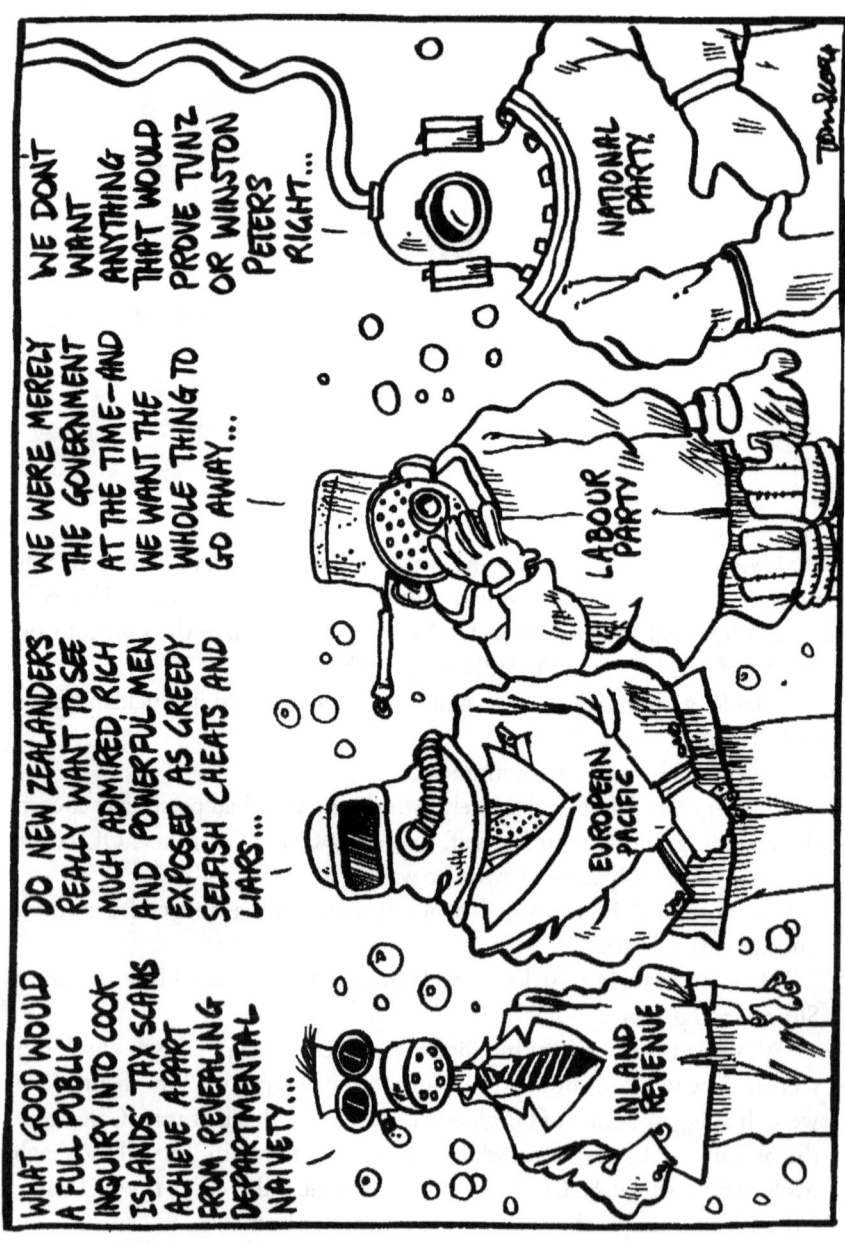

The latter was none other than international tax haven company European Pacific Group, whose activities lay at the heart of the inquiry, and which had occupied offices in the very same building that was now hosting the inquiry. If only the walls could talk: they may well have had a better memory than many of the executives who worked there.

The neighbours included Fay Richwhite's merchant bank, and the Bank of New Zealand, just down the road – both of them previous part-owners of European Pacific.

Carruthers shuffled a pile of papers on the desk as his colleague entered the room, lawyer Suzanne Clark.

In an adjoining room, just visible through a glass partition, was the man who would later be dubbed "The Lion King" – former Chief Justice Sir Ronald Davison. It was to be his task to get to the bottom of the winebox. Davison was peering at me knowingly, and I grinned to myself as I wondered whether the boardroom had been wired with hidden microphones for his listening pleasure.

"Thank you for agreeing to see us," began Clark.

I shrugged agreeably. "No problem. How can I help?"

"Well, coughing up your documents and files would be a start."

I erred and aahhed for a moment. European Pacific had just taken me all the way to the Court of Appeal in an unsuccessful bid to get their paws on my files and material. Nor would TVNZ be impressed at one of their staff co-operating with such a request.

"We can always serve you with a Section 4 compulsion notice," added Carruthers with a grin.

"Charmed," I grunted. Was that a smile just tweaking the corner of Sir Ronald's mouth? I couldn't be sure.

They were heady days in that summer of '94, and we all had such high hopes that, for once, a Government inquiry would achieve something.

In 1981 the Cook Islands, a tiny Pacific Island state with limited independence from New Zealand, declared itself a tax haven. The event passed with barely a whisper in the New Zealand media, but it was marked by a flurry of top-level correspondence between the Cook Islands and New Zealand Governments.

As it was effectively illegal at the time for New Zealand residents or companies to transfer money offshore without Government approval, the prospect of a tax haven on New Zealand's doorstep that operated in New Zealand currency raised all sorts of possibilities and implications.

"You will, therefore, understand our wish to monitor fairly closely," wrote

NZ Deputy Prime Minister Brian Talboys in July 1981, "the development of offshore banking in your country and any impact on the New Zealand financial system.

"My Government's concerns centre on the stability and the international reputation of the New Zealand dollar. Bearing this in mind, we would want your Government to place a general restrictive condition on all [banking] licences issued to the effect that all transactions made by the offshore bank must be in a currency *other than* the New Zealand dollar. [Talboys' emphasis]

"We are also somewhat concerned at the possibility of an offshore bank operating out of the Cook Islands carrying out unorthodox transactions which may bring disrepute on both the Cook Islands Government and the New Zealand Government."

Perhaps Talboys had a crystal ball, as both events would eventually come to pass.

The tax haven laws in the Cooks had been drafted with the significant input of one David William Lloyd, an Englishman who wanted to create a new Empire. Having helped write the laws, Lloyd then set up the Cooks' only tax haven bank. For him, money was growing on palm trees.

In 1985/86, Lloyd brought in three New Zealand corporates to invest in his dream. Fay Richwhite merchant bank, Brierley Investments Ltd and the NZ Government-owned Bank of New Zealand. Together, they created what became known as the European Pacific Group.

The operations of European Pacific were highly secret, each staff member concentrating on their own area of responsibility and information passed on a "need to know" basis.

Although the key details about European Pacific can be found in *The Paradise Conspiracy I*, for the sake of a refresher here's what happened.

In 1988 the New Zealand Government finally passed a law that made any tax haven company with a 50% or higher NZ ownership liable for New Zealand tax.

This had a huge impact on European Pacific, not least because its majority New Zealand ownership would bring it under the scrutiny of the Inland Revenue Department, even though the company's trust and banking group was domiciled in the Cook Islands.

The thought of NZ tax inspectors getting hold of EP's records and client information was horrific, so the company's shareholders voted to sell a majority stake in the group to a Cook Islands company called Laverton, which was allegedly owned by David Lloyd.

Fay Richwhite and Brierleys would have a reduced shareholding, and the BNZ would eventually sell out altogether. Provided the selldown of a majority stake in the group to Laverton was legitimate, and not just a con to fool the tax department, then none of European Pacific Group's activities need be declared in New Zealand.

Obviously Fays, Brierleys and the BNZ would still pay tax on the money they earned as shareholders in European Pacific, but as they were now only entitled to less than half of the profits, not 86% (the remainder was owned by small shareholders and institutions) their tax bill wouldn't be as high.

The issue of whether the selldown was, in fact, a con-trick, would later become very significant at the Winebox Inquiry.

Having restructured the company, European Pacific's executives came up with new ways to generate money now that the usual tax haven trick of simply hiding money from the revenue had been made more difficult.

What they devised was a product known as "tax credits".

If a New Zealand individual or a company earns income in the United States as well as New Zealand, for example, the tax departments of both countries might scrap over who should get the tax, or even force the person to pay double tax. To avoid this, the revenue departments of many countries have come to an arrangement.

If the taxpayer pays tax in the United States, he or she is given a US tax certificate to prove the money has been deducted, and this can be offset against their tax liability in New Zealand.

What happened in the Cook Islands was simple: European Pacific effectively controlled the Cook Islands Government. They convinced elements in that Government to approve a scheme whereby companies would be encouraged to pay tax in the Cook Islands, and get a Cook Islands tax certificate in return.

At first glance this may seem strange – paying tax in a tax haven – but there was a lucrative twist. Thirty seconds after paying the tax to the Cooks Government, the Government would hand the money back *under the table*, as well as giving the company a Cooks tax certificate to say that tax had been paid.

Specifically, in regard to the highly controversial Magnum transaction in the Winebox, $2 million was paid upstairs in the main Cook Islands Government building in Rarotonga, and then returned to the company downstairs as they left, along with a tax credit certificate to the value of $2 million.

Although, as you will discover later in this book, the transaction itself was deviously simple, the paper trail they created turned tax money laundering into an art form.

On paper, the tax was paid to the Cook Islands IRD, but refunded in disguise. That disguise involved getting another Cooks Government Department, the Property Corporation, to make a pre-arranged (but supposedly coincidental $2 million loss in a financial deal with European Pacific that afternoon.

With the money in its back pocket, a European Pacific subsidiary company then handed the Cooks tax certificate to the New Zealand IRD, and received a further $2 million dollar tax rebate in New Zealand. In basic terms, there is a strong case fpr saying the money was stolen from the NZ IRD under false pretences.

If the NZ IRD had known that the Cooks Government had refunded the tax allegedly paid in the Cooks, it would not have given European Pacific a $2 million rebate in New Zealand. But the IRD was never told, despite requirements under section 301 of the Income Tax Act which states:

> *"A credit for foreign tax shall not be allowed unless ... the taxpayer claiming the credit ... furnishes to the Commissioner all information (including information in relation to any amount to which the taxpayer is entitled in respect of any relief or repayment of the foreign tax) necessary for determining the amount of the credit."*

The decision to undertake individual transactions rested with those directly involved on European Pacific's trust and banking teams, and obviously their clients in various major corporates. But approval for the tax credit schemes in general came from European Pacific's board of directors.

At a board meeting in early 1988 those directors, including Chairman David Richwhite, voted in favour of raiding the Australian and other treasuries via the use of Cook Islands "tax credit certificates".

It is significant that the directors, and European Pacific's staff, had been put on notice prior to the meeting that the deals could be illegal. An internal EP memorandum released at the Winebox Inquiry reveals that:

> *"A criminal barrister, Mr [Brian] Oslington QC was approached and his response focused upon one critical issue. One element of a 'tax' is that the money raised by the taxing authority is used for 'public purposes'.*
>
> *"In the structure devised, the Cook Islands Government Property Corporation pays to an EPBC subsidiary a premium that is calculated in direct proportion to the tax that has been levied. In Mr Oslington's view as the premium paid for purchase of the note by the Property Corporation*

is essentially for a smart business dealing by the Government, it is not for public purposes.

"Therefore, the Cook Islands withholding tax is not a 'tax', promotion of the note constitutes a criminal offence by company officers and those knowingly involved in a conspiracy to defraud the Australian revenue."

Two other lawyers consulted by European Pacific took a different view – that the Cook Islands Government could do what it liked with its tax money including giving it back, so therefore the deals would be OK. Probably.

"None the less," the internal EP memorandum warned, "there remains the chance that if the matter ever went to court it may well be that a judge could side with the view taken by Mr Oslington."

Why is this "warning" to EP's directors significant? Because under New Zealand law it is not simply enough for a law to have been broken – to make a prosecution at a criminal level one must prove that the offender intended to commit the act. In legal terms, it is known as "mens rea".

If a law is broken by accident, that is one thing, but if a law is broken with deliberate intent, that is quite another.

At the end of this book, when all the evidence has been presented, I believe you will find there can be no doubt that there is strong evidence of criminality although – as I warned at the beginning – the question of individual guilt is a matter for the courts to decide, not me as an author or you as a reader.

The highest court in the world, the Privy Council, has already indicated that the transactions may be fraudulent, as has New Zealand's Court of Appeal. Which begs the question: how is it that the people responsible managed to avoid being investigated by the IRD and Serious Fraud Office, and then received a clean bill of health from a Commission of Inquiry whose Commissioner – as you will discover – was *privately* describing the deals as "criminal … grand larceny"?

Is the Winebox merely the tip of the iceberg? Is the truth so devastating that it must never be revealed? In my view the Mafia's "Teflon Don", John Gotti, has nothing on these people in terms of the inability to make anything "stick".

At the height of the Winebox Inquiry, I was disturbed to discover a conversation between two [inserted text follows: deletion] lawyers.

"Don't worry about the Winebox Inquiry," one reassured the other, "[politician's name deleted]'s in up to his neck on some forestry deals."

The implication being that a key political figure could be relied on to ensure that the Winebox Inquiry did little damage.

TVNZ's *Frontline* programme had attempted to investigate [inserted text follows: alteration] some forestry deals in 1993, and reports that some politicians may be involved, but the programme and investigation were canned after corporate and political pressure on TVNZ.

After *The Paradise Conspiracy* was published I was contacted by a National Party electorate chairman who was disturbed at a briefing he and his officials received from their local MP in private.

Asked why the Government had refused to investigate the BNZ affair, the MP explained that National's largest corporate political campaign donors had categorically stated they would withdraw their funding of the party if an investigation took place.

On the face of it, this appears to be a blatant case of corruption, where elected officials do not carry out a public duty because of financial inducements. I say on the face of it because no agency exists that can credibly investigate this kind of allegation.

It is interesting to note that this information came to me a year or so before the Serious Fraud Office's Chief Investigator, former police Detective Inspector Geoff Downey, testified on oath to the Winebox Inquiry that the then SFO Director Chas Sturt had shut down an SFO investigation into the BNZ – allegedly for political reasons.

"[Sturt] indicated to me that he did not want the matter to go any further, whatsoever," said Downey. "He told me that our friends in Wellington would not appreciate the office inquiring into the Bank of New Zealand."

He who pays the piper calls the tune. And one has to wonder whether the tune was the America's Cup anthem *Sailing Away*.

The evidence that a legitimate inquiry into the BNZ was shut down for political reasons, whilst circumstantial, is in my view absolutely damning.

Which brings us to another point: the next time that you see Judy and Richard on *One Network News* telling you what a "corruption-free" country New Zealand is according to the latest international survey – have a little chuckle and disregard the credibility of the story entirely. There is no agency in New Zealand designated to investigate corruption – unlike many other nations – and so the New Zealand Government simply files "nil" returns in the OECD surveys.

The joke, I guess, is on the naïve journalists and news producers who trot the story out every six months. One can only hope that Judy and [inserted text follows] Richard will read this and refuse to lend their own credibility to this "lies, damned lies and statistics" farce.

The Winebox Inquiry verdict has been used by some to rewrite history.

One of those to wield it in this fashion is Charles Sturt, the disgraced – in my opinion – former Director of the Serious Fraud Office.

He writes[1] of New Zealand First leader Winston Peters' parliamentary attacks on the credibility of the SFO and IRD thus:

> "*Peters bit his tongue for a few months but by mid-1994 was back on his feet in the House and sounding more desperate than ever. Charges were not being laid, he said, because of collusion between the Government and its business network. I [Sturt] was supposed to be the Government's hired gun to combat fraud but I 'couldn't hit a barn at ten paces'.*
>
> "*There were further calls for [Inland Revenue Commissioner] David Henry and me to be suspended, and then came an extraordinary claim: 'I [Peters] have had contacts from senior investigators from both Inland Revenue and SFO who say their bosses are plainly wrong. Some say they are lying when they claim these schemes are within the law.'*
>
> "*This was a serious and damaging claim [says Sturt of the staff-leak claim]. I knew it couldn't be true.*"

As you will see shortly, despite Sturt's attempts to gloss over the truth post-verdict, a number of SFO and IRD staff gave incredibly damning testimony against their bosses, just as Peters and others said they would.

And so, let battle commence. *The Paradise Conspiracy II* will now take apart the Winebox Inquiry verdict point by point, and you can decide for yourself whether the points Sir Ronald Davison raised in his report were right, or whether his report was a waste of millions of dollars.

---

1 *Dirty Collars*, Charles Sturt, Reed Publishing 1998.

Chapter 2

The Old Mongolian Yak Trick

"A Commission to inquire into and report upon whether the Commissioner of Inland Revenue and his staff ... acted, in the course of their official duties, in a lawful, proper and competent mannerin dealing with the transactions."
– *Terms of Reference, Winebox Inquiry*

When he raised the issue in Parliament, Winston Peters had hypothesised on why the Winebox documents had not been acted upon. The investigating agencies were either incompetent, or corrupt.

As a point of logic, this is almost a truism: if a crime is not investigated it is either a result of incompetent investigators or a deliberate act. However, the statement also presupposes that a crime has taken place, or at least a prima facie one.

Before the Winebox Inquiry could reach a conclusion on incompetence or corruption, it first had to determine whether there was an issue that should have been investigated.

As the Inquiry began in 1994, it quickly became apparent to the public that the IRD and Serious Fraud Office had done very little with the Winebox papers. And what they had done was often confused and ineffective.

In August 1996, the Inland Revenue Department came under heavy questioning at the Winebox Inquiry over why it hadn't prosecuted Brierley Investments for tax offences.

The IRD officer in charge of the Brierleys audit, Chris Cunniffe, told the inquiry the company had failed to file CFC tax returns for up to 30 subsidiaries since 1988.

One company, Oscar Mindy Investments Ltd, hadn't filed a tax return since 1986, leaving Brierleys open to a potential $20,000 fine.

Brierleys executives earlier told the inquiry they'd forgotten they owned Oscar Mindy.

The problem, according to the company, was that a lot of the records of the tax haven subsidiaries were sold to new owners along with the companies, leaving Brierleys unable to meet its statutory tax filing obligations. This was despite evidence that Brierleys knew it had an obligation to file those tax returns.

"If the department is unable," posed counsel assisting the Commission, Colin Carruthers QC, "to identify the income with the result that no return may be filed, what is the department's policy in relation to enforcement of the obligation to file returns?"

"I would be most surprised if we had a policy," replied Cunniffe.

"Well," continued Carruthers, "what is the department's policy in relation to prosecution in the situations we are discussing?"

"Again, I don't know if a situation, such as we have with BIL, has ever arisen, so there would be no stated policy that I am aware of. Which isn't to say that we don't view the matter with great seriousness," said the tax inspector, helpfully.

Chris Cunniffe told the inquiry that while prosecution was a live issue, there were several preliminary steps to go, such as asking the company formally for an explanation.

Like other IRD staff before him, the picture he painted of the Brierleys audit was a bleak one.

Those witnesses, such as Michael Spelman, told of stonewalling by the company and being given page two of a document but not pages one or three.

"If a report was requested which was in the minutes of the company," said Spelman, "we would be informed that this in fact did not exist because it was an oral report by one of the chief executives."

Other excuses for non-compliance included "that the documentation had been destroyed, or that the documentation belonged to a member of the company and the records were not in fact those of the company and therefore they could not be provided to us."

When tax investigators did manage to get an answer, it didn't usually take the form of written English.

"[Paddy] Marra preferred to advise us verbally of what the answer was, and that was about it. If, in fact, we sought to verify what he had told us, he seemed to become agitated that we were in fact casting aspersions on his integrity."

In a revealing day of cross-examination, Spelman said that if the tax team wanted to photocopy a document, the photocopying had to be done by a Brierleys employee.

"It would be fair comment," asked counsel for Winston Peters, Brian Henry, at one point, "to say that the management of Brierleys were in control of your audit at that stage, not yourself?"

"We were beginning to consider that was possibly the answer, yes!" acknowledged Spelman.

The IRD witness also accused Paddy Marra's successor in BIL's tax division, Gerald Gibbard, of continuing to obstruct IRD investigations.

"He may provide page three of a document but would not provide pages one and two," complained Spelman, who added that Mr Gibbard's selective co-operation extended to simply ignoring IRD requests for information, apparently when it suited him.

"With regard to the ignoring of information, these were the areas which were possibly more embarrassing to the company, or may have been areas where the company felt they were exposed, and just ignored the requests."

Throughout this time, the tax department failed to bring to bear its considerable arsenal of statutory powers to deal with the non-co-operation, and instead tried to talk its way around the intransigent corporate. This path failed as well, when Brierleys took legal action against the IRD, preventing any further investigation pending a judicial review.

Chris Cunniffe told the Inquiry that the legal action taken by Brierleys in the early 1990s had ground the audit to a halt, and things didn't get moving again until the IRD struck gold in the winebox papers delivered to it in February 1993.

With 16 years of experience in the IRD under his belt, Chris Cunniffe raised some eyebrows when he said he'd never come across a case of corporate tax evasion. He defined evasion as having a "wilful" element, whilst avoidance was only "frustrating" the Revenue.

As readers of *The Paradise Conspiracy* and *Lawyers, Guns & Money* will be aware, corporates and their tax and legal advisors routinely took the route of most resistance when dealing with the IRD, everything from playing word games to allegedly blackmailing the tax department into submission.

The measure of competence in this context would surely be found in the nature of the IRD's response.

Unfortunately, it was more akin to *Fawlty Towers* than *The Bill.*

News feature, 13 July 1996

Have you ever wondered, at the end of a long hard day filling in GST returns, PAYE slips or other taxation paraphernalia, if there was an easier way of dealing with the IRD?

Boy, do I have some cracker news for you! Fresh from the Winebox Inquiry this week we've managed to assemble an easy to understand Simpleton's Guide to Winning Friends and Influencing the IRD.

"Dear Ian," writes Paddy, "I'm a busy executive running a multi-billion dollar multi-national investment company. I don't have the time to deal with those pesky so-and-so's at the IRD, always ringing up wanting documents. What should I do?"

Well Paddy, I'm glad you asked. My panel of advisers on the media bench at the Winebox Inquiry picked up some tips only this week on how Brierley Investments Ltd handles problems like yours.

Firstly, you must allow a decent interval to pass before responding. Tax inspectors are like impatient lovers, they just want to do one thing to you – remember, you can still say "no!" and mean no.

After a suitable time has elapsed, drop them a line or – better still – commit nothing to paper and instead ring them from an unmarked payphone. If they start asking tricky questions, just open the door of the phone box so that the sound of a passing bus drowns out the substance of your answer.

"Dear Ian," writes Jerry, "but what happens if the IRD actually want to see the documents that support what Paddy told them in the phone booth?"

Well Jerry, it's like this. You can either tell them that the key papers on the transaction were consumed by a hungry Yak on a recent field trip to Mongolia or – and this is one of my personal favourites – you can improvise the way the Brierley boys did.

The IRD wanted to get hold of a report in the company's board minutes. Well, after some lengthy consultation with some high-powered lawyers and a linguist, they managed to convince the boys over at IRD "that this in fact did not exist, because it was an oral report."

Failing that, you could try giving away some of your more sensitive documentation – perhaps sell it on a peppercorn basis to one of your employees. Then you can explain to the tax inspectors "that the documentation belongs to a member of the company and the records are not, in fact, those of the company and therefore they can't be provided to you."

"Yeah, sounds great," Jerry writes back, "but we can't give all our documents to one employee – that's why we've got tax havens for heavens sake!, so poor old Bill in accounts doesn't have to keep all this stuff in a shoebox under his bed."

Yes Jerry, but the Privy Council's ruling on tax haven secrecy isn't going to protect you for much longer now, is it? No, once again I recommend one of the BIL tips.

Suppose the IRD is asking a specific question about a transaction, and demands to see the transaction documents relating to the point they're querying. Instead of bogging down those poor tax inspectors with needless paper work, just give them page three of the transaction blueprint, and not pages one or two.

"Dear Ian," writes Paddy, "I've just returned from the phone box, and the boys from the IRD have turned up wanting to use my photocopier, what should I do?"

Well Paddy, it's simple really. It's the IRD's job to be fair, and this is the era of user pays. Frankly, I think it's only fair if you charge them for every sheet they use but, seriously, these people are trained to sniff out tax rorts, not operate expensive office equipment like photocopiers.

You really have no idea how much damage a tax inspector could do to one of those, and just think of the deductibility problem if they break it, let alone the ACC levy issues if they harm themselves on your property.

No, you are far better to offer – nay, insist – that one of your own secretarial staff handle all the photocopying. That way you can also keep an eye on what they're copying, and perhaps set them on the right track if they start getting excited about silly little things of no consequence.

"Dear Ian," writes Denny,[2] a high-powered tax lawyer, "unfortunately my clients didn't have the benefit of your sage advice, and the Revenue ended up with all these documents on a movie they invested in. The IRD claims the movie was a fraud, and they've been scaring my clients with stories about what happens to white collar criminals in the penal system. How can I make the Revenue see that this is really a misunderstanding?"

How do I say this Denny – you've got your work cut out for you! It's very important that you don't blackmail the IRD. They get very huffy about people trying crude shakedowns on them.

You should never "threaten" to take a course of action which would ultimately tie up their resources for three years if they don't back off – they might misconstrue that as an attempt to pressure them. Instead, you should "explain" to them that you will take a course of action which would ultimately tie up their resources for three years if they don't back off.

As an example, you would never say that you "have something embarrassing on a certain senior tax inspector", but you might say that "there were soft spots in the conduct of the IRD in its investigations which were potentially embarrassing to senior officials."

---

2   A parody of Russell McVeagh lawyer Geoffrey Denis Clews, who allegedly attempted to blackmail the IRD.

Remember Denny, you're a professional tax lawyer at a prestigious firm. You were born to rule, and frankly you're just going to have to make the drones at the IRD understand. You should bring to bear the "influence of experience, the influence of argument and the influence of logic."

That is what your clients expect of you in these negotiations. That, and nothing more.

If it wasn't so amusing you'd probably cry. But even taking Chris Cunniffe's yardstick of "wilfulness" for tax evasion, is it wilful to sell the tax records of 30 companies, and then fail to file tax returns despite knowing you had an obligation to do so?

Could this be Cunniffe's first case of tax evasion in 16 years' experience? If so, he still could not see it.

Is it a case of departmental incompetence?

The Brierleys men were also unhelpful when it came to one of the Winebox's other major issues – the Laverton Adjustment.

Three Brierley Investments executives testified. The then Chief Executive Paul Collins, and senior staff Paddy Marra and Gerald Gibbard.

The trio suffered badly from a dose of CMS – Cooks Memory Syndrome – the symptoms of which include an inability to remember much more than one's name.

They were also experts in the game of pass-the-parcel. Brierleys weren't involved in the tax credit deals, and Paul Collins couldn't remember a hell of a lot about the meetings where the deals were discussed, so one of the main issues Commission lawyers were trying to focus on with Collins was a mysterious payment of money.

As we noted in Chapter 1, European Pacific's biggest shareholders, Fay Richwhite and Brierleys, had been forced to sell their majority stake in the company in 1988 so as to avoid having Cook Islands-based EP declared a New Zealand Controlled Foreign Corporation, or CFC, for tax purposes.

The selldown should have been the end of the matter, but the Commission's lawyers discovered a mystery $2 million payment to Brierleys and Fay Richwhite several years after the sale. Intriguingly, the money was paid to them by Laverton – the Cook Islands company that had apparently purchased their shares.

Laverton's true owners remained hidden behind a secret trust and Cook Islands secrecy laws, although Fay Richwhite eventually coughed to having an interest in Laverton.

The key period of 1988 to 1990 however stayed shrouded in a corporate mist, and yet here was Laverton, paying what appeared to Commission lawyers to be a shareholders dividend of $2 million to the two corporates.

If the Commission could establish that European Pacific's restructuring was a snow-job, then all of the profits from the $2.4 billion JIF deals would have been liable to New Zealand tax.

In short, proof of an ownership cover-up would be de facto proof of tax evasion on a grand scale.

Unfortunately, Paul Collins couldn't explain Brierley's share of the mystery payment, and suggested asking Gerald Gibbard – the company's tax specialist. Gibbard said it was a mystery to him, and perhaps Paddy Marra could provide the answers.

Alas, no. And having just survived this little run-around with their sanity intact, Commission lawyers were stunned when the next question they asked of Marra was met with the response: try asking Paul Collins, he might know.

It wasn't something the SFO had bothered to investigate ever, despite the fact that the ownership of Laverton had been raised and questioned in TVNZ's award-winning *Frontline* documentary on European Pacific in 1994.

All of a sudden, however, the SFO decided it had better take a closer look.

News feature, January 24, 1997

The Serious Fraud Office is turning up the heat under tax haven company European Pacific and two of its former owners – Fay Richwhite and Brierley Investments.

In a surprise revelation as the Winebox Inquiry resumed this week, SFO Assistant Director Gib Beattie said a formal investigation has been launched into a mystery payment of almost two million dollars shared between Fay Richwhite and Brierley Investments in early 1990.

The transaction is called the Laverton adjustment, and was made by a Cook Islands company associated with European Pacific principal David Lloyd, which ostensibly owned a 49% stake in the European Pacific Group.

Laverton had originally purchased 51% of the tax haven group in March 1988 to ensure that European Pacific stayed outside New Zealand's CFC clutches, but soon after sold a two percent interest to another Cook Islands company. This left the New Zealand corporates, through the original holding company European Pacific Investments, holding just 49% of the group.

Last year the inquiry discovered evidence of two payments of almost US$600,000 each, which executives from Fay Richwhite and Brierleys were unable to explain at the time.

BIL returned its windfall for tax purposes. Fay Richwhite did not, which has only added to the confusion over whether the payments reflected capital or revenue items.

One of the big questions at the inquiry has been whether the selldown to avoid the CFC regime was genuine or just a warehousing operation. The downstream implications for European Pacific and its former owners could prove extremely serious if the tax haven's operations are brought back within the CFC ambit.

Beattie is refusing to discuss the progress the SFO has made in its investigations of the matter, but significantly it has not graduated at this point to a "Part 2" level inquiry, where an offence is suspected.

However, in reconstructing the selldown, the Serious Fraud Office has calculated the payments could reflect a secret shareholding by FR and BIL totalling 16.6%, although Beattie was at pains to point out that both corporates have denied any such holding, and that it was merely a scoping exercise.

As you will discover later in this book, there is evidence that the SFO's entire experience with the Winebox was merely one big scoping exercise.

The IRD meanwhile had been caught by surprise by the Commission's discovery of the Laverton payments, and was reserving its position on their implication.

News feature, November 10, 1996

A key Inland Revenue official has conceded the department could be looking at tax evasion if it turns out the IRD wasn't told the truth about tax haven company European Pacific's ownership.

Senior audit manager John Nash admitted last week that the Winebox Inquiry's discovery of mystery payments to Brierleys and Fay Richwhite relating to European Pacific had caught the tax department by surprise.

Nash says he still doesn't believe that European Pacific's Cook Islands subsidiaries were secretly owned or controlled from New Zealand, but he admitted that it's an issue still under investigation.

"Is a second issue," asked counsel assisting the Commission, Colin Carruthers QC, "that the department may have been misled by the taxpayers involved?"

"Oh certainly, yes," replied Nash. "Even more than that, it could well be outright evasion."

The IRD official also conceded that "there is an element of tax haven in New Zealand" for major corporates, both in the lack of a capital gains tax but more significantly in a little-publicised section of the NZ tax Act, section 106, which includes clauses allowing large tax deductions for some corporate money deals.

Nash denied, however, that the IRD wasn't living up to its motto "it's our job to be fair".

"Do you think there is room for the view by the man in the street that there isn't a level playing field in relation to the treatment of taxpayers?" asked Colin Carruthers, after earlier criticising the department's handling of Brierleys.

"No, I don't," disagreed Nash. "The man in the street doesn't get investigated like we investigate Brierley Investments."

Tell that to the late Ian Mutton and his son.

In October 1996, the Inquiry heard how an Inland Revenue Department goof-up in its winebox investigation may have cost the tax department more than three million dollars in lost tax.

It transpired that the IRD's Corporates Unit rubber-stamped a request by the BNZ to liquidate one of its subsidiaries, even though the company was under active investigation for possible tax avoidance.

The subsidiary involved was BNZ Finance Deposits Ltd, which had been involved in a series of tax driven investment deals designed by Fay Richwhite and European Pacific, and catalogued in the winebox.

Documents on the deals had been in the Revenue's hands since February 1993, but when the BNZ made a request to wind up five subsidiaries in March 1994, the IRD did not object.

"Is the position," asked Colin Carruthers QC, "that in what was really the middle of the IRD investigation into the winebox transactions, the department gives permission to the liquidation of a company that it subsequently decides is liable to the department for tax in excess of, what, $12 million worth of income?"

"Yes," admitted IRD audit manager John Nash. "Procedures weren't followed. It was pure human error."

Nash told the inquiry that he didn't discover that IRD had approved the 1994 wind-up until 1995, when he was issuing income assessments for the 1989 and 1990 years totalling $13 million. The mistake happened despite a set of internal IRD measures designed to stop companies under investigation from slipping through the cracks.

"The FIRST [IRD computer] system should have noted [the existence of an investigation], such that any response to a winding up letter of application would be referred, immediately, to the officer heading the investigation," said Nash.

"That wasn't done. Secondly, the correspondence should have been lodged against all five companies. It was not. Procedures in our manuals say that that should have happened, but that didn't happen."

Despite the blunder, the IRD began pursuing the now defunct BNZ Finance Deposits Ltd under section 276 of the Income Tax Act, which allows the IRD to assess taxes on wound-up companies.

Taxpayer confidentiality requirements mean it is unlikely the public will discover the end result.

Unfortunately for Nash, he was later caned by Carruthers for failing to take the same sort of legal action against Fay Richwhite, which was involved in the very same transaction.

The IRD could have gunned for a company called Fay Richwhite Investment Management Ltd, (FRIML) which had helped mastermind the deal for the BNZ.

John Nash admitted that he had never done an in depth investigation of the Fay company's potential tax liability, because he chose instead to hit the BNZ. Nash also argued that FRIML didn't have any assets left to pay the tax.

Commission lawyers argued that the IRD could, however, hit Fay Richwhite itself if it could prove that the parent company exercised a controlling influence on FRIML. John Nash tried to claim there was no evidence of such a relationship.

Hang on a minute, protested Colin Carruthers.

"If Fay Richwhite Investment Management Ltd was a company that had a share capital comprising 100,000 shares of which [Fay Richwhite] owned 99,000, that's probably fairly compelling evidence that it consists, substantially, of the same shareholders as an original company, don't you think?"

"Yes," admitted Nash, "it is pretty good."

"And if the directors of FRIML," continued Carruthers, "were Messrs Birnie, Poole and Richwhite, with the secretary Balgarnie[3], do you think there is evidence worth investigating as to whether it is under the control of the same persons as an original company?"

"Yes," conceded Nash again, "that's certainly worth looking at."

"Do we get to the position," asked Carruthers, "that the facts in relation to the Fay Richwhite companies have not been investigated?"

"No," agreed John Nash. "Not in relation to applying section 276."

As the IRD moved heaven and earth at the Inquiry to avoid getting labelled incompetent, its answers were at times downright misleading. An example of this came in regard to Witness A, a former European Pacific

---

3 All directors and/or senior executives of the parent company.

executive who helped blow the whistle on the company's activities. Nash was asked why he had never bothered to interview Witness A about the winebox documents when his team received them in 1993.

He told the inquiry that Witness A had "stolen" the winebox papers from European Pacific – an allegation that has never been proven. He told the inquiry that Witness A had serious tax problems himself, perhaps involving up to half a million dollars of unreturned income, and this was why the IRD felt he had a credibility problem from the start.

Serious allegations indeed. Sounded very convincing to the waiting media. Just a pity that John Nash wasn't aware of Witness A's alleged tax problems in 1993 when he was assessing whether to approach the man.

In fact, evidence at the Inquiry shows the first time the IRD raised the matter with Witness A was in 1996, and only a month or so before Nash's cross examination began in October of that year.

John Nash was forced to admit that he hadn't even formed an initial view on Witness A's affairs until the middle of 1994 – 18 months after the Winebox papers first surfaced!

Attempts to kick for touch with teflon answers to tough questions can be dangerous, as the IRD witness found out. When the Commission lawyers finally obtained traction after scraping away the teflon, they bit back a lot harder than they otherwise might have. Not to mention the impact such testimony should have on the credibility of any witness in the eyes of the Commission.

"Competence". It's a pretty straightforward concept. In the case of the Winebox papers, one would assume that competent investigators would immediately review the papers, assess them, and begin following leads and interviewing witnesses before the trails got cold.

News feature, February 8, 1996[4]

To some, the Winebox Inquiry is a collection of dark-suited men in a room full of computer screens debating the arcane niceties of tax law.

To me, the undercurrents of the Winebox Inquiry are starting to resemble an African jungle, full of wild animals and hidden dangers, where only the fittest survive.

Up in the treetops, Tarzan the Taxman has had a relatively easy ride in the past couple of months as attention focused more on the activities of the other jungle inhabitants, but all that came to a very painful end for the

---

4   Reprinted from *Ian Wishart's Vintage Winebox Guide*, Howling At The Moon Productions Ltd, 1996

IRD this week, as a passing gorilla landed a well-aimed kick in Tarzan the Taxman's soft parts.

The gorilla, in this context, was Spyros Papageorgiou, the Bank of New Zealand's taxation manager, a man who bears more than a passing resemblance to American actor Danny de Vito and who obviously shares the colourful sense of culture unique to the Mediterranean lands.

When a computer keyboard alarm was accidentally triggered, Spyros Papageorgiou broke off what he was saying and nervously looked around to see if he should be diving for cover under a desk.

"Don't worry," reassured Sir Ronald Davison, "it's not a warning. Yet."

"Oh, that's all right," laughed the witness sheepishly, "it's just that some of my cousins are Sicillians!"

To complete the mental picture of the gorilla's clash with Tarzan however, imagine Johnny Weismuller as Tarzan the Taxman – senior IRD investigator John Nash – and the scene unfolds at the end of a liana vine high above a swamp full of treacherous sinkholes, quicksand, vicious crocodiles and lawyers.

The jungle analogy, whilst colourful, arises because a sense of desperation is becoming apparent among some of the parties to the inquiry. They have realised that saving their own skins may require dealing some "bush justice" to others. Gone is last year's veneer of civility.

For the IRD and the BNZ, the grudge match now being played out dates back to last July, when IRD investigator John Nash underwent what some commentators cynically labelled a "road to Damascus" conversion, and started throwing the dreaded "evasion" word around whilst poking significant borax at many of the corporates in the winebox.

Among those on the receiving end was the BNZ, accused of massive tax avoidance and a failure to co-operate with IRD requests.

This week Spyros Papageorgiou saw his chance for revenge and seized it. He revealed that IRD had begun a general audit of BNZ's affairs back in May 1992, but says IRD didn't raise winebox issues with the bank until April 1994 – more than a year after first getting the winebox documents, and a month after Winston Peters had tabled them in Parliament and accused the IRD of failing to investigate them properly.

All of a sudden, Papageorgiou told the Inquiry, the BNZ was deluged with a whole raft of winebox related inquiries from the tax department – the volume of which threatened to derail the main audit as winebox issues suddenly took priority. The BNZ claims the IRD's requests were "driven by influences in the political arena relating to the winebox," and later described the IRD's late investigations as more of a public relations exercise than a serious tax investigation.

Creeping up the liana vine, away from the snapping jaws of the Commission's crocodiles, Papageorgiou the Gorilla waited until Tarzan the Taxman swung close, and then kicked with all the force he could muster. Tarzan felt the pain instantly.

The pain came in the form of BNZ file notes of discussions with Tarzan the Taxman. They revealed the IRD felt "pressured" by Winston Peters' allegations and were looking for help from the BNZ to refute them. One note contained an alleged admission by John Nash that "the process we were going through was basically an attempt to placate the Commissioner in respect to Winston Peters' allegations."

Nash had allegedly already told the BNZ that he was satisfied the $200 million captive insurance scheme was not tax avoidance, but later requested all the BNZ's papers on the issue. When Papageorgiou asked why, Nash allegedly said that he needed to actually review the papers just "in case a subsequent internal quality review (IRD) was undertaken by either the Audit Office or some other organisation."

Nash allegedly added that if the IRD was asked, the department had to be able to state that it had reviewed the papers.

Tarzan the Taxman was then quoted as saying the winebox was "a pain in the neck".

Clearly aiming to limit further collateral damage to their sensitive regions, tax department PR staff swung into action, approaching journalists during an adjournment to add their own spin to the evidence.

While admitting they hadn't approached the BNZ about winebox matters until after Winston Peters opened fire on them, the IRD spin-doctor reminded the media of IRD working papers which indicated the department had been working solidly on the winebox behind the scenes ever since it received it in 1993.

And just how "solid" was that work?

News feature, August 31, 1996

It had been a really bad day for the Inland Revenue Department. A really bad day.

In the witness box at the Winebox Inquiry was the head of the department's Tax Intelligence Unit, Tony Loo, and at the back of the hearing room, one of his bosses sat motionless – as if stricken by some illness.

Loo's ordeal had been going since Thursday morning, his boss's had begun only half an hour before the Commission closed for the day, but what a nightmare half hour!

Loo, you see, was the IRD analyst given the task of sorting through the winebox transactions in 1993 after the papers were obtained from the Serious Fraud Office, and the transactions he was to report on included "Magnum" and the "JIF" deals.

These were what have come to be known as tax credit transactions, and they are arguably the most controversial, possibly criminal, deals in the winebox.

When the then Minister of Revenue Wyatt Creech told Parliament on March 30, 1994 that "an Inland Revenue project team of senior specialists has carefully analysed those papers", he was referring to Tony Loo and his Tax Intelligence Unit team.

When the then IRD Commissioner David Henry told his Minister on the same date that each of the 59 deals was "thoroughly and progressively reviewed" by the project team between March 1993 and February 1994, he was referring to Tony Loo and his analysts.

Those statements were used to allay public concern about the winebox deals in 1994, and they were used by European Pacific as a weapon in its legal fight to stop TVNZ from broadcasting a *Frontline* documentary on the winebox.

So now, the question has to be asked: if the IRD and the National Government were pinning their winebox credibility on the Tax Intelligence Unit, would it come as a shock to you to discover that TIU boss Tony Loo only found out how the tax credit deals really worked when he watched the *Frontline* programme?

I kid you not.

For a year, the TIU toiled with the winebox deals, and Loo happened to be the analyst in charge of reviewing the Magnum and JIF deals.

On Thursday afternoon, August 29, he confirmed what many observers have long suspected: that the IRD investigators didn't have a clue how the Magnum and JIF deals really worked, and that the 1994 Ministerial statement wasn't – in my opinion – worth the paper it was written on.

"At the time I did my analysis in March 1993," Loo said, "I didn't understand how [Magnum] operated."

Even worse, the man from the IRD who had all the Magnum documents under his nose in 1993, and whose job it was to analyse the transaction, was shown on Thursday afternoon the main planning document for the transaction.

"I don't particularly understand it because I have never read the document before," he told Commission QC Colin Carruthers.

"I'm sorry?" queried a clearly startled Carruthers, "You have never read the document before?"

"No, I just, no," the witness stammered.

By now it wasn't just Colin Carruthers looking like a stunned mullet – lawyers for some of the corporates had spun their heads around as well.

Here was the head of the IRD's Tax Intelligence Unit revealing that when he "carefully analysed" the Magnum deal, and passed a judgement that failed to detect that $2 million tax rort, he hadn't even read the blueprint planning document for the transaction.

In Loo's defence, he told the inquiry he didn't understand the deals and found a wiring diagram confusing.

"All I am saying is that I never sat down, at any stage, and analysed these papers in absolute detail. I perused them, identified what I thought were the pressure points, and I passed it on to [another analyst] to do the work for me."

Unfortunately, there's no evidence that the other analyst managed to crack the winebox code either.

Asked by Carruthers how he finally found out how the deals worked, Loo revealed his knowledge had come from the TV documentary in mid-1994.

Loo's boss, Tony Bouzaid, watching from the back, was looking more and more shattered as the afternoon wore on.

Towards the end, he wasn't even looking at the witness. Instead, his face was in his hands, and still the embarrassment for the IRD came in never-ending waves.

"Is it fair to say," challenged Carruthers, "that you had not, in fact, 'thoroughly and carefully analysed' those papers on the transaction, in that you hadn't made the connection between the Magnum papers and various other papers in the winebox dealing with tax credits."

"Yes, that is correct," admitted Tony Loo. "I personally have not." Nor was he aware of anyone else in the department who had either.

Nor had the head of the Tax Intelligence Unit been informed that the IRD had been warned about the possibility of "false Cook Islands tax certificates" being in circulation.

"Is that the sort of information that you would have expected to have received in the TIU?," asked the QC.

"I presume so, yes," said Loo.

For a Commission of Inquiry set up to examine, among other things, whether the IRD had been competent in its handling of the winebox, Loo's evidence has been a goldmine.

Of one thing we can be sure: the surprise quotient is sure to grow when the inquiry resumes in a fortnight with the cross examination of top officials from the Inland Revenue Department.

When John Nash was questioned about this latest revelation from the head of the Tax Intelligence Unit, he said he'd been flabbergasted to hear that Tony Loo didn't know how the tax credit deals worked until he saw them explained on TV in mid-1994.

Loo's answer, Nash said, was "absolutely staggering". Especially as Nash claimed to have understood the tax credit deals as far back as April 1993.

Nash had not previously claimed to have understood the deals when he first appeared before the Commission in late 1994, but was now making that assertion in his cross-examination at the end of 1996. During the intervening period the IRD had taken a pounding for failing to recognise how the deals worked and do something about them.

Although Nash says he instructed staff to investigate the tax credit arrangements, there is no documentation to suggest this was ever done. Nor, in a department where many conversations are recorded on filenotes, is there any documentation to suggest the instruction was ever given.

IRD lawyers, in their closing submissions, claimed I had wrongly criticised Nash over this, and quoted two documents to support Nash's statement. One document is a handwritten attempt at doing some calculations on the Magnum deal, the other is a memo from Tony Loo, dated March 1993, asking another IRD employee to check out the tax credit aspect of the Magnum deal.

Given that Loo testified he didn't suss out the full story behind the deal until he saw it on TV, this document does not illustrate an "understanding" of how Magnum worked. Nor is it an instruction from John Nash that shows he understood it.

The document, signed by Loo, was read at some point by Nash who then forwarded it to another investigator, Mike Spelman, without any covering letter. Was that an "instruction" that shows Nash understood the arrangement?

Instead, the IRD's own closing submissions note in regard to Magnum:

"The offsetting of the cost of paying tax is the objectionable element in the tax credit transactions.

"The offsetting of tax was implemented so that in the absence of direct evidence (almost impossible to obtain from a tax haven) or voluntary disclosure by the taxpayer seeking the benefit of the credit, identification of the tax credit itself would not lead to identification of the objectionable element."

So, even if the IRD had identified the use of a tax credit back in early 1993, where is the evidence that they identified the "objectionable element" – the tax refund mechanism?

For one purpose in their submissions, the IRD say the refund mechanism was impossible to detect, but for another they claim the Magnum deal was understood.

The documents indicate to me that only one IRD employee, senior inspector John Trezise, had apparently understood the tax credit rort. His analysis, in February 1993, noted a "novel" scheme involving Cook Islands tax certificates and a double benefit. Unfortunately, once again, there's no evidence that anyone else in the IRD followed up Trezise's discovery.

So, whether or not John Nash knew how the Cook Islands tax credit deals worked in 1993 is irrelevant, as the IRD did nothing further to investigate the tax credit transactions until February 1994, when news media publicity revealed exactly what the transactions were and how they worked.

If John Nash really had figured out that the IRD had been rorted to the tune of $2 million, why weren't the issues immediately investigated then? Nash, as the officer in charge of the Winebox Project Team, is the man responsible at the end of the day.

Sir Ronald Davison heard all of this evidence, of which the preceding pages are a mere appetiser, and reached the following conclusion about the Inland Revenue Department:

"There can be no substance to an allegation that it was incompetent."

You will be reminded of this judgment throughout this book, because the evidence you're about to read paints a vastly more disturbing picture.

Chapter 3

Political Interference

"A Commission to inquire into and report upon – whether ... the Director of the Serious Fraud Office and his staff acted, in the course of their official duties, in a lawful, proper and competent manner in dealing with the transactions."
— *Terms of Reference, Winebox Inquiry*

Apart from competence, other aspects for consideration by Sir Ronald included whether the IRD acted lawfully or properly. Now this can range from doing something that is obviously unlawful, to neglecting one's statutory duty, to doing something unethical, such as allowing politicians to have a say in things.

One of the more interesting developments that was never fully pursued by Sir Ronald Davison was the Western Samoan tax credit scheme.

Witness A, the former European Pacific employee who originally had the Winebox papers, had begun helping a Western Samoan tax haven company set up. This company was a potential rival to European Pacific, and the latter used private investigators to try to find out more about it.

Curiously, the New Zealand Government suddenly announced in 1993 that it was outlawing a new "tax credit" scheme, emanating from Western Samoa. Suddenly, European Pacific's opposition was conveniently blown out of the water, courtesy of some National Government legislation.

News feature, October 5, 1996

The pin has been pulled from a grenade at the Winebox Inquiry this week as the Inland Revenue Department and the Davison Commission's lawyers play a deadly game of catch.

IRD senior audit manager, John Nash, set the tone when the inquiry resumed this week, shedding his "Tarzan" image in favour of a more aggressive "Rambo the Taxman".

Describing how the New Zealand Government had legislated swiftly to outlaw dodgy tax certificates from Western Samoa in 1993, John Nash colourfully described the IRD strategy.

"Schedule 17a action was taken against Western Samoa. That is the equivalent of dropping a nuclear bomb on a sovereign [government], because you have one sovereign saying 'your tax credit paper isn't worth the paper it is written on'.

"We nuked Western Samoa ... so that really put a clear end to the Western Samoan scheme. End of story," said Rambo.

Contrast the nuking of Western Samoa with the slow as a tortoise approach on the winebox tax credit deals. Documents presented to the inquiry tend to suggest the IRD didn't discover how the tax credit deals worked until after TVNZ's legal fight against European Pacific in February 1994.

However, John Nash claims to have worked the deals out in April 1993, but has been unable to explain why the dodgy tax certificates weren't investigated and dealt with in the same way and speed as the Samoa scheme. Nash says he asked staff to look at the tax swizz, but this wasn't done.

One explanation given by Nash for not pushing it faster was that work was, by mid 1993, now underway to legislate against foreign tax credit abuse.

However, an internal IRD memorandum released by the Commission this week casts a worrying political light on that issue.

Dated March 18, 1994, the memo is from IRD's Legislative Affairs manager David Partington, and addressed to "John Nash, Trouble Shooter".

"The Government agreed in principle to a disallowance provision for dodgy foreign tax credits," writes Partington. "We never followed through with legislation last year as the Government became nervous about controversial legislation with the election looming."

Now, call me an old-fashioned cynical journalist, but the question going begging here is this: So far, the only company known to have used dodgy tax credits in New Zealand is European Pacific. It was hardly widespread or even a widely known rort. At that time nobody knew about European Pacific's tax credit deals. Why, on earth, would legislation cracking down on "dodgy foreign tax credits" be too controversial for the Government to handle prior to the 1993 election?

Did the Government know something about tax credits that the rest of us didn't? And should the Government have politically meddled in a genuine IRD attempt to clamp down on the problem? Questions with no obvious answers yet.

And the answers never came. The lead was never followed up. What a lucky break for European Pacific and its corporate shareholders: first the

New Zealand Government acts unilaterally and swiftly to make dodgy tax certificates from Western Samoa illegal, but Cook Islands ones are left alone and the IRD is warned off cracking down on other dodgy tax certificates because the Government was worried it might be too "controversial".

Remember, the Cook Islands tax certificate deals were valued at around $2.4 billion in today's dollars.

In his closing submissions to the Inquiry in 1997, Colin Carruthers QC appears to doubt John Nash's claim that he knew about Magnum's tax credit swindle as early as 1993.

Carruthers highlights the urgent action taken by New Zealand to combat the Western Samoan scheme. The IRD's Tony Bouzaid exploded into writing when he heard of Samoa's plans, saying "We are very concerned with the potential enormous cost to our own tax base ... by means of a series of paper transactions, corporate groups using Western Samoa as proposed could virtually write their own tax credits."

Carruthers then quotes from an urgent briefing paper sent by the IRD to the Government in March 1993, less than a month after Samoa's plans were discovered:

"The essential point of this scheme for New Zealand is that the scheme produces a foreign tax credit where in substance little or no tax is paid."

Another IRD strategy paper a week later urged the Government to deny the use of foreign tax credits from Samoa, apply a test of "substance over form" to tax credit claims, and introduce penalties for taxpayers who use the schemes and those who promote them.

The report also recommended, said Carruthers, "that the Commissioner of Inland Revenue be permitted to alert all OECD countries of the existence of the scheme."

In other words, it was the IRD equivalent of "battlestations". The klaxon horns were sounding and the big guns were coming out.

The IRD's Legislative Affairs section was immediately ordered to begin work on combatting the problem but, writes Carruthers, "the existence of a similar foreign tax credit scheme occurring in the Cook Islands was not drawn to the attention of Mr Partington in Legislative Affairs during 1993 while the Western Samoan issue was being dealt with.

"Two issues arise from this: first, whether Mr Nash indeed worked out that the Magnum transaction involved a [similar] refunding mechanism ... and second, if so, whether Mr Nash should have drawn Legislative Affairs' attention to the existence of a similar scheme in the Cook Islands."

Carruthers then ominously notes that when Legislative Affairs became aware of the Magnum deal a *year* later, the alarms went off. David Partington fired a memo to Bouzaid, suggesting Nash hadn't told him about a problem with Cook Islands tax credits.

"The allegations being made by Mr Peters in the House," writes Partington, "and the attached cable that I received from Ministry of External Relations and Trade suggest that foreign tax credit abuse may also be occurring in the Cook Islands.

"Are you able to tell me whether we have any firm evidence of what is happening in the Cook Islands in relation to foreign tax credits?

"If there is evidence that the Cook Islands is generating tax credit certificates where the tax is not in substance paid, I would be very keen to bring it to our Government's attention."

By this stage, in early 1994, so were those of us working on the *Frontline* documentary, but the Government didn't want to know.

Just how involved were the politicians? Sir Ronald Davison's Inquiry catalogued numerous spectral sightings but never called in the "Ghostbusters" to haul them in.

In July 1996, two senior National Party politicians were named in dispatches at the Winebox Inquiry. It came just three months before the election and, if he had had the power to actively pursue it (it was outside the Terms of Reference), could have been potentially explosive.

In the first "tagging", Cabinet Minister Wyatt Creech, a former Minister of Revenue, was named in relation to an alleged attempt by a Russell McVeagh lawyer to intimidate an IRD senior investigator.

The allegation was made in 1995 by Denese Latimer, who was investigating alleged fraud in the David Bowie movie *Merry Christmas Mr Lawrence*.

Latimer claimed that in 1991 she was being heavied by Russell McVeagh tax lawyer Geoff Clews, a man who subsequently spent several days in the witness box denying any threats or blackmail attempts.

"He commented that he was concerned that the Department would walk away from the negotiations," Latimer had told the inquiry, "and if we were not prepared to continue the discussions he would have to go to a higher power.

"I asked who the higher powers were, and he replied they were the Commissioner [of Inland Revenue, David Henry], the Minister of Revenue and the Minister of Finance."

Geoff Clews said he "can't remember" using the phrase "higher power", but admitted he did invoke the Commissioner's name and a Minister of Revenue. He's told the inquiry that the Minister he meant was Trevor de

Cleene, a former Labour Cabinet Minister who's now reportedly supporting both ACT and the National Party.

He said de Cleene had indicated to some delegates at a tax conference in 1988 that he wanted the film partnership issues "settled", according to Geoff Clews.

That explanation wasn't good enough for Winston Peters' counsel, Brian Henry.

"In the context that [Latimer] has written this note," probed Henry, "it could only be referring to the current Minister of Revenue, which at that time was Mr Creech, and the Minister of Finance – the current Minister of Finance at that time – which was Mrs Richardson?"

"If that was what was said, Sir," replied Geoff Clews, "that would be a fair inference, but I put my position clearly on that.

"I certainly intended to convey to Mrs Latimer that a Minister had made those comments in the past and that I knew – or understood – that the Commissioner wanted to settle."

Was it a statement of fact or a veiled threat? Those were the questions being pursued by Brian Henry.

"Weren't you always wishing to make it very clear to Mrs Latimer that you did have access to the Commissioner, the Minister of Revenue or the Minister of Finance if you desired?"

"I have already indicated, Sir," responded Clews, "that I certainly had access to those people. If I can just clarify again, I don't recall mentioning the Minister of Finance and I don't think that would have been a natural reference in the context. The Minister of Finance had little, if anything, to do with tax administration."

"But you do accept," concluded Brian Henry, "the Minister of Revenue is a name that would have been there?"

"Yes, I would have to do that. Yes," confirmed the Russell McVeagh lawyer.

But if Ruth Richardson had little, if anything, to do with tax administration, why was her name found in documents suggesting a direct knowledge of Fay Richwhite's tax affairs?

The reference in the documents is intriguing, and this one did fall within the Inquiry's power to subpoena her.

It comes in an internal IRD memorandum dated December 10, 1992, which records a meeting between a senior tax inspector and a group of Fay Richwhite executives and their lawyer, Dr Geoff Harley – who also testified at the Winebox Inquiry.

The tax inspector notes discussion about $400 million dollars worth of

Cook Islands deals carried out by Fay Richwhite and the BNZ.

The IRD told the inquiry it was now alleging massive tax avoidance in the deals to the tune of almost a hundred million dollars. Back in 1992, however, Fay Richwhite's lawyers were allegedly trying to talk the IRD out of investigating.

"Mr Harley asked if it was worth pursuing this," wrote the tax inspector, "as he said the deemed repatriation rules covered the situation now. He said that Ruth Richardson was furious about the situation i.e. their use of the deals, and that the rules were changed in July to prevent this sort of deal.

"Later in the meeting," the IRD official continued, "I further asked about R Richardson's comments and was told that she was at a meeting at Fay Richwhite Wellington and made some comment in relation to the issue. [She] said to G Harley that he was aware what she was talking about, then turned to [Fay Richwhite executive John] Balgarnie and said so was he.

"They said that she was really angry about the matter."

Ruth Richardson was never called to give evidence on what she knew or when, nor was Wyatt Creech.

Given the number of times Cabinet Ministers have said they're not allowed to get involved in individual tax cases, however, the evidence does pose questions that Ruth Richardson, Wyatt Creech and Trevor de Cleene should have the right – in my view – to reply to what did they know, and when?

News feature, July 27, 1996

At the same time as National MPs were rubbishing Winston Peters' winebox allegations in 1992, at least one senior Minister knew the truth about the deals.

Russell McVeagh tax lawyer Dr Geoff Harley confirmed he'd been attacked at a Fay Richwhite function by the then Finance Minister, Ruth Richardson, who berated him over $400 million worth of winebox deals involving Fay Richwhite and the BNZ.

The Minister angrily called the deals "tax avoidance".

Dr Harley, a man with a wicked sense of humour and a great sense of theatre, enthralled the inquiry on Tuesday as he described the Minister's demeanour.

"This wasn't a conversation that permitted any explanation [of Fay's side of the story]," he told lawyer Brian Henry.

"The only reason she could be angry," said Mr Henry, "is if she thought something wrong was being done, surely?"

"There's no doubt that's what she thought – and communicated in clear terms!" replied Geoff Harley as a smile began to play at the corner of his mouth.

"Do you recall the exact words she used?" continued Brian Henry eagerly.

"No," said Dr Harley, seizing the moment, "I was more surprised at having her finger stuck in my ribs, several times, with emphasis."

On the media bench, hoots of laughter could now be heard openly as Geoff Harley fought to keep a straight face and an even tone in his voice. Elsewhere, lawyers were sheltering behind computer screens to stop Sir Ronald from seeing their smiles.

"She was basically going ballistic about it, is that it?" asked Henry, his own voice breaking.

Geoff Harley, with masterful understatement, kept his answer short and to the point.

"I understood that she was *displeased* with me."

It was too much. The hoots had become long, gut-wrenching, eye-watering howls that rolled uncontrollably throughout the hearing room, the mental image of the short, feisty Minister with the *Split Enz* hair-do scolding the naughty tax lawyer had become too much to bear. Even Sir Ronald's mouth was twitching.

None of which explains how Richardson knew about the deals, or why the Government kept taunting Peters and telling him "where's the evidence?" when the Minister of Finance already knew.

And then there is the curious case of the Serious Fraud Office.

"Decisions by the SFO and IRD not to prosecute," Peters had angrily claimed in Parliament in 1994, "have been made behind closed doors.

"Who knows what favours are being called or bribes are being paid even as we speak to save the reputations of some of New Zealand's so-called leading business figures and top political campaign donors?"

The statement, made under parliamentary privilege, incensed SFO Director Charles Sturt, who presumed he was personally being accused of taking bribes. But what if the statement was meant to be interpreted more widely?

As you read earlier, there appears to be clear circumstantial evidence that large companies donating money to the National Party had ordered the Government not to investigate the BNZ, at the peril of losing their funding. The Winebox documents are intricately linked to the mysterious BNZ affair. If politicians decide not to have an inquiry because they won't get campaign donations (bribes, for the sake of this argument), and then make that view known to the two Government departments, isn't that corruption? It is in my view.

Of course, there was never any evidence presented to the Inquiry to indicate that any politician had attempted to influence either of the department chiefs. In fact, when they were on the stand, both denied such a thing.

So it was with a keen interest that I discovered in Charles Sturt's book allegations that former Attorney-General Paul East had interfered in several other SFO investigations.

> "One effect of the grandstanding by [accused Equiticorp boss Alan] Hawkins came from an unexpected quarter. I received a visit in my office from the Attorney-General, by this time Paul East.
>
> "He was concerned ... wanted to know why I had not sought the opinion of a senior Queen's Counsel before deciding to prosecute, and was clearly concerned about the SFO taking on another major fraud prosecution of this kind in the future.
>
> "I told Paul East quite firmly that I was the expert in this area, and that I had not intended wasting six months by having a Queen's Counsel run over my work. My thinking was that I didn't need his advice as to which cases I would take on."

That's incident number one. Then, a little later in the book, a claim that the investigation into Sports Foundation boss Keith Hancox came under East's scrutiny.

> "The Attorney-General, Paul East, telephoned to ask whether it was correct that I was investigating Keith Hancox. Told that I was, he queried how much was involved, which at that stage was approximately $70,000. He then questioned whether a fraud of that value warranted an SFO investigation. I informed the Minister that my investigation would continue and that it was becoming more serious every day."

If Sturt's allegations were true, then in my view they are very serious indeed, as it is a fine line between a Minister being briefed on an investigation and a Minister offering advice that a department head may feel compelled to act upon.

I had been told of occasions where the Inland Revenue Department had been used by certain politicians as a weapon against troublesome people, and in *The Paradise Conspiracy I* the case of former Cabinet Minister Aussie Malcolm is laid out: he suffered a police and an IRD investigation just weeks after indicating that he was prepared to re-enter Parliament at the head of a National Party faction unhappy with the party's leadership hierarchy. He was also suspected of helping leak the Winebox to Winston Peters (he didn't).

So while the IRD's appearance in the political arena didn't surprise me, it was fascinating to see the former head of the SFO publicly claim to have evidence of the old-boys network in action.

East, for his part, denied any impropriety and claimed in a Parliamentary personal statement that Sturt had got his facts wrong.

The Winebox Inquiry heard from three former or current SFO staff who gave crucificial evidence against Sturt. As an investigative journalist I had interviewed two further SFO staff, one of them second only to Sturt in the office. All had chilling stories to tell, both about the way the office was run, and about the way controversial investigations were nipped in the bud by Sturt.

One of my sources revealed how the Serious Fraud Office had been investigating the allegedly fraudulent film and bloodstock deals[5] carried out by lawfirm Russell McVeagh.

Then, said the source, Charles Sturt received a visit from Lyn Stevens, a lawyer associated with Russell McVeagh and the son of Sir Laurence Stevens – the Chairman of Fay Richwhite. Almost overnight, said the source, the atmosphere inside the SFO changed and the bloodstock investigation was effectively shelved. Lyn Stevens then became a contracted prosecution barrister for the SFO. In the view of my source this sequence of events reeked of conflict of interest.

In his book, Sturt attempts to explain away the SFO's lack of action on the deals by claiming that Chris Dickie and Dr Tony Molloy QC, lawyers acting for disgruntled investors in the schemes, had not found any evidence of fraud.

Interestingly, their evidence was sufficient to get Russell McVeagh to cough up in full to the tune of almost $20 million dollars in a civil case, and when Molloy's book *Thirty Pieces of Silver* was published he was inundated with comments from leading QC's and even judges who believed the evidence was more than proven to a criminal standard.

On the other hand, Molloy laid a complaint with Peter Preece, at the Auckland Police fraud squad, and so far nothing has been done. Preece was one of the officers involved in prosecuting Citibank's false complaint against computer dealer Paul White before he was killed.

But the Serious Fraud Office is making a name for itself by finding every reason in the world not to tackle controversial issues, as you will see.

---

5 See *Lawyers, Guns & Money*, Ian Wishart, Howling At The Moon Productions Ltd, 1997

Chapter 4

Boomerang Chickens

"Never confuse movement with action."
– *Ernest Hemingway (1899–1961), US author.*

The seeds of the SFO's destruction (in the eyes of everybody else except the SFO and Sir Ronald Davison, it seems) had been sown years earlier when the Winebox was first delivered to the office. But by early 1996 those seeds were growing into thornbushes.

In March 1996, somebody within the SFO apparently leaked confidential timesheets to the *Independent* that disclosed the SFO had spent the grand total of 42.5 hours assessing the Winebox deals – one person-week – before tossing them aside.

The SFO was highly embarrassed at the security breach and tried to take legal action against the paper. In response, journalist Jenni McManus revealed just how good her sources were by printing details of a confidential SFO staff meeting.

"*Monday at the Silly Fraud Office. It's getting to be a ritual. Every Monday morning Serious Fraud Office supremo Chas Sturt addresses his troops ... waving a copy of the Independent – the enemy.*

"*Behind this scene of intense paranoia there's a witchhunt for the person or persons who leaked the SFO's 1992-1993 timesheets.*

"*Not that these Monday get-togethers lack their lighter side. Why, only recently our Chas (referred to fondly by some staffers as Charlie) turned Truman-esque and advised his troops, 'If the oven's too hot, stay out of the chicken.'*

"*This set off an avalanche of chicken jokes and sent some of the SFO's super sleuths flapping the right wing and clucking surreptitiously.*"

A year later, it looked as though the SFO was all but dead and buried.

News feature, January 26, 1997

A top Serious Fraud Office administrator has denied that investigations into the winebox deals may have been influenced by bad blood between SFO director Charles Sturt and NZ First leader Winston Peters.

In an electric exchange at the Winebox Inquiry on Friday afternoon SFO assistant director Gib Beattie shadow-boxed with Peters' lawyer, Brian Henry.

Much of the questioning was ruled out of bounds by Commissioner Sir Ronald Davison, as Brian Henry searched desperately for a chink in the SFO armour.

It began with a question about whether there had ever been discussion of Winston Peters at internal SFO staff meetings.

"There may have been," acknowledged Beattie.

"In what ways did the Director describe Mr Peters at those forums?" asked Henry, but before the witness had a chance to answer the SFO's counsel, Nick Davidson QC, was on his feet with an objection.

"Commissioner, this is quite outside the scope of this inquiry," he protested. "It is on a very personal level, Sir."

Called upon to referee the scrap, Sir Ronald Davison wanted to know why the cross-examination was heading down this path.

"Well Sir," explained Brian Henry, "I am endeavouring to ascertain whether or not there have been attitudes indicated by the Director to members of the staff which could have an effect on how they view the winebox because of Mr Peters involvement."

Sir Ronald ruled that questions could be asked about whether the Director of the SFO had influenced staff investigations, but he indicated that questions about Charles Sturt's views of Peters were "not helpful".

After a long period of silence, Brian Henry tried again.

"Has Mr Peters, over the years 1992–93, raised a series of matters including complaints to the Serious Fraud Office, to your knowledge, and have any of those matters, including the winebox, been discussed in staff forums?"

"They have been discussed," confirmed Beattie.

"Now, in any of those forums, has Mr Sturt indicated his views of Mr Peters as a factor?"

"Mr Sturt's view of Mr -" began the SFO witness, but he was cut off by his lawyer.

"Sir," pleaded Nick Davidson, "I object to the question!"

"I disallow that question," confirmed Sir Ronald.

"Has Mr Sturt made known his views of Mr Peters," pushed Brian Henry, "in a manner that could stifle debate and discussion by the staff as to the merits of the transactions in the winebox?"

"No," answered Beattie.

Earlier, the SFO witness had been taking a hammering from Counsel assisting the Commission, Colin Carruthers QC, over his statement that the Magnum tax credit deal is not a fraud.

After suggesting a series of possibilities as to why the deal may well be fraud, Carruthers decided to test the issue in a personal way.

"Would you have been prepared to sign the [European Pacific] tax return?" he asked Beattie.

"Thank you for that question, Mr Carruthers," said the witness as laughter broke out in the hearing room at the curved ball that had been thrown. "I would have to satisfy myself as to the legality of the return."

"You know what the circumstances are, Mr Beattie. Would you have been prepared to sign the return?"

"Knowing what I know now," conceded the SFO Assistant Director, "no."

Interestingly, Sir Ronald Davison refused to allow lawyers for Winston Peters to probe whether the attitude of Charles Sturt towards Peters had tainted the SFO's willingness to investigate Peters' allegations. This was an issue that my own SFO sources had been strong on – that staff were left in no doubt what Sturt thought of Peters and his allegations, long *before* Winston Peters had ever attacked Sturt.

The issue wasn't going away, as the next report shows.

News feature, February 2, 1997

Serious Fraud Office Director Charles Sturt looks set to undergo what could be the heaviest cross-examination he's ever had to face when he takes the stand at the Winebox Inquiry this week.

Assistant SFO Director John Hicks last week managed to turn what was already a steady heat under his boss into a blast furnace, with a series of shock revelations that were pinned back to Sturt.

They included:

1) Charles Sturt appeared to have a deep animosity towards Winston Peters at the time of the MP's original winebox, BNZ and film fraud allegations in 1992, long before the MP attacked the SFO for being possibly corrupt or incompetent in 1994.

2) Sturt described Peters as a liar in front of SFO staff as they discussed

how to handle the MP's formal complaints, and Hicks says the complaints were treated as "irritants". The thrust of Sturt's comments "was his personal dislike" of the MP. John Hicks said the Director often used the words "rat, mongrel liar, cheat" to describe people like Peters that he didn't like.

3) Charles Sturt instructed his staff to make what Commission lawyers allege were misleading or dishonest statements about the status of the winebox investigation both verbally and in writing.

Other areas of major concern being explored by the Davison Commission include the apparent alteration of SFO filenotes, discrepancies in SFO timesheets relating to the amount of time spent working on the winebox investigation, and claims by SFO staff that they understood the key winebox transactions as far back as 1992, when evidence they gave to the inquiry in 1994 does not appear to support that claim.

As an example, John Hicks underwent a grilling on Friday that was, at times, painful even for observers to watch. He told the Commission he had figured out the tax refund mechanism in the allegedly fraudulent Magnum tax certificate deal, but couldn't explain why there was no hint of this understanding in previous evidence.

He told the Commission that while the mechanism was interesting, he didn't regard it as more significant than other parts of the deal, and that's why he didn't mention it earlier.

The Commission has already heard evidence showing the Magnum deal hinged totally on the tax refund mechanism, and couldn't have proceeded without it.

Hicks is expected to finish his cross examination tomorrow, and he'll be followed by former SFO Deputy Director Denis Pain and finally Charles Sturt himself.

And then, a week later, more bombshells.

News feature, February 9, 1997

A top prosecutor in the Serious Fraud Office was allegedly warned off when she tried to discover why the SFO was not laying criminal charges over the winebox deals.

In more shattering evidence to emerge last week, the personal diaries of SFO Assistant Director John Hicks were seized and published.

They show that SFO lawyer and senior prosecutor Susan Pilgrim went to see Hicks in June 1994 to ask why charges were not being laid under s229A of the Crimes Act.

Hicks told Pilgrim that it was "not prudent to discuss at present", and noted in his diary afterwards that Pilgrim was concerned if an inquiry into the SFO's actions occurred.

Evidence in the diaries and in Hicks' testimony continues to fence in embattled SFO Director Charles Sturt, who was last week fingered by Hicks as the mastermind behind a series of what Commission lawyers label "misleading and dishonest" statements on the winebox.

Hicks says he was told to make the statements on the orders of his boss, apparently as a tactical manoeuvre to keep people in the dark about what the SFO was doing.

The tactics included the creation and documentation of a fictitious conversation.

Elsewhere in his diary, Hicks had drawn up a list of criticisms of the Director, including that he provided bullets for his staff to use that he wasn't prepared to fire himself, that he tended "towards favouritism" inside the office and that he abused staff in front of others.

The inquiry has already heard that Sturt was making derogatory remarks about Winston Peters inside the office at a time when SFO staff were deciding whether the MP's complaints were worthy of investigation or not.

Former SFO Deputy Director Denis Pain, now a High Court judge in Fiji, told the inquiry last week that he had been unaware of the strategy to mislead people about the winebox, and he was visibly shaken when evidence of what had taken place was put before him. He called the SFO's actions "incredible" and "inexplicable".

It was Charles Sturt's turn to take the witness stand at the Inquiry, but if you believed the claims in his book, he was being picked on over a word being taken out of context.

"Unfortunately, in a report to the Attorney-General that was read to Parliament," he writes, "I said that having examined the papers I could not see the need to 'further investigate'. My inadvertent use of these two words on two separate occasions would later be seized on to accuse me of having misled Parliament into believing that an 'investigation' had been carried out when only an 'examination' of documents had taken place. It was playing with words, but by then it would be all they had to go on."

As the reader will probably by now have gathered, it was a lot more serious than that.

News feature, February 21, 1997

The future of Serious Fraud Office boss Charles Sturt appears to hang in the balance following his devastating admissions to the Winebox Inquiry this week.

In Parliament, Alliance leader Jim Anderton was looking for Sturt's scalp, but he'll probably have to take a ticket and stand in line behind Sir Ron Davison's Commission of Inquiry.

In a major coup for Commission lawyers, they established that:

1. A Sturt press release on the winebox contained more inaccuracies and information described as misleading.

2. Sturt claimed to have "investigated" the winebox, but didn't.

3. Sturt was the self-appointed sole SFO lawyer to check the winebox for fraud, despite a view among his own staff that he was incompetent.

4. Sturt was the self-appointed sole SFO "investigator" on the winebox.

5. Charles Sturt accused winebox whistleblower Stephen Lunn of trying to sell the winebox for money in 1992, but had to admit to the inquiry he had no proof to back up his allegations.

6. The director claims to have spent 40 hours analysing the winebox papers but has no worksheets or written notes to support the claim.

7. Sturt did not attempt to analyse the transactions for himself in any "deep" sense.

8. The SFO considers it is acceptable for law enforcement agencies to mislead when required.

9. Sturt authorised the return of the original winebox documents to European Pacific, despite rules that require prosecution agencies to keep the "originals" for possible evidential purposes.

10. The SFO believes it has no power to retain documents leaked to it by unauthorised persons.[6]

11. Sturt did not believe references to illegality in some documents were sufficient to arouse statutory suspicion in terms of the SFO Act.

12. Sturt allowed a statement to go to Parliament knowing that it contained incorrect information.

13. Sturt's statement to Parliament said he copied the winebox documents by virtue of his statutory powers.

14. Sturt told the Winebox Inquiry on oath that he had no statutory power to photocopy the winebox.

Tuesday was the first time in more than two years that Charles Sturt has faced questioning over his examination of the winebox, and it started badly for the SFO director.

Within seconds, Counsel assisting the Commission, Colin Carruthers

---

6 Author's question: is there any such thing as an "authorised leak"?

QC had taken Sturt to one of his press releases, dated March 18, 1994, and proceeded to cane him with it.

The release referred to a team of 'investigators' who'd examined the documents.

"Who were the investigators to whom you were referring?"

"I was wearing an investigator's hat for that particular purpose," replied the Director.

"There is only one of you, Mr Sturt. Who were the investigators to whom you were referring?"

"In the plural sense," admitted the SFO boss, "that would not be correct."

"It really is an abuse of language to call you an investigator in that capacity, Mr Sturt," said the QC at one point.

After a further work-over, Carruthers asked whether "we get to the position that one accountant looks at the papers for, at the outside, 31 hours, over a period at the outside, of three weeks?"

"Yes."

"And do you say that that state of affairs is accurately recorded and reflected to the New Zealand public by a statement that the winebox contained hundreds of documents which were examined by accountants and investigators in this Office over a period of several months?"

Sturt maintained it was a fair statement, but he came to grief only moments later as the QC found more inaccuracies, this time in a paragraph stating "the investigation satisfied me that there was no evidence of criminal fraudulent offending."

"There never was an investigation by the SFO involving accountants and investigators over a period of several months, was there?" asked Carruthers.

The SFO Director attempted to weave around the blunt probe, but eventually answered after a ticking off from Sir Ronald Davison.

"There was never an investigation carried out, no" he admitted.

He was accused of trying to discredit whistleblower Stephen Lunn, who'd given the winebox to the SFO in October 1992, with press statements suggesting Lunn had tried to hawk the winebox around town and sell the documents for a hundred thousand dollars.

Sturt admitted those issues had no relevance to the SFO's examination of the winebox, but denied it was an attempt to besmirch Lunn or play down the whole winebox affair in the public's eyes.

Asked then whether he had any hard evidence to back up the damaging allegations, Sturt had to admit he did not, apart from hearsay provided by a couple of media contacts.

In a statement to be used in Parliament, Sturt said "the Director was not prepared to make any offer of payment of public funds to Mr Lunn." He was then forced to confess that Lunn had never once asked him for money.

Sturt told Parliament that the SFO did not seek to hand back the winebox documents to tax haven company European Pacific within days of receiving them.

Yet, in testimony before the Winebox Inquiry, SFO Assistant Director John Hicks has admitted he was seeking permission from whistleblower Stephen Lunn to hand the winebox back, telling Lunn the SFO had finished with it.

Charles Sturt has now admitted he knew of this before the statement was sent to Attorney-General Paul East.

"Do you agree," asked Carruthers, "that at the stage you drafted the reply for Parliament you knew what Mr Hicks had said?"

"Yes."

"So you knew, when you drafted the reply, that paragraph one of the reply was wrong?"

"In terms of my particular view on the matter, yes," confirmed Sturt.

The SFO boss claimed to have spent 40 hours assessing the documents, but couldn't back up the claim.

"Do we get to the position," asked Carruthers, "that there is no written record of the time that you, in fact, spent on the winebox papers?"

"There is no written record," confirmed the Director, who hadn't even made notes from the analysis and was basing his 40-hour claim on memory.

Sturt hadn't bothered to make any real analysis of the deals themselves when he looked at them either, saying SFO accountant John Hicks had done that. But Hicks' testimony earlier this month indicates his analysis was cursory, at best.

The Director could not recall instructing Hicks to lie to European Pacific or Stephen Lunn about progress with the winebox in October and November 1992, but claimed that it was OK for law enforcement agencies to make misleading statements if necessary.

Apart from the obvious, the astute reader may also have picked up that Sturt prepared a statement to be read out in Parliament implying that Stephen Lunn had asked for public money and been turned down, when Lunn had never made such a request of Sturt. Not only had the SFO director got his facts wrong, again, but he was deliberately smearing Lunn through innuendo.

Charles Sturt is a liar.

For the record, Lunn offered me the Winebox papers and never once asked for money. Even if Lunn had asked others for money, as transcripts of evidence would later suggest, he never asked Sturt or the SFO, and for a law enforcement agency to publicly imply that he had – without first checking their facts – was not only incredibly incompetent detective work but also utterly misleading.

Sturt's claim that he was qualified as the expert investigator – and lawyer, as he would also tell the Inquiry – should be viewed in the context of this admission about his understanding of the Magnum deal:

> *"I found the deal particularly complicated when I first saw it and, as I have said, I never carried out a sophistication – a sophisticated analysis of it. That was beyond me, it was beyond – either as a lawyer or an investigator."*

His perusal of the Magnum documents, however, was enough for him to conveniently declare that there was no evidence of fraud, at a time when the Government and European Pacific still believed there was a chance that the public would never get to see the Winebox documents.

Sturt told the Inquiry that he relied on the Magnum transaction document and its accompanying wiring diagram in making his decision. In making this admission he again proves to my mind his utter incompetence as a lawyer and a fraud investigator: as revealed in *The Paradise Conspiracy* four years ago, the documents contained what appeared to be a deliberate error. If you take the main transaction document and the European Pacific wiring diagram at face value, the two million dollar tax swizz is not visible.

The SFO boss couldn't even detect the discrepancies in the documents in front of him, nor was he capable of matching them up with the real transaction documents.

Nor, importantly, was Sturt able to define "fraud" in any meaningful sense, when asked.

"Well, the features that are essential are certainly – without going into the actus reus and mens rea – how can I easily explain it?

"It's acting dishonestly in terms – and without entitlement. That is the – I think the basic definition that one can actually make of it."

Pressed on what this meant, Sturt was vague, but perked up when asked how he might recognise fraud.

"What would alert me to an issue of illegality would be a document containing reference to a dishonest dealing. What I am referring to here are comments by the author – or authors of these documents.

"That is what gets behind – what does, in fact, trigger one's particular attention to a deal that then follows."

In other words, the SFO needed a written admission from criminals before they could recognise fraud in documents.

News feature, February 22, 1997

There are weeks at the Winebox Inquiry when things go from the ridiculous to the even more ridiculous. This has been one of those weeks.

Leaving aside, momentarily, the self-inflicted destruction of Serious Fraud Office director Charles Sturt, let's turn to an example from the man who once told his staff: "If the oven's too hot, stay out of the chicken!"

Sturt is a man whose weapon of choice at this inquiry appears to have been "boomerang chickens", the kind that come home to roost more rapidly than most, with the added advantage that they'll return right to the hand of the thrower.

One such boomerang-chicken clucked its way free of wherever Chas Sturt keeps his chickens cooped up, and promptly proceeded to dive-bomb its owner with eggs. It came as Sturt was trying to prove that he understood a key winebox deal involving Australia's notorious Bond Corporation and what Sturt says was a Cook Islands money-laundering loop.

"These were all loans," said the SFO director, putting on his expert winebox investigator hat and tone, "that were involved with Bond through a subsidiary of Bond Corporation called BellSouth."

Hold the phone? Did he say BellSouth?? The journalists on the media bench, and certainly most of the assembled lawyers, presumed that Sturt meant a Bond Corp subsidiary called Bell Resources, not in any way connected with the multi-national phone company. But no, Sturt was adamant.

"We were looking at the figures that were into many millions of dollars," he said knowledgably, "and I said this is all tied in with DFC and, of course, BellSouth which, as I say, is a subsidiary of Bond."

By this time we were wincing, as the country's top corporate fraud cop kept firing at an innocent corporate.

"It involved a money laundering type situation using DFC as the ticket puncher, in terms of receiving and simply forwarding on through to BellSouth what had been perpetrated by BellSouth in terms of transfers of some $50 million odd."

Poor old BellSouth. Up to its eyeballs on most days with claim and counter-claim against rival cellphone giant Telecom, I imagine the Winebox Inquiry was the last place not only on earth but in the entire galaxy that BellSouth figured it could possibly suffer any collateral damage or ambush attacks.

By now I had a mental image of BellSouth's PR chief James Norman – a likeable fellow – caught like a possum in Charles Sturt's headlights, as if he'd suddenly been beamed straight from his office into the middle of the SFO's road to hell at the Winebox Inquiry.

By now, the corners of the journalists' mouths were beginning to twitch. And still the SFO director continued.

"The situation regarding BellSouth ... was a matter of considerable concern and after discussion with the [Australian Securities Commission] they welcomed the evidence which they maintained was strong evidence of criminality."

This couldn't continue. Someone, anyone, please throw Chas Sturt a line. Any kind of line will do (except perhaps a phone line).

"You referred to BellSouth being involved," said Colin Carruthers QC. "Were you referring to Bell Resources?"

In a word, nope.

"I seem to have BellSouth on my mind," said the director. "I am sure it is BellSouth."

Later on, Sturt referred to another company involved in the deal called "Weeks".

"I might add at this stage," he said helpfully, "that this Weeks involvement – no pun intended but it does ring a bell."

"Resources or South?" teased the Davison Commission QC gently, obviously unable to resist the temptation.

"South" said Sturt definitively, "because what strikes me straight away is the monies involved ... in tranches of $50 million odd."

It was too much. By now the packed media bench was in hysterics, along with grins from many of the lawyers and those members of the public gallery familiar with mobile phones. And still the director of the Serious Fraud Office hadn't twigged. He had to be rescued a few minutes later, as his besmirchment of the cellphone network threatened to get out of hand.

The exchange, to me, neatly sums up the quality of the SFO's winebox examination: a turkey, not a chicken, and singularly lacking the 11 secret herbs and spices that could have made it a successful recipe.

With every day that passes at the inquiry, the Serious Fraud Office is looking more and more like law enforcement's answer to *Dad's Army*.

As the week ends, we now have on the record that the SFO director allowed a statement to go to Parliament that he knew was wrong, and that in general terms he believes it's OK for a law enforcement agency to be misleading in some circumstances.

We have an admission that, after Charles Sturt had tarred and feathered winebox whistleblower Stephen Lunn and basically accused him of being an extortionist trying to sell the winebox documents for profit in 1992, Sturt now admits that he has no proof of this and, what's more, Lunn never once demanded money from the SFO.

We now know Charles Sturt was using the Royal "we" when he said in 1994 that a team of SFO investigators – note the plural – had investigated the winebox. Under cross examination he admitted that he personally was the only investigator – singular – who looked at the winebox, as well as being the only SFO "lawyer" to examine it – a kind of lone corporate Rambo against the winebox. "I regarded myself as wearing various hats," said the director.

There was also an admission that his use of the word "investigation" in a statement released to Parliament had also been injudicious, given that "there never was an investigation carried out, no."

The SFO gave away the original winebox documents to European Pacific, despite what's known as the "best evidence rule" which requires prosecution agencies to hold the originals as exhibits of evidence for possible prosecutions down track.

There is far, far more which I shall recount next week, but for now I offer a sage piece of advice to the director of the Serious Fraud Office: People in ovens should not throw chickens.

It should have been the SFO's darkest hour, but that was still to come.

Chapter 5

Mayday! We're Going Down

"I was court-martialled in my absence, and sentenced to death in my absence, so I said they could shoot me in my absence."
Brendan Behan (1923–64), Irish playwright. The Hostage

The game, as far as the media, Commission lawyers, many politicians and the public were concerned, was up. The issue of Serious Fraud Office and IRD incompetence had been soundly proven. All that was still up in the air was the murky topic of corruption.

Sturt, after finding himself being bested by Carruthers on the witness stand, had a nervous breakdown and took a break to recover.

In his absence, meanwhile, another SFO staff member who plainly believed his boss was wrong was taking the witness stand, and it would be arguably the most damaging testimony that the SFO would face. We touched on it briefly earlier, now here's the detail.

The SFO's Chief Investigator, Geoff Downey, told the Commission he'd been authorised to follow up allegations of fraud within the BNZ from mid-1992 onwards.

There were suggestions of senior bank executives receiving "kickbacks" in return for approving large loans to corporates, and allegations of other foul play.

Downey explained that his inquiries took him to London in March 1993 for an interview with a former senior bank executive, identified only as "Mr B.", who suggested he should be looking at certain areas and certain people within the Bank. The informant was unable to provide any corroborative evidence of his own, but did pass on the names of two executives who he said would be worth talking to.

When Geoff Downey, previously a police Detective Inspector with 16 years' experience, returned to New Zealand he briefed Sturt on his progress, and asked to continue following up the leads.

"He indicated to me," Downey told the inquiry, "that he did not want the matter to go any further, whatsoever.

"He told me that our friends in Wellington would not appreciate the office inquiring into the Bank of New Zealand and, in particular, he did not want to give Winston Peters any further ammunition or cause in regards to his call for an inquiry into the Bank."

"What did you understand from the reference to 'our friends in Wellington'?" asked Colin Carruthers QC.

"I clearly took that, and had no doubt, that he was referring to members of the National Party who were then in Government."

Sturt and Downey had been friends for nearly 30 years. The decision to testify against Sturt had not been taken lightly, and had only come about as a result of a Commission subpoena.

News feature, March 8, 1997
Memo: To Charles Sturt, SFO Director
From: Susan Pilgrim & Geoff Downey
Re: Winebox Appreciation Society Dinner

"How would you like your goose cooked, Sir?"

And that, folks, just about sums it up. Two and a half years after it began, the Winebox Inquiry is within days of finishing its public hearings, subject only to the possible return of the aforementioned Charles E. Sturt to face the conclusion of his cross-examination.

Back in 1994, Parliamentary pugilist Winston Peters, wearing the attractive multi-million dollar wine-boxer shorts, suggested that a full Commission of Inquiry would hear evidence from staff within the IRD and the SFO testifying against their bosses.

At that time, the two Government departments were a lot tighter, and the general consensus was that they would ride out any inquiry unscathed. Slowly but surely, however, the cracks appeared. First it was a string of rebel IRD staff who alleged some of the winebox deals were fraud, who questioned the propriety of secret settlements with a major lawfirm involved in film deals, and who alleged the department had been blackmailed.

Now, SFO director Charles Sturt gets his chance to say "Et tu, Bruté?", in the wake of damning evidence from two of his formerly most-trusted lieutenants. First, former Senior Prosecutor Susan Pilgrim told the inquiry that staff were worried about the way the SFO had investigated the winebox, and believed that Sturt was incompetent.

Then the director himself had to admit misleading Parliament albeit, he claimed, unintentionally. But for king-hits you can't really go past the SFO's Chief Investigator Geoff Downey, a former Detective Inspector with 16 years' experience in the NZ police who joined the SFO in 1990.

Subpoenaed to appear by the Commission, he was asked about investigations he'd made into allegations of fraud at the BNZ. The allegations had come to the SFO in mid-1992, and Downey had been given the task of working through them.

His inquiries took him to darkest Africa – Gambia, in fact – where he located a former senior BNZ executive who'd spent 25 years in the world's top banks, including the Bank of America, the First National Bank of Chicago and a subsidiary of Natwest, Royal Bank.

Hired on a five year contract in 1986 to work for the BNZ he left only a few months later, concerned that fraud may be taking place. He described the BNZ as "alien" and told Downey at an interview in London in March 1993 that the BNZ didn't "smell" right.

Downey came back from his London sojourn with no hard evidence of fraud, but with several leads to follow including the names of two more senior BNZ executives who could help the SFO with its inquiries.

On taking his findings to Sturt, however, the former top policeman found a frosty reception.

"He indicated to me that he did not want the matter to go any further, whatsoever. He told me that our friends in Wellington would not appreciate the Office inquiring into the Bank of New Zealand and, in particular, he did not want to give Winston Peters any further ammunition or cause in regards to his call for an inquiry into the Bank."

Well, I'm sorry. In my opinion, that evidence is perhaps some of the most damning testimony to emerge at the inquiry. At the stage that you have the head of a law enforcement agency quashing further inquiry into allegations of fraud, on the basis that it might upset "our friends in Wellington", then in my view you have corruption.

If you can't trust your law enforcement authorities to do their job without fear or favour, who can you trust?

It is important to remember, of course, that there is no evidence before the inquiry to show that any political pressure was brought to bear on the SFO.[7] However, it is enough that Sturt apparently gave it as a reason to

---

[7] It's academic now, in 1999, but if Sturt had "coughed" at this point to the alleged contacts by Paul East in other investigations, it probably would have been sufficient to get the Attorney-General subpoenaed to

shut the inquiry down. This shows a major flaw in Sturt's character, to my mind, that he would even consider it.

Senior SFO counsel Willie Young QC attempted a novel and obviously untested form of damage control. Three times, Dr Young asked whether Downey was "intending to suggest that Mr Sturt had acted in an improper way?"

Not content with Downey's attempts to be diplomatic, the QC's tone became more acerbic.

"Just listen to the question and answer it," he snapped. "Were you *intending* to suggest that Mr Sturt had acted in an improper way."

"Yes," sighed Downey.

The sinking of the BNZ investigation, apparently for political reasons, is a telling indictment on the morality of the Serious Fraud Office in my opinion. The fact that it became public right at the end of the inquiry was ironic, especially as one day earlier European Pacific's QC Richard Craddock had lambasted both Winston Peters and the Inquiry for failing to find evidence of fraud and corruption.

Arguably, the BNZ issue per se is not a winebox one. However, its relevance is unquestionable, given that BNZ informants had gone to the SFO and tipped that office off about certain matters which later turned up in the winebox. Those matters were never investigated by the SFO, even though the winebox documents gave them the documentary evidence to substantiate some of the earlier claims.

If the SFO failed to properly investigate the BNZ winebox deals because of a dodgy decision to leave the bank alone for political reasons, then it brings the matter smack bang within the Inquiry's terms of reference.

Interestingly, prior to the 1990 election that swept National into power, the part had indeed been planning to hold an inquiry into the BNZ. The MP co-ordinating it was Ian McLean, and Brian Henry was the barrister he approached to help. After the election, the Government backed rapidly away from the inquiry idea.

But it wasn't just alleged corruption that surrounded the BNZ issue. There was also a suggestion of SFO incompetence.

Sturt, already under pressure from a devastating cross-examination by Counsel Assisting the Commission, was then sent reeling by lawyers for Winston Peters, who were keen to score a technical knockout on points.

---

appear at the Inquiry. At the time, however, Sturt was keen to emphasise that politicians didn't attempt to influence him.

Barrister Brian Henry honed in on the BNZ captive insurance scheme which had been set up by tax haven company European Pacific, and highlighted the fact that New Zealand law at the time required companies promoting insurance schemes to pay a half million dollar bond to regulatory agencies.

Asked if he'd checked the matter when examining the scheme as the self-appointed SFO lawyer on the winebox, Sturt told the inquiry that he failed to see the relevance.

"Well, Mr Sturt, if someone is marketing an insurance policy in New Zealand, they need to comply with New Zealand law, don't they?"

"Yes."

"And if they are required to pay a $500,000 deposit and have not, it goes to honesty, doesn't it?"

"Yes," admitted the SFO director, who also agreed that it was the SFO's task to look at issues regarding honesty.

It's a pretty basic point: if European Pacific failed to comply with insurance law then how could the $200 million scheme to hide BNZ losses stack up? The SFO Director was so incompetent, in my view, that he hadn't even considered the point.

Henry then tackled the director over a letter Sturt had received from a former top BNZ executive, Dr Brian Perry, in July 1992.

The letter warned that the BNZ appeared to have loaned the Fay Richwhite group more than a billion dollars by mid 1989, in a series of transactions deliberately hidden from Reserve Bank scrutiny. Dr Perry said such an exposure to a customer was excessive by world standards.

International banks normally keep lending to any one customer under a limit of up to 15% of the bank's shareholders funds.

"Do you know that the Bank of New Zealand shareholders funds at March 1989 were $389 million?" asked Brian Henry. "Do you know that that represents an exposure of 257% of the Bank's shareholders' funds?"

"I accept what you say," said Sturt.

Dr Perry also suggested that some of the BNZ money loaned to Fay Richwhite may have been used to help the merchant bank buy its 30 percent stake in the BNZ in 1989, which would have made the buy-in illegal under section 62 of the Companies Act.

Sturt admitted he had not investigated Dr Perry's allegations, even though he knew the BNZ had collapsed the year after the buy-in and required a massive taxpayer bailout. Sturt said he *overlooked* the matter when he told his Minister the SFO had found nothing to investigate regarding the BNZ.

"What is the use of an intelligence file if you overlook it?" railed Brian Henry.

Significantly, Sturt attempted to retract his earlier admission that he mislead Parliament and the Commission when he said the SFO had not attempted to hand back the Winebox to European Pacific in 1992, but the reader can make up their own mind based on the contents of Sturt's documents.

When Sturt finally returned to the witness box on the Ides of March, 1997, though, the SFO Caesar was left to contemplate the frenzied stabbing he'd received from previously loyal lieutenants.

"I, like every other manager of any organisation, will have malcontents in the Office," muttered the Director, "who, for their own reasons, may see fit to exploit a particular situation. I have always believed that I have 90 percent a very good staff and 10 percent who may not be as loyal and competent. And the same applies to former staff."

Judging from the evidence presented to the hearing much of the alleged disloyalty appeared to be concentrated in the upper ranks, if that was the case.

As just one example, the SFO's Deputy Director, Terence Healey, bumped into me in the corridor at the Winebox Inquiry.

"The man is dangerous. He's got to be stopped," Healey said of his boss.

Healey, while Sturt had been on sick leave, had assessed the BNZ information and decided to launch a formal inquiry into the Bank of New Zealand. Sturt, on his recovery, quashed the investigation and arranged for Healey to resign.

But Sturt's alleged 'malcontents' did not exactly rush forward to give evidence voluntarily, however. Against their wishes they were summonsed by order of the Commission to appear and tell all. Hardly, as Colin Carruthers QC pointed out to Sturt, "exploiting" a situation for their own ends.

On oath, Charles Sturt said that he found Downey's BNZ suggestion preposterous, and appalling. He would not, however, say that Downey was lying.

"Are you suggesting that Mr Downey is not telling the truth on this point?" asked Carruthers.

"All I am suggesting," said the Director, "is that I find it quite absurd.

"I think if you looked at my record, you'll find that I investigated two politicians in the National Government. I initiated it myself. I have investigated close friends of very senior politicians.[8]

"I have investigated, on my own initiative, the former Auditor-General.

---

8 The willingness to investigate something is not a 'badge of courage', in my view. It is the willingness to prosecute such a matter in the face of political opposition that would be the test. As Sturt did not prosecute the Winebox, his comments are irrelevant. He has never put his office to the test.

Again, take that on board. Now I have always been independent and the integrity of my office is dependent on that independence."

Sturt suggested Downey's recall of the incident, which took place four years ago, was incorrect and very different from the way Sturt remembered the conversation.

But Caesar himself ran into memory problems, when he was asked to recall a conversation he had with broadcaster Paul Holmes only the previous week. There were two conversations with Holmes – the first initiated by the TV performer, but the origins of the second shrouded in memory fog.

"Are you telling us," asked Colin Carruthers, "that you can't remember whether you rang him or he rang you?"

"I can't," replied the Director. It was around this time that Sturt had one of his last contacts with the Attorney-General.

> *"Out of the blue came a call from the Attorney-General, Paul East, who wanted to stress that I was not to continue with my direction of the Aotearoa Television investigation. This was a political hot potato, given the allegations being made against former broadcaster and New Zealand First MP Tuku Morgan.*
>
> *"As a former director of the Maori television channel Morgan was being accused of spending company funds for his own personal benefit – there was talk of wining and dining, overseas trips and, of course, the purchase of those now famous underpants.*
>
> *"East had already told Parliament that I was off the case. This had been yet another body blow, as I had always held rigidly to the guiding principle that as Director of the SFO I could not be subject to political interference. That principle was reflected in the Serious Fraud Office statute, and I had always contended that the Office would only retain its integrity if it retained its independence.*
>
> *"Yet here I was getting instructions from the Attorney-General in a government whose Deputy Prime Minister also happened to be leader of the alleged offender's party. It left a sour taste in my mouth."*

Sturt gave in, and a few weeks later resigned.

In my view, there was a simple explanation for the SFO's failure to properly investigate the Winebox. I believe it was corruption, motivated by ill will.

To test that, one must first determine what "corruption" is.

Microsoft Bookshelf, using the resources of *The American Heritage Dictionary*, defines corruption as follows:

cor·rupt (ke-rùpt*1*) *adjective*
1. Marked by immorality and perversion; depraved.
2. Venal; dishonest: *a corrupt mayor.*
cor·rupt·ed, cor·rupt·ing, cor·rupts *verb, transitive*
1. To destroy or subvert the honesty or integrity of.
2. To ruin morally; pervert.
3. To taint; contaminate.[9]

I note the reference to "subverting the honesty or integrity of".

Comptons Reference Collection echoes the suggestion that corruption can include immorality or even behaviour that deteriorates from what is expected.

cor·rupt (k rupt) **adj.** [[ME < L *corruptus*, pp. of *corrumpere*, to destroy, spoil, bribe < *com-*, together + *rumpere*, to break: see RUPTURE]] 1 orig., changed from a sound condition to an unsound one; spoiled; contaminated; rotten 2 deteriorated from the normal or standard; specif., *a)* morally unsound or debased; perverted; evil; depraved *b)* taking bribes; venal *c)* containing alterations, errors, or admixtures of foreignisms (said of texts, languages, etc.) vt., vi. to make or become corrupt **SYN**. DEBASE **cor·rupt er** or **cor·rup·tor n. cor·rupt·ly** adv. **cor·rupt·ness n.**[10]

For further context, there is Burmese Nobel Prizewinner Aung San Suu Kyi, whose definitions of corruption were tabled into the record at the Winebox Inquiry.

In 1991 she wrote:

> *"It is not power that corrupts but fear. Fear of losing power corrupts those who wield it, and fear of the scourge of power corrupts those who are subject to it.*
>
> *"Most Burmese are familiar with the four a-gati, the four kinds of corruption.*
>
> *"Chanda-gati, corruption induced by desire, is deviation from the right path in pursuit of bribes, or for the sake of those one loves.*
>
> *"Dosa-gati is taking the wrong path to spite those against whom one bears ill-will, and Moha-gati is aberration due to ignorance.*
>
> *"But perhaps the worst of the four is Bhaya-gati, for not only does Bhaya, fear, stifle and slowly destroy all sense of right and wrong, it so often lies at*

---

9   *The American Heritage ® Dictionary of the English Language*, Third Edition copyright © 1992 by Houghton Mifflin Company. Electronic version licensed from InfoSoft International, Inc. All rights reserved.
10   Excerpted from *Compton's Reference Collection* 1996. Copyright © 1995 Compton's NewMedia, Inc.

the root of the other three kinds of corruption.

"Just as Chanda-gati, when not the result of sheer avarice, can be caused by fear of want or fear of losing the goodwill of those one loves, so fear of being surpassed, humiliated or injured in some way can provide the impetus for ill will."

There is bucketloads of evidence that Charles Sturt nursed an almost pathological hatred of Winston Peters, that pre-dated Peters' attacks on Sturt.

I believe that Sturt didn't believe that Peters or anything he said was credible, and certainly disliked the MP attempting to make political capital out of topics that fell into his own serious fraud domain.

"I'm the expert," Sturt might have told himself, much as he said when Paul East questioned him over the Equiticorp case.

And so when Peters claimed something was fishy, maybe the SFO looked for evidence that would prove Peters wrong. After all, there are two sides to every story, maybe the SFO took a devil's advocate view of Peters' allegations and convinced themselves that prosecutions could never succeed.

The thought of delivering a political victory to Peters was probably anathema to Sturt, based on the evidence I've seen.

Failing to do one's official duty because of malice or political favouritism is still a form of corruption[inserted text follows], based on the definitions I've read.

A comment in Sturt's book speaks volumes about this, in my view. He writes:

"Life after the SFO has not been easy. Any work or appointments that I could reasonably expect, as a barrister, to have derived from Government evaporated when Winston Peters received his appointment as Deputy Prime Minister and Treasurer."

Is this how the system works in New Zealand? Do senior civil servants do their jobs in the expectation that retirement will bring lucrative Government contracts for them to work on as a reward?

Do the expectations that people like Charles Sturt have of some taxpayer-funded gravy train influence them in their duty to apply the law without fear or favour?

Is there an implicit message from political parties to top public servants: do a good job in our eyes and you'll be rewarded later?

I think so. I think the New Zealand system is inherently corrupt. Sturt clearly believed that he might get some Government contracts thrown his way, but that the appointment of Winston Peters spoiled all that.

Wow!

Significantly, corruption and bribery of a law enforcement officer is a criminal offence under section 104 of the Crimes Act. Under section 99 of that Act, the word *bribe* means 'any money, valuable consideration, office, or employment, or any benefit, whether direct or indirect'.

Under this definition, I believe Sturt's expectation of further employment could be an issue, if it was a motivating factor.

I also believe that there are wheels within wheels as far as the Winebox and related topics are concerned, and that the Inquiry's narrow terms of reference were simplistically interpreted as being an inquiry into whether a large, overarching, grand conspiracy existed.

Instead, maybe the Inquiry should have broken the concept down into smaller units: There is evidence suggesting corporates applied financial pressure to prevent a BNZ inquiry. This doesn't mean those same corporates conspired with the SFO and IRD to cover up the Winebox.

And yet Sturt's alleged dislike of Peters and desire not to give him more ammunition would dovetail nicely with the aims of those who didn't want to be investigated, even though there was no direct connection between the parties.

In another corner, there is evidence that the IRD was effectively blackmailed into signing an arguably unlawful document promising not to prosecute a group of influential people. But that doesn't mean that the SFO's reasons for not thoroughly investigating the issue were influenced by other parties.

And so on it could go.

Sir Ronald Davison, however, sat through all of the evidence that you've just read, and decided that:

"No evidence of unlawful conduct on the part of the SFO was detected. No impropriety on the part of the SFO was detected. The SFO cannot be held to have been incompetent."

Chapter 6

The Peters Factor

"If you know somebody is going to be awfully annoyed by something you write, that's obviously very satisfying, and if they howl with rage or cry, that's honey."
— *A. N. Wilson (b. 1950), British author*

No tale of Winebox intrigue could be complete without an appearance by the Master of Intrigue himself, Winston Peters. It was his allegations, after all, that had set the ball rolling all those years ago.

In analysing Peters' parliamentary speech of March 22, 1994[11], Sir Ronald Davison broke it down and measured it against his terms of reference. In that speech, Sir Ronald found:

Allegations Against SFO:
Impropriety – lying to the people of NZ
Incompetence – Finding nothing criminal in the documents. Mr Sturt claiming he cannot investigate tax fraud.
Incompetence – Failing to find evidence of fraud in the Magnum transaction.
Unlawfulness – Possible corruption by the SFO.
Impropriety – Being judge and jury in respect of decisions that should have been taken to prosecute in relation to the Magnum transaction.
Unlawfulness – Granting favours or accepting bribes.
Allegations Against IRD:
Incompetence – Finding no evidence of tax fraud in the Magnum transaction.
Unlawfulness – Conspiracy to pervert the course of justice.
Impropriety – Being judge and jury in respect of decisions that should

---
11 See The Paradise Conspiracy, p240

have been taken to prosecute in relation to the Magnum transaction.

Unlawfulness – granting favours or accepting bribes.

At the time Peters made the speech, there was no inquiry. In fact, the Government had made it abundantly clear on numerous occasions that it had no intention of setting up an inquiry into the BNZ, the Winebox, the Paul White affair, film and bloodstock deals or other similar matters.

As he told the Inquiry, he was being advised by sources to dig deep, and he would find a secret IRD agreement promising not to prosecute a group of Russell McVeagh lawyers for tax fraud. This agreement, they said, resulted from Russell McVeagh blackmailing the IRD into backing off.

It is illegal in this country to pressure a public official into not performing their duty. Section 309 of the Crimes Act states:

> *"Everyone is liable to imprisonment for a term not exceeding 2 years who conspires with any other person by force or intimidation to prevent the collection of any rates or taxes the levying of which is authorised by law."*

Two Russell McVeagh lawyers or associates were on the board of the Bank of New Zealand, and the BNZ itself was part controlled by Fay Richwhite, who had a long relationship with both Russell McVeagh and the BNZ in the promotion of various tax schemes, such as the ones in the Winebox.

Peters told Parliament "Who knows what favours are being called in or bribes being paid, even as we speak, to save the reputations of some of New Zealand's so-called leading business figures and top political campaign donors?"

In later private conversations, his lawyer Brian Henry has lamented the way the statement was deliberately taken out of context when the Winebox terms of reference were drafted.

"Winston honestly believed, when he said that, that corporate campaign donors had put pressure on the Government not to investigate certain matters. As far as he's concerned, campaign donations with strings attached are bribes," said Henry.

And yet the Inquiry, and the corporates, would be able to nail Peters to a cross if the comments were treated as referring specifically to the heads of the IRD and the SFO, and specifically in regard to the Winebox deals and nothing else.

For the corporates and Government strategists – and as you shall shortly discover they were the same person in some cases – the issue was a simple con-job on the public. Pin Peters down on something he didn't actually mean, force him to publicly justify it and crucify him when he can't prove it. Peters did, however, make their task easier. On June 1, 1994 he took his knowledge of the secret IRD non-prosecution agreement on the film deals, and his belief about campaign donors pressuring the Government and, by virtue of Fay Richwhite and the BNZ's role in European Pacific and Fay Richwhite's role in the BNZ, lumped them all together.

> *"Sturt and Henry should be suspended immediately. An inquiry should hear evidence linking these men to a criminal conspiracy involving Michael Fay, David Richwhite, Paul Collins [there because he was Brierley's rep on the EP board] Peter Travers and Lindsay Pyne, formerly of the BNZ. This conspiracy involved secret agreements by the IRD and SFO not to prosecute EPI."*

Unfortunately, as noted earlier, Sir Ronald Davison's Inquiry raised the possibility of corruption, particularly in regard to the SFO within the terms of reference, but did not pursue it beyond a he says/she says battle between two witnesses. The non-prosecution film deal, which even SFO lawyers acknowledged at the Inquiry was probably unlawful, fell outside the terms of reference, leaving Peters vulnerable to a technical knock-out.

This then, is the background to the appearance at the Winebox Inquiry in June 1996 of one Winston Raymond Peters.

News feature, June 1, 1996

An American General once recalled how, as a young platoon commander in World War II, he'd managed to get himself and his troops trapped on the business end of a vicious German assault.

Faced with insurmountable odds, the platoon commander and his boys kept pumping lead into anything that moved on the perimeter, at the same time dodging the massive volleys of return fire.

"What the hell's going on?" crackled headquarters over the radio.

"It's alright sir," replied the future General optimistically, "they've surrounded us again, the poor bastards!"

This coming Wednesday, as he takes the witness stand at the Winebox Inquiry amid a roomful of hostile lawyers, New Zealand First leader Winston Peters will be seeking inspiration from such lessons in history.

The showdown between the high-flying MP and lawyers for European Pacific, Fay Richwhite, Inland Revenue and the Serious Fraud Office is shaping up to be the grudge match of the decade: four years of pent-up fury desperately searching for an outlet.

If the crackle and spark could be harnessed, it could probably power the national grid several times over.

As the lone gunfighter facing overwhelming odds, Winston Peters goes in minus one "pop" in his gun – after Commissioner Sir Ronald Davison ordered him to open the chamber of his six-shooter and remove the bullet with the BNZ's name on it.

At a special hearing on Tuesday, the Peters legal team tried to argue that the BNZ captive insurance scheme, which resulted in a Securities Commission report in 1993, was a fraud on both the Reserve Bank and the BNZ's shareholders. They alleged the proceeds of the "insurance" scheme were used to cover up losses which, had they been declared, would have breached the bank's capital adequacy limit – which governs how much the BNZ is allowed to lend out.

They also managed to table, in support of their application to broaden the inquiry's scope to look at the deal, a damning affidavit from former BNZ property manager Larry Johnson, who alleges BNZ lawyers gave seminars to selected staff on how to sanitise bank files prior to court hearings.

It stemmed, said Dr Johnson, from the sharemarket and property market crashes in the late 1980s, and by 1990 the BNZ had set up an internal hit squad – the "recovery unit" – whose task it was to undertake "damage control in the event that litigation ensued at the behest of creditors."

He alleges the law firm Buddle Findlay taught recovery unit staff how to "record any file notes of an adverse or sensitive nature by using yellow Post-It stickers which could be easily cleansed from the bank's files."

Comforting news, I'm sure, to all of you who've ever tried to take legal action against a bank and seen them present a pristine and damaging file on you in court.

Dr Johnson also claims that he was part of a management team, including consultants Booz Allen Hamilton, who'd been asked to go through the BNZ's accounts and work out how big the 1990 loss was going to be.

When they finally came up with a number, Larry Johnson claims it was rejected by chief executive Lindsay Pyne because it was too high for him to "sell" to the Government. Several times, claims Dr Johnson, the team was asked to go away and think again.

"We started to consider how or if we could get a number acceptable to upstairs. I was surprised. We had done a proper analysis and reached the accurate figure we should be using, yet here was a recently appointed chief executive officer with no in-depth knowledge of the bank, in cavalier fashion telling us, apparently for political rather than commercial reasons, that the figure was still unacceptable.

"Someone at the meeting correctly made the comment that we are now inventing arbitrary figures."

Eventually, said Dr Johnson, a loss provisioning figure was plucked from thin air, about 25% or 30% below what he claims was the accurate one. This figure was more politically correct.

In an apparent side-swipe at the poor memories of his former BNZ colleagues, Dr Johnson's affidavit also included this gem about senior manager Ron Diack, who testified to the inquiry last year.

"Ronald James Diack was the real brain behind the bank. It was common comment that [General Manager] Peter Travers would sign off any deal provided Ron Diack told him it was good for the bank.

"Ron Diack has a very good banking knowledge and memory. He wasn't known as 'Sharp as a tack Ron Diack' for nothing!

"Ron Diack was the wiring diagram expert. One joke in the bank was he wrote up wiring diagrams and rubbed them off with his sleeve as he wrote. This was because he would always meticulously pick up all wiring diagrams and shred the paper or clean the whiteboards himself."

In response to the Peters push, BNZ counsel, Alan Galbraith QC, noted that Peters was really trying to use the insurance deal as a "ladder" to get stuck into the bigger issues of the BNZ's relationship with Fay Richwhite and the Government, issues outside the scope of this inquiry.

After much legal argument, including mutterings from Fay Richwhite QC, Rhys Harrison, about "conspiracy theories", Sir Ronald Davison ruled the BNZ deal was out of order because it didn't bear enough relevance to the inquiry's terms of reference – which focus on the SFO and IRD's competence in dealing with the winebox deals.

While Peters' counsel Brian Henry argued that the Securities Commission and a subsequent QC's report didn't address the issue of criminality, Sir Ronald appeared to adopt suggestions from his counsel, Colin Carruthers QC, that it was a little unfair to expect the SFO to investigate the deal after two reports recommending no further action.

Winston Peters says that while he understands the reasons for the Commission's ruling, it shows the need for an inquiry with wider terms of reference than the current one.

It is here that one of the most telling pieces of evidence arises that casts into doubt, to my mind, the integrity of both Sir Ronald Davison and his Winebox Inquiry judgment.

Unable to discuss the BNZ captive insurance deal, even though it was a winebox transaction, unable to discuss the BNZ itself, Brian Henry applied to Sir Ronald aside and sought permission and funding to call tax QC Tony Molloy as an expert witness to give evidence on Peters' behalf about the winebox tax deals.

Sir Ronald's answer was a firm "no".

"This is a criminal case," said Sir Ronald, "that does not need the public to meet the expense of Tony Molloy QC. The Americans, Brian, have a term for this: grand larceny."

Davison refused permission for Winston Peters to call Molloy as an expert witness, but then had the cheek in his report to say:

"Neither Dr Molloy nor Mr Darvell was called by Mr Henry to give evidence."

Sir Ronald then went on to attack Henry for failing to call witnesses to back up Peters' allegations.

Sir Ronald Davison is playing some kind of game, in my view. Sir Ronald knew he had refused permission for Peters to call Molloy, but then criticised Henry and Peters for not calling Molloy in his report. Criticising them for failing to call lawyer Paul Darvell as a witness was a little rich, as well, because Darvell had died of cancer some six months before Winston Peters was allowed to open his legal case at the Inquiry.

Darvell, a Rudd Watts & Stone partner, had been one of those who helped European Pacific set up its tax credit schemes. Ironically he was also the one to blow the whistle on them. As one of Winston Peters secret sources, Darvell told Peters, Henry and lawyer Chris Dickie that "if Equiticorp was a fraud, then this is doubly so."

Darvell had also been interviewed secretly by the Commission of Inquiry, but at that stage he was still practising as a lawyer and did not suggest to them that the deals he had helped design were fraudulent. Instead, he told Davison that having examined the Winebox documents he "could not see, on the face of it, any documents that particularly disclosed anything improper."

Contrast Sir Ronald Davison's]"grand larceny ... criminal" comment with his verdict saying there was "no fraud". Look at it also in the light of Peters being told which witnesses he can and cannot call, when no such restriction to my knowledge applied to the corporates, who did indeed call their own tax experts.

Given that Davison then lashed out at Peters and Henry in his final report for failing to provide evidence of tax fraud in the Winebox, doesn't this raise a very big issue about natural justice and improper behaviour by the Commission itself? It does to me.

Going into the Inquiry room that day, however, Peters and his lawyers knew they'd been nobbled by the terms of reference, but they were heartened by the fact that Davison's Inquiry had so far been robust. It was up to Brian Henry to launch the opening volleys of the MP's case.

Brian Henry said:

> *"The tradition of the civil service is one of neutrality. By choosing to enter the public debate [SFO director Charles Sturt and then-IRD Commissioner David Henry] stepped out from that neutrality and showed for whatever reason that they had a public view of the events.*
>
> *"Having stepped into the public arena, the clearances by the two civil servants stood as an absolute rebuttal of alternative debate. Mr Peters will give evidence he weighed the circumstances, the constitutional position of these civil servants was considered, their breach with tradition by entering into the public arena was considered along with the applicable law.*
>
> *"Mr Peters formed the view that the only explanation of all the events, of which the winebox transactions are but a part, is that they were either incompetent or corrupt. It was one or the other.*
>
> *"We do not regard this as a tax case, we regard it as a criminal case.*
>
> *"The intent throughout is to deprive the revenue of money that is rightfully its own. Put shortly: you make a lie, you tell that lie, someone acts on that lie, you gain from that lie – there can be no issue but that you intended to benefit by the lie."*

Far from backing away from the corruption allegations, Winston Peters ladled it on thick when he finally took the stand, claiming there was an orchestrated "attempted cover-up inside and outside of Parliament in respect of the winebox" which, taken in tandem with the BNZ issue, alleged fraud in the bloodstock and film partnerships and "the role of the Director of the Serious Fraud Office in respect of the Paul White affair", led to serious conclusions.

> *"I suspected that the civil servants of both the Serious Fraud Office and the Inland Revenue Department were not carrying out their statutory duties as required by law[12] and that, if my suspicions were true, they were protecting certain influential individuals associated with the winebox transactions."*

Peters told of the now infamous meeting at the vineyard of tax QC Tony

---

12 See *Lawyers, Guns & Money*, p218, "Incompetent? Or Corrupt?"

Molloy in April 1992 to discuss the alleged film and bloodstock crimes.

Also present, he said, were lawyers from McVeagh Fleming, the Auckland lawfirm hired to investigate the alleged frauds, an IRD officer named Alan May, and two staff from the Serious Fraud Office.

> "Dr Molloy recounted a detailed narrative of how tax fraud was deliberately and systematically perpetrated by certain Russell McVeagh McKenzie Bartleet & Co. tax partners. I understand these schemes were the work of a small clique within that lawfirm and not known to the wider partnership."

Peters said the meeting also discussed a settlement that Russell McVeagh's Geoff Clews had managed to nut out with the IRD – a settlement that the inquiry has already heard described as "blackmail" by another IRD staff member.

"The result of the vineyard meeting," continued Peters, was that both the Serious Fraud Office and Inland Revenue Department personnel had heard

> "A compelling suggestion that the Inland Revenue Department was being manipulated and improperly influenced by Russell McVeagh McKenzie Bartleet & Co."

Peters was later surprised to discover that the IRD's Alan May had apparently been "potted" to his bosses by the SFO, who he claimed had told the Revenue of the vineyard meeting.

> "The meeting was essentially an indictment of the Commissioner of Inland Revenue's decision, yet the director of the Serious Fraud Office – rather than investigating the statements of eminent Queens Counsel, appeared to have tipped off the Inland Revenue Department."

The MP says he laid a formal complaint with the SFO about the secret non-prosecution agreement in the *Merry Christmas Mr Lawrence* film partnership, and asked for an investigation of whether the IRD was covering up a crime. He claims the SFO failed to properly investigate his complaint.

Challenged by Willie Young QC to produce a shred of evidence to support claims of Serious Fraud Office corruption, Peters then waved the *Merry Christmas Mr Lawrence* settlement document between the IRD and Russell McVeagh.

> "Mr Young, I produced an agreement, an agreement which I told [Mr Sturt]

I believed was in existence. Why did he not find out about it?"

Willie Young later admitted

> "There may well be a real issue as to the enforceability of an agreement not to prosecute in this context. From the position of the SFO, we understand the argument that an agreement not to prosecute is, at the very least, highly likely to regarded as unenforceable."

Young told the MP it was one thing to say the agreement shouldn't have been entered into, but it was another thing to say "that anyone who enters into that agreement is corrupt, guilty of a criminal conspiracy and appropriately the subject of all the other florid epithets you use."

Young continued to question whether the MP had any evidence for his sweeping allegations, or whether his source was just "a man called Harry you met in a pub?"

"You asked me did I get my information from people like Harry," responded Peters a little later. "I did get information the other day from a person like Harry. In fact, it came from a legal personality in Christchurch. It relates to a court case in which the judge felt compelled to make a comment as to why the Serious Fraud Office had not prosecuted a certain party for conviction he felt would have been a certainty.

"I was alarmed to learn that the person acting for that certain party was the same person acting for the Serious Fraud Office, namely yourself."

"So the cover-up and the conspiracy gets ever wider, does it?" sneered Young.

Again, on the face of it, an alleged conflict of interest for the SFO, but again outside the terms of reference. This time relating to the Fortex trial and the SFO's decision not to prosecute a man that the judge felt should have been charged.

Peters told the inquiry that the lawyer advising the SFO, and the lawyer representing the man the SFO *didn't* prosecute, was the same lawyer, Willie Young QC, now a judge himself.

Based on what the Inquiry was told, in my view it is a shocking conflict of interest that casts little credit on Justice Young.

News feature, June 8, 1996

The sweet little old lady gazed around the packed Winebox Inquiry hearing room as they adjourned for the day, and shared a sweet little old lady thought with a passing journalist.

"The sods," she exclaimed, "they're just trying to trick him, but Winnie's too clever for them!"

If she'd had an umbrella, she probably would have poked it at someone. Under normal circumstances, the hapless victim would probably have been a journalist. But these were not normal circumstances, and today anyone dressed like a lawyer was fair game.

She and 50 others had bussed up from Tauranga on Wednesday to see New Zealand First leader Winston Peters in action at the inquiry, all of them wearing NZ First campaign buttons and not afraid to show a little verbal solidarity for the man whose parliamentary speeches caused this inquiry.

Added to a 150 strong crowd of other interested observers, the tour bus contingent completed a sizeable welcoming force for the MP – spontaneous applause marking his entrance, and fellow NZ First MPs Tau Henare and Jack Elder providing the honour guard.

At one time, 25 media personnel, including three television crews and a battalion of newspaper photographers, were darting all over the hearing room looking for vantage points and photo-opportunities.

Wednesday was definitely Winston's day. From the moment the bell rang and Winston came out of his corner, the MP took time between punches to play his audience like a piano, talking easy to understand concepts like "one tax law for everybody".

Every time he scored a point against his foes, it was as if a Mexican wave was surging through the public gallery.

"Good on yer, Winston!" rang one voice in the midst of one particularly telling exchange.

At times, also, it took on the flavour of a tennis final at Wimbeldon, as the politician and the SFO lawyer served and rallied to the ooh's, ahh's and tut-tut's from the back of the room.

Not that SFO QC Willie Young was working from Dale Carnegie's book on winning friends and influencing people.

"I meet people every day around this country," Peters had said, "possibly I have spoken to 180,000 of them in the last year at public meetings. I have not had one get up and say: 'Mr Peters, you should not be saying those awful things about the Serious Fraud Office.'"

"Perhaps you mix in the wrong company," said Willie Young, forgetting for a moment that some 200 ordinary New Zealanders were sitting behind him.

They hissed, booed, and sucked in their breath as one, leaving Winston Peters to capitalise on the moment.

"Well, if you regard the New Zealand people as being the wrong company,

I can understand that given the circles you mix with," the MP snapped back.

Surprisingly, there were no more NZ First busloads for the rest of the week, but nevertheless a large cross-spectrum of ordinary people managed to fill the public benches, and still managed to tut-tut in the appropriate places.

The big mystery, at the end of the week though, is not whether Winston Peters will end up getting six of the best from Fay Richwhite QC Rhys Harrison, but rather: who was the person that fluently signed themselves in on the visitors' log as "Oliver Stone – film director", and was the signature related to the American man in the elevator who asked for directions to "this Winebox Inquiry"?

News feature, June 9, 1996

They wanted bread and circuses, they got Christians and a lion at the Winebox Inquiry this week.

The inquiry took a decidedly political and primal turn with the appearance of New Zealand First leader Winston Peters, and rather than a biblical Daniel entering the lions' den, it was more akin to Rome's Christians inviting 300kgs of furry, slavering trouble into their midst.

Trouble wasted no time making his presence felt.

His counsel, Brian Henry, started proceedings by declaring open season on Serious Fraud Office boss Charles Sturt and former Inland Revenue commissioner David Henry. The reason? Both men had made public statements pouring cold water on Peters' winebox allegations.

"It is the decision not to investigate, not to inquire and ultimately not to prosecute for which there is no check or balance in New Zealand society, save the integrity of the civil servants and their staff," explained Peters' lawyer.

Like a big cat feeling confined by the inquiry's narrow terms of reference, Peters first tested those limits and then sprang right over the top of them.

He talked of the BNZ bailout and the flow-on financial trouble it caused – Sir Ronald Davison stepped in and told Brian Henry to put Peters back on his leash.

"Mr Henry," warned Sir Ronald, "I notice there are references being made to the Bank of New Zealand which I have ruled is not the subject of the inquiry."

The leash didn't hold for long. Winston Peters said there was a much bigger background picture to his corruption and incompetence allegations than the one he was being allowed to paint.

He questioned "the role of the Director of the Serious Fraud Office in respect of the Paul White affair", before quickly adding "however, I'm advised by my counsel that this simply can't be brought within the terms of reference."

Even so, like flies to fly paper or lions to a carcass, the MP and SFO lawyer, Dr Willie Young QC, couldn't leave the mysterious death of Paul White alone.

"With respect to the Citibank tapes," said Dr Young, "Phillip Roigard [of the SFO] made contact with you on the 11th of September 1992 … and he would, if necessary, say that he asked you four times whether you had evidence [of fraud], was unable to get a straight answer and concluded that you didn't!"

"With respect," retorted Peters, "here is a Serious Fraud Office that uplifts a series of tapes which an expert in that technology told me would take about two weeks to clear. They cleared it in 48 hours."

The lion-tamer running the show cracked his whip again.

"Mr Peters," intervened Sir Ronald Davison, "this is not relevant."

"But he asked me, Your Honour," said Winston plaintively.

"Whether he asked you or not, I am telling you it is not relevant," said Sir Ronald in a tone of voice that indicated Winston Peters would be sent back to his cage if he didn't behave.

The MP also alluded to the "orchestration of an attempted cover-up inside and outside of Parliament in respect of the winebox," and "the sad public televised spectacle" of the Government preventing the documents from being tabled.

But Winston Peters roared longest and loudest about the document that he says proves his claim of corruption – the infamous, previously secret, agreement by the Inland Revenue Department not to prosecute partners in the law firm Russell McVeagh for their role in the Merry Christmas Mr Lawrence film partnership.

This was a document that one senior IRD officer refused to sign – she told the inquiry last year she felt the IRD was being "blackmailed". When she refused to agree to the terms of the deal, including a promise not to prosecute, it was signed on her behalf by her boss, Tony Bouzaid, in Wellington.

"I believe such an agreement is unlawful," growled the NZ First leader at the SFO QC, Dr Willie Young.

"In this country we have tax laws and they are for everybody, not one law for one group of people and a different set of tax laws for others.

"A serious criminal conspiracy has been wrongfully covered up in circumstances where the Commissioner of Inland Revenue knew he had, and still has a duty, to initiate a prosecution. I am talking here about the law being applied equally, identically, to everyone."

Winston Peters laid a formal complaint with SFO director Charles Sturt about the alleged cover-up by the IRD, but says the SFO never even picked up the phone to ask the IRD for a copy of the settlement document before clearing it.

Dr Young later acknowledged that there was a "real issue" as to whether a non-prosecution agreement was legally enforceable, but he said that was a different matter entirely from suggesting that parties to such an agreement were criminals.

I suspect, however, that both sides in this primal struggle will be claiming victory. Winston Peters keeps on punching in words of one syllable that most people can understand. The SFO and IRD lawyers, on the other hand, have also scored points, showing an MP with a sometimes inaccurate memory when it came to chronology.

Peters told the inquiry that he hadn't had time to familiarise himself with previous evidence or transactions, and it showed. When it came to detail on some issues, he was out of his depth, a casualty – he said – of having to run a political party and having to fight off up to 14 current lawsuits.

"Mr Peters," asked Willie Young at the close of his questioning, " isn't the position here that in this respect and in other respects, you have made allegations of dishonesty and corruption where you simply haven't understood what was done and why, and can't even explain it now?"

Winston Peters, for his part, says he was never a financial "whizz-boy" and took expert advice on transactions, basing his views on that advice.

Nevertheless, the politician showed consistency. He began this quest by asking hard questions. He came to the inquiry still asking those questions, not offering answers. That, he maintains, is the job of the inquiry.

Peters had started the week well, but around 3pm on the Friday his blood sugar levels must have dropped, and he allowed Fay Richwhite's dangerous QC Rhys Harrison to back him into a corner.

Steering clear of the wider allegations of illegality in the winebox deals themselves – Harrison repeatedly asked Peters to produce any evidence specifically showing his clients had been responsible for the alleged corruption of the IRD and SFO.

"Mr Peters, you have made the most serious allegations of criminality over many years against those two civil servants and my clients. You don't have the courage now to acknowledge that those allegations have no factual basis whatsoever, do you?"

"Yes I do Mr Harrison, with respect. We have sat here for month after month, over two years, looking into the most serious transactions which were given preferential treatment by the Serious Fraud Office and the IRD, and no amount of shouting at me is going to change that!"

Harrison's biggest coup came by accident however, when he badgered an angry Peters into repeating some hearsay evidence which he said showed SFO boss Charles Sturt knew Sir Michael Fay. Little did Peters know it, but he'd inadvertently grabbed one of Chas Sturt's "boomerang chickens".

Peters promised to find the source of the claim and bring her to the Inquiry the following week, so in the interim Fay Richwhite's cross examination on other matters continued.

Peters had, of course, failed to have the BNZ issue placed on the Inquiry's agenda, after strenuous opposition by all parties except the Inland Revenue Department.

Trying to rectify some of the collateral damage suffered by David Richwhite and Sir Michael Fay during Peters' brief unauthorised sojourns into the BNZ affair, Rhys Harrison wanted to take Peters to task on some of those matters, but only succeeded in creating more collateral damage, mostly at the expense of the SFO.

On the subject, for example, of the 1989 BNZ sale to Capital Markets and the 1990 bailout, Peters said the SFO should have investigated given the huge public controversy and concern.

"My evidence, Mr Harrison, is that on [the SFO's] formation, presumably for very similar issues like this, it did nothing. That's evidence of neglect, slothfulness, idleness!"

"Mr Peters," snapped back the QC with a hard edge to his voice, "if this was a matter of such moment to you, why did you not write a letter of complaint?"

"Because, Mr Harrison, when I became a member of Cabinet, I had become a member of a Cabinet that had promised a full scale inquiry into this very matter, and when the National Government got into power it did exactly nothing on this matter … I would have thought in that situation, the Serious Fraud Office would have done that investigation."

It was all too much for SFO counsel Nick Davidson, who interjected to ask for the issues to be brought back within the terms of reference. Sir Ronald's response was swift.

"Mr Harrison, I am going to put a closure on this line of inquiry as far as the Bank of New Zealand is concerned. I have allowed it to go on, but I have had enough."

The ruling is understood to have provoked furious discussions within the

Fay Richwhite team as to how to deal with the Peters problem.

David Richwhite was seen arguing loudly with Harrison as they walked up Auckland's steep Shortland Street a few minutes later.

"Shut it down! We've wasted enough money on this already. If we can't ask the questions just shut it down."

Across the city, Sir Michael Fay was enjoying lunch in a chic restaurant when his mobile rang. His conversation indicated he agreed with Richwhite.

The result of those discussions was revealed on the following Tuesday afternoon.

"Commissioner," began Rhys Harrison, "I am instructed to terminate my cross-examination of Mr Peters at this point ... in view of your direction that I am unable to cross-examine Mr Peters on any issues relating to the Bank of New Zealand which are not winebox-related."

Harrison set out a number of areas in the transcript where Fay Richwhite or its directors had taken hits outside the terms of reference.

"In view of Your Honour's ruling, I am prevented from testing the credibility of those allegations. I simply wish to record that those allegations are emphatically rejected by the parties whom I represent."

The irony of Fay Richwhite finding itself restricted by the narrow terms of reference hadn't been lost on Winston Peters either.

"If you think that this matter requires further investigation," he'd growled during one of their earlier arguments, "why didn't you join me and my counsel in opening this matter up, but you did your best to shut it down and, more importantly, you asked for a secret inquiry Mr Harrison. Now you are on your back saying something else!"

Of all those to take a tilt at the MP however, it was arguably Brierleys' QC Jim Farmer who scored the most points on behalf of his client, and he did so without beating Winston Peters around the ears.

In a largely relaxed, sometimes humourous and mostly gentlemanly exchange, Winston Peters and Jim Farmer appeared to strike a rapport with results that satisfied both sides.

Peters said he accepted the word of BIL chief executive Paul Collins that the company hadn't been involved in the captive insurance transactions, although he expressed a strong opinion that Collins, as a director of European Pacific, should have known about the $200 million dollar insurance deal that EP carried out for the BNZ, and said he couldn't believe that Collins didn't know.

Nevertheless, he agreed with Dr Farmer that he had no evidence with which to challenge Collins.

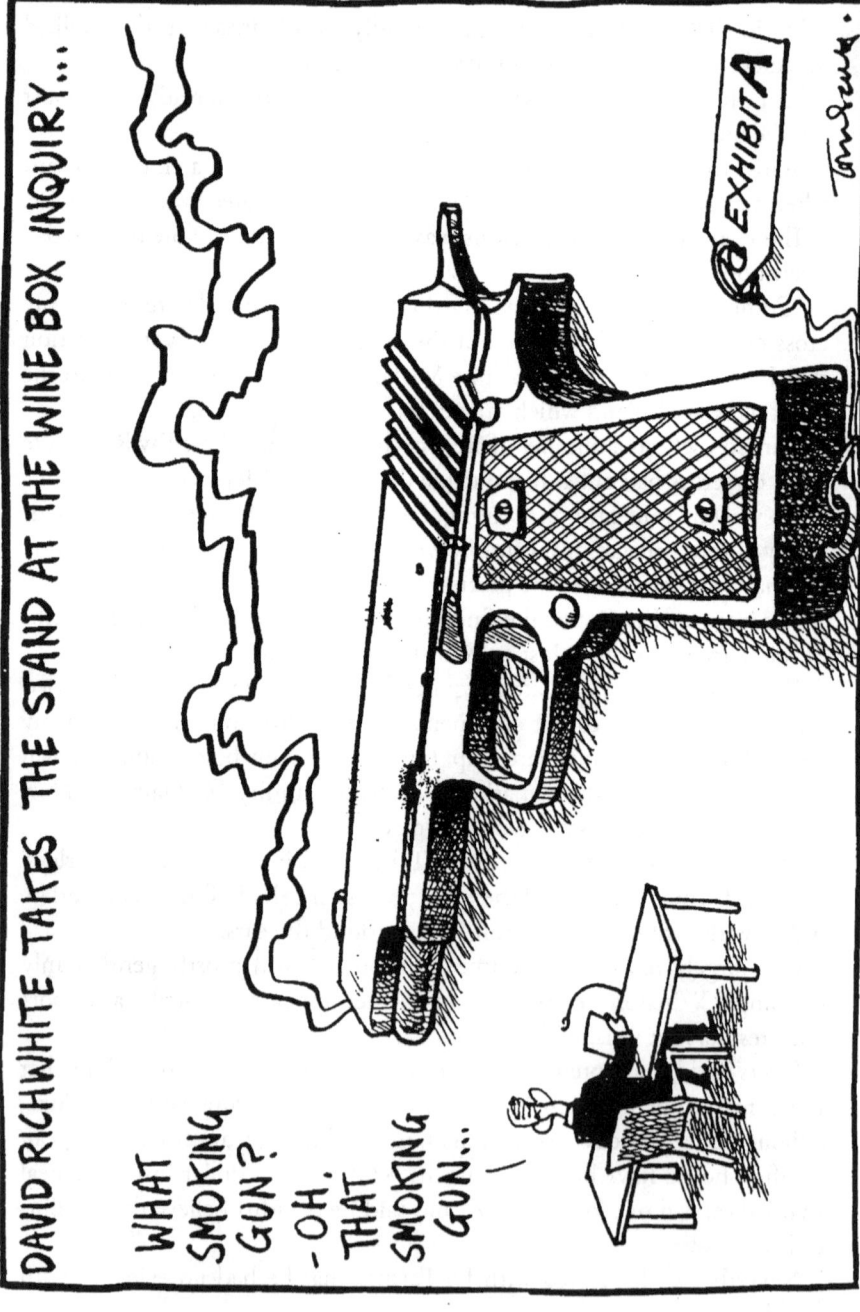

Peters also provided an assurance that his allegations about fraud in the winebox related to the tax credit deals, not Brierleys transactions.

Alone among the cross-examining QC's, Dr Farmer was the only one to go to the heart of Peters' concerns about alleged fraud in the tax credit deals, effectively saying that even if the deals were illegal, Collins and the other non-executive directors had acted on good faith on legal opinions from respected QC's, just as Peters had relied on expert legal opinion in coming to the view that they were criminal deals.

While the QC and the witness remained at odds on the issue of how much criminal intent flows from acting on a legal opinion there was, even on this crucial issue, no shouting.

European Pacific QC Richard Craddock, widely expected to take a swing at Winston Peters, followed the Fay Richwhite lead and decided not to cross-examine, partly because the MP's parliamentary speeches were out of bounds but also because some of their questions had already been answered.

But the boomerang chicken was hovering above, and Peters was about to get clucked.

Victory for Fay Richwhite came the following Thursday afternoon, when the woman who'd passed the hearsay about Fay and Sturt and the babysitter to Peters was called as a witness.

News feature, June 14, 1996

Merchant bank Fay Richwhite is claiming victory against New Zealand First leader Winston Peters in the latest skirmish in their long running battle.

Peters yesterday retracted an allegation that Sir Michael Fay and Serious Fraud Office director Charles Sturt had met each other at Sir Michael Fay's house, chaperoned by a babysitter.

The NZ First leader had relied on information that he said came in a phone call from the former head of the Phobic Trust, Marcia Read.

"I mentioned to Mr Peters," Read told the inquiry yesterday, "that I believed that Mr Sturt's second wife had previously been a nanny to Sir Michael Fay's children and had met Mr Sturt via that position.

"She had later run a child daycare centre where Sir Michael Fay's wife occasionally took her children. I had been told this in a social context previously and had no direct personal knowledge of it.

"I acknowledge that it is possible that Mr Peters may have taken my remarks as having been from personal knowledge."

Winston Peters, recalled to the witness stand afterwards, later acknowledged that in fact the information was wrong, and it related instead to

David Richwhite, not Sir Michael, and he retracted his allegation about Sir Michael Fay and Sturt meeting.

Richwhite's two children went to a private creche run by Sturt's wife, Leonie, although Peters now accepted that the two men had not spoken to each other. David Richwhite told reporters afterward that there was "no evidence whatsoever" to support claims that he or Sir Michael Fay had corrupted the SFO or Inland Revenue Department.

"There is no conspiracy, there is no fraud, there is no bribery and there is no corruption," he said, before launching a stinging attack on Peters, accusing him of "fabricating evidence to suit his political agenda," and "lying to Parliament and this Commission."

Those of you who have read *Lawyers, Guns & Money* will of course know that Sir Michael Fay and Charles Sturt did in fact meet, after private investigators working for Fay Richwhite managed to misappropriate a copy of the unpublished manuscript of a book called *The Paradise Conspiracy*. At a meeting between the two men in 1995, a year prior to Peters appearance at the Inquiry, Fay revealed to Sturt that he had taken care of it, and the SFO director wasn't to worry, because "steps have been taken to stop it from being published."

I alerted the Winebox Inquiry to the existence of this meeting, but it was never raised in evidence.

Evidence of corruption? To my mind yes.

News feature, June 15, 1996

QUESTION: What's the difference between the US WWII officer who once told his commanding officer "they've surrounded us again, the poor bastards!", and Winston Peters?

ANSWER: The US officer proceeded to pull the pin and hurl a grenade at the advancing Hun hordes, Winston Peters grabbed a grenade and threw the pin at advancing winebox lawyers.

As the soot clears, Winnie-the-singed-battered-but-not-broken-Pooh will undoubtedly pause to reflect on the vagaries of war – after numerous bombshells under numerous winebox witnesses to date, it was Winston's turn to take some of the punishment that he's revelled in seeing others suffer up until now.

It began Friday a week ago when, finding himself in stormy seas courtesy of Fay Richwhite QC Rhys Harrison, Peters reached out for a cement lifebouy.

Harrison had been badgering the MP over whether he believed the SFO and IRD had been corrupted by Fay Richwhite. Repeatedly, Peters had answered no, qualifying it by saying that he believed the two Government departments had effectively been intimidated at the thought of investigating Fay Richwhite, and he described that as a form of corruption.

In one of the more esoteric twists of the inquiry to date, Peters found support for his definition of corruption from the currently besieged Burmese Opposition leader, Aung San Suu Kyi, in her essay *Freedom From Fear*.

"*It is not power that corrupts but fear,*" she wrote in 1991. "*Fear of losing power corrupts those who wield it and fear of the scourge of power corrupts those who are subject to it.*

"*It would be difficult to dispel ignorance unless there is freedom to pursue the truth unfettered by fear. With so close a relationship between fear and corruption it is little wonder that in any society where fear is rife corruption in all forms becomes deeply entrenched.*"

Moral of the story? If things get chucked in the "too hard" basket for the wrong reasons, that's corruption.

Needless to say, the wisdom of the east failed to save Peters from himself. Cleverly baited beyond his endurance, the MP finally lashed out at Rhys Harrison, saying he knew a woman who'd seen Sir Michael Fay and SFO director Charles Sturt together at the Fay home in the company of a babysitter.

Given, he said, that Sturt had previously testified to never having met Sir Michael, he suggested Sturt may have lied to the Commission.

Had the MP not taken the bait, he would have sailed through his six day stint in the witness box largely unscathed. Instead, Peters found himself forced to call an unscheduled witness, the head of the Auckland Phobic Trust, Marcia Read.

Read confirmed she'd passed the information to Peters, but said there appeared to have been a communication breakdown.

"I mentioned to Mr Peters that I believed that Mr Sturt's second wife had previously been a nanny to Sir Michael Fay's children and had met Mr Sturt via that position. She had later run a child day care centre where Sir Michael Fay's wife occasionally took her children.

"I had been told this in a social context previously and had no direct personal knowledge of it. I acknowledge that it is possible that Mr Peters may have taken my remarks as having been from personal knowledge."

So where the MP had thought he had an eyewitness, he simply had a woman passing on information which she said was hearsay, and needed further investigation.

Worse still, the evidence would show that in fact Leonie Sturt ran an

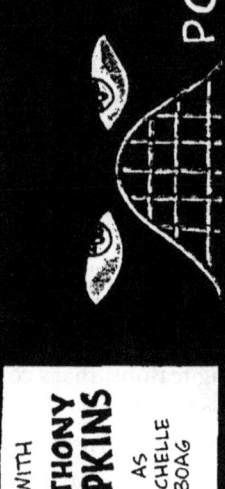

exclusive creche attended by David Richwhite's children, not Sir Michael's. Right hearsay, wrong man. Even so, there was no evidence that Charles Sturt and David Richwhite had actually met, let alone spoken.

Like Wylie Coyote's eternal quest for culinary supremacy over the Roadrunner, Winston Peters gulped, looked down at the fizzing explosive he found himself holding, looked up to see a grinning Rhys Harrison go "beep-beep", smiled weakly and went bang.

Peters said he accepted Read's testimony, and accordingly retracted his allegations about Sir Michael and Charles Sturt. He also accepted that Sturt had not met Richwhite through the creche.

It would be churlish to suggest that Peters failed to bring evidence to the inquiry. After all, he was responsible for the winebox papers tabled in parliament and delivered to the inquiry. Commission investigators are asking pretty specific questions about those deals, including whether the Crimes Act has been broken in three places.

Nevertheless, asked whether he had specific evidence on the more nebulous issue of whether Fay Richwhite had actually corrupted two Government departments, Peters chose to turn his "no" answers into a "yes", and suffered accordingly.

It is certainly not the end of civilisation or the western world as we know it, and when the sun rises on Tuesday, the Winebox Inquiry will still be there, still churning through the detail as it endeavours to find out who did what with the winebox and why.

For Peters, however, the publicity damage was done. Boldly snatching defeat from the jaws of victory the MP watched as his public approval rating tumbled. And so it would have stayed, possibly, had it not been for National Party election strategist, Fay Richwhite PR woman and TVNZ board-member Michelle Boag.

Chapter 7

Boagus Film Crews

"Every thing secret degenerates, even the administration of justice; nothing is safe that does not show how it can bear discussionand publicity."
– Lord Acton (1834–1902), English historian.

When Winston Peters took the stand at the Inquiry, there was naturally a large media contingent on hand. Unusually however, in a country with only two TV news services, there was a third TV crew.

Unlike the TVNZ and TV3 cameras, which were manned by only one person for reasons of cost, this third camera was manned by two, sometimes three people.

To the journalists on the already crowded media bench, this was even more unusual.

"Who the hell can afford to spend money on three-person crews these days?" muttered *One Network News* reporter John Stewart as he was forced to give assistance to his own over-worked cam-op.

"We're doing work for the National Archives," one of the strangers explained.

The other unusual thing about this TV crew was that while TV1 and TV3's cameras only filmed small portions of Peters' fortnight-long evidence, this other crew rolled tape on every second. Every single thing Peters said was recorded.

"My God!" stammered Stewart at one point, his mind reeling at the thought of having to wade through 100 video tapes of Winston Peters giving evidence.

But there were two members of the media who took their inquiries a little further. For yours truly, it was just a case of suggesting to Commission Executive Officer Susan Evans that she look more closely at the crew. For

North & South journalist David McLoughlin, however, there was more digging involved and it paid off big-time.

News feature, July 26, 1996

Senior Fay Richwhite executive and TVNZ board member Michelle Boag flies from the frying pan heat of Fiji into the fire of the Winebox Inquiry today, when she appears to face questions about a covert plot directed at NZ First leader Winston Peters.

The inquiry was rocked on Wednesday when Commissioner Sir Ronald Davison announced he was launching an inquiry into a bogus film crew, hired by Fay Richwhite but smuggled into the hearings under false pretences.

"That sequence of events," warned Sir Ronald as he outlined what had transpired, "has given me cause for concern."

"Approximately one week before Mr Peters gave evidence," said Sir Ronald, "the Commission received a request for permission for a camera crew from Zee Films to be present throughout the duration of Mr Peters' case.

"Permission was granted on the basis of the representation made, that the purpose of the filming was for archiving purposes. The impression given was that there was an official connection with National Archives."

Using his wide contempt powers, which allow Sir Ronald to impose penalties ranging from a slap on the wrist to a term of imprisonment for those involved, the winebox Commissioner dragged executives representing the film company into his hearing, as well as ordering the appearance of Michelle Boag and Russell McVeagh lawyer Mark Gavin.

The inquiry heard that the film company had initially approached the Commission using the name "Hauraki Films", a name that film producer Cathy White later admitted was fictitious.

"Hauraki Films wasn't the correct name of the production company I was representing," she said under cross examination. "Because the client wished to remain anonymous, we felt it was best that we use this name."

"Do I understand from your answer," pressed Colin Carruthers QC, "that there is no body or company called Hauraki Films?"

"That is correct," White confirmed.

According to the story, Fay Richwhite public relations executive Michelle Boag approached Zee Films producer Richard Riddiford, asking him to send a camera crew into the inquiry to get video footage of everything Winston Peters said. Among the reasons given, Boag said Fay Richwhite were considering making a TV programme on the MP.

"After discussions with [Sir Michael Fay]," wrote Michelle Boag in a

memo released to the Commission, "I commissioned Richard Riddiford of Zee Films to carry out the filming. I advised Richard that because we were uncertain whether the film would ever be used, we wished to film anonymously through a third party.

"His instructions were to seek accreditation on the basis that his client was considering making a programme but this was dependent on the content of the evidence."

Riddiford, in turn, hired Cathy White – a freelance producer – whose job it would be to organise the video shoot.

White claims she was never told that Fay Richwhite was the client, but she was told that the client had requested absolute anonymity. For that reason, they'd hatched up the false company name and a false cover story.

The crew, which on normal freelance TV rates would have been paid somewhere in the region of $1,000 a day, was present throughout the almost two weeks that Winston Peters spent on the witness stand.

The flag only went up after inquiries from other journalists about the secretive video crew, and a formal request from lawyers for Winston Peters who wanted to know who the crew was filming for.

Documents released by the Commission, despite a request from Fay Richwhite QC Rhys Harrison that "it is not to be published", show it took Commission investigators more than a month to pierce the veil of secrecy.

Commission executive officer Susan Evans demanded on June 18 that Zee Films "identify your client", and "outline the form and content of the proposed programme."

On June 27, Zee Films producer Richard Riddiford wrote back "I have spoken to my client who at this stage would prefer not to be identified. However, I can advise that my client does not currently intend to produce a programme as originally anticipated."

On 11 July, Susan Evans turned up the heat, stating it was now obvious the Commission "has been under a misapprehension" about Zee Films' role.

"From the information given previously, the Commission had understood that your company had an official role in obtaining material for film archives. If the Commission had understood the position as it now appears, you would not have been allowed to film.

"The present situation is unsatisfactory," she warned. "The Commission is not prepared to allow use of the material without its permission. You are required to answer [the earlier questions] within 7 days of receipt of this letter.

"Failing this, the Commission will require you to deliver up for destruction all copies of the film in your possession and to provide an affidavit to the Commission confirming you have done so."

Finally, on Tuesday this week, one of Fay Richwhite's lawyers, Russell McVeagh partner Mark Gavin, wrote to confirm that his client was the mystery puppeteer behind Zee Films. He told the inquiry that the merchant bank had wanted to film Peters because of all his previous allegations against the company.

He intimated that the footage was considered useful for the Fays legal team as they prepared a strategy on dealing with the MP in the witness box, and added that "depending on the nature of the reporting of Peters' evidence, there was the possibility that a programme could be developed around his evidence ... the publicity surrounding his evidence was such that it is now considered no longer necessary or appropriate to utilise the film for the purposes of a programme."

With a sting in the tail, Gavin's letter ended with a request that the Commission keep the whole issue confidential, so as "to ensure that the issue of the filming of Peters' evidence does not develop unnecessary political overtones."

Michelle Boag, a former National Government press secretary, has previously had her dual role as TVNZ director and Fay Richwhite PR woman questioned by the National Business Review. This week TVNZ was distancing itself from the scandal – spokesman Alistair Carthew describing management as "baffled" by the revelations and saying TVNZ played no part in the planning for a possible Fay Richwhite TV documentary on Winston Peters.

News feature, July 28, 1996

Merchant bank Fay Richwhite and film company Zee Films have until noon tomorrow to decide whether to plead guilty to charges of contempt of the Winebox Inquiry, or try and defend the charges.

In a devastating blow to both companies, inquiry head Sir Ronald Davison found that a prima facie case of contempt existed.

"The contempt alleged is this: falsely misleading the Commission for the purpose of obtaining the consent of the Commission to the filming of the evidence of Mr Winston Peters given before the Commission, by deliberately suppressing the fact that the person for whom the filming was to be done was Fay Richwhite ... and by falsely stating the purpose for which such filming was to be done."

Both Fay Richwhite and Zee Films have been told to make up their minds by midday on Monday as to whether they wish to "admit their contempt and purge it by appropriate apology and then be further dealt with by the Commission, or they may proceed to show cause why they should not be held in contempt and they may call such evidence and make such submissions as are appropriate."

Sir Ronald's finding came despite Fay Richwhite executive – and TVNZ board member – Michelle Boag's bid to explain the company's way out of the scandal.

Boag, also working alongside the Prime Minister and National Party president on devising this year's election campaign strategy, said the idea of secretly filming Winston Peters had been hatched during discussions with Sir Michael Fay, but she said David Richwhite and the company's lawyers were also present when it was discussed.

Fay Richwhite wanted a complete video record of the Peters evidence so that if the chance arose, even up to two years down the track, the footage could be resurrected and used against Mr Peters in a TV programme of some kind produced by Fay Richwhite.

"May we take it," asked Counsel assisting the Commission, Colin Carruthers QC, "that the programme would not be aimed to be a flattering one to [Winston Peters]?"

"I think you can take it," said Boag, "that our response to Mr Peters' allegations about us would be of a similar nature to the sort of things he had said about us."

The Fay Richwhite pr executive claimed the decision to go incognito was because of Peters "paranoia", and the fact that he might "make political mileage" out of the fact that Fay Richwhite were filming him.

She said the instructions to Zee Films had been to keep Fay's name out of it, but Boag maintains she wasn't aware that Zee Films had used a fictitious identity to gain media accreditation.

In an admission that shocked media representatives at the inquiry, the public relations expert admitted lying to a journalist, David McLoughlin, who'd asked her at the time whether Fay Richwhite was involved with the mysterious third TV crew filming Winston Peters.

"What was your response [to the question]?" asked Colin Carruthers.

"I said I don't know," answered Boag.

"And was that a correct response?" queried Carruthers.

"No, it wasn't," admitted Boag.

She later apologised to the Commission for what had transpired, saying neither she nor Fay Richwhite had intended to mislead the inquiry.

McLoughlin, the journalist who'd been lied to by Boag, was furious. Boag, on the other hand, wanted my blood. She stormed out of the lift on one occasion, spotted me in the crowded foyer accusing me of calling her a liar during a radio interview – her evidence being that her elderly mother had heard me say it.

"We're watching you, Wishart. You be very careful."

"Well, for the record Michelle, I did not call you a liar on the radio this morning."

"My mother heard you," she snapped waspishly.

Great, I thought. This was a conversation I couldn't win. She was now going to think I was calling her mother a liar.

"I think you'll find she misheard," I soothed. "When you get a transcript, you'll find that was not what I said about you."

Boag, to borrow from Geoff Harley's Ruth Richardson anecdote, was "displeased" with me.

The pressure was on, thanks in part to my radio interviews where I was telling anyone who'd listen that Boag's roles as Fay PR mouthpiece, Prime Ministerial advisor and would-be Winston Peters movie director were in major conflict with her position as a TVNZ director.

I'd raised the issue on previous occasions but this time the wheels gained traction, and "Should She Stay Or Should She Go?" became the dominant talking point for the country for the next few days.

Boag, however, didn't see it that way. She spent the weekend bluntly telling journalists she would not be stepping down as she saw no conflict of interest, even though she had a key position as one of National's election strategists for the upcoming election, working alongside the Prime Minister and the National Party president, Geoff Thompson.

As a measure of Boag's confidence, her comments came despite news reports suggesting SOE Minister Phillip Burdon would be approaching TVNZ chairman Norman Geary to discuss her future.

Geary swung in behind her, telling the *Herald* that Michelle Boag had behaved "impeccably" as a TVNZ board member and had, at all times, respected TVNZ's editorial independence.

Which wasn't true. Boag had played a role in hastening my own departure from TVNZ, ringing up news staff while she was a director and expressing her views on my position. Her complaints, on behalf of Fay Richwhite, were sufficient that I was sidelined as the reporter on an *Assignment* programme investigating Fay Richwhite's massive borrowing from the BNZ. I was replaced by Terence Taylor, now the producer of *20/20*, and Fay Richwhite executives then boasted about my removal.

Did I, as Boag complained, have a conflict of interest because I was about to publish *The Paradise Conspiracy?* That's in the eye of the beholder, I guess. My position was no different from that of investigative journalists for *Time* magazine or the *Wall Street Journal* who published similar books on other banking scandals. Those journalists got pay-rises. I got dumped. But enough of the digression.

By Monday morning, like a slow-acting poison, Sir Ronald Davison's prima facie contempt finding was clearly taking its toll, as Boag announced she was taking three months leave from both the TVNZ board and her National Party duties.

By Tuesday, the contempt issue became a mortal blow.

In front of a packed hearing room, Fay Richwhite's lawyer Rhys Harrison QC told the inquiry his clients were pleading guilty to the charges of contempt laid against them for arranging the covert filming of Winston Peters.

"I might indicate," continued Harrison, "that Fay Richwhite expressed no interest whatsoever in exploring any possible legal defences available to it.

"Its sole concern has rested in tendering an immediate apology."

That apology had been delivered to Sir Ronald Davison on Monday. In it, Sir Michael Fay and David Richwhite said "the company sincerely regrets its action and unreservedly apologises to you and the Commission staff."

Rhys Harrison tried to argue that the contempt was a minor one and unintentional, but it was an argument Sir Ronald wasn't buying.

"With respect to Mr Harrison," opined the winebox Commissioner, "that is far too simplistic an interpretation to be placed on the events.

"This contempt lies not just in falsely obtaining a discretionary permission, it lies in deceiving the Commission with a view to obtaining film evidence which it would not have otherwise obtained for use against Winston Peters in a programme yet to be produced."

In sentencing Fay Richwhite and Zee Films, which had also pleaded guilty, Sir Ronald let fly with a carefully-worded missile – far more deadly in its totality than the $23,300 in fines and court costs he eventually imposed.

"I deal first with the case of Fay Richwhite," said Sir Ronald. "It is clear that Michelle Boag ... initiated the filming of Mr Peters' evidence by Zee Films Ltd on terms that the identity of Fay Richwhite, as the client, should not be disclosed and in such a way that the true purposes of the filming were not revealed."

Sir Ronald ruled that Boag "clearly intended to deceive the Commission for the purpose of obtaining permission to film and her actions must be regarded accordingly as amounting to an intended contempt of the Commission and a serious one at that."

Rubbing it in, Sir Ronald later talked of Boag's "guilty actions".

Dropping a $15,000 fine on Fay Richwhite with $5,000 in costs, and a fine of $2,500 plus $800 in costs levied against Zee Films, the Commission closed the book on the sordid affair.

Within two hours, Michelle Boag had walked the plank from the state television network.

News feature, August 3, 1996

A sound thrashing followed by squeals of pain, the whole of New Zealand listened in morbid fascination this week as the Winebox inquiry delivered six of the best to Fay Richwhite and its PR woman, Michelle Boag.

Caught out by the Commission, secretly filming Winston Peters under false pretences, Michelle Boag and the boffins from the merchant bank single-handedly delivered the New Zealand First leader the smoking gun loaded with silver bullets that he's always craved.

"Take that!", exclaimed Whipmeister Sir Ronald Davison as he administered justice winebox-style, sentencing Fay Richwhite to a fine and court costs totalling $20,000.

"Aaarghhh!," screeched interested parties inside TVNZ and the National Government, as Sir Ronald singled out Boag for a special mention in dispatches.

He accused the then-TVNZ director and National Party election strategist of having "clearly intended to deceive the Commission for the purpose of obtaining permission to film, and her actions must be regarded accordingly as amounting to an intended contempt of the Commission and a serious one at that."

Now it would be fair to say, before I continue with this little tale, that Michelle Boag and I differ, and have crossed swords before, on issues like conflict of interest and the like. As one might imagine, *The Paradise Conspiracy* went down like a square pill at Fay Richwhite's Auckland head office.

Even after the Commission's prima facie contempt findings Friday-week ago, Boag still believed she had done nothing wrong, that the media and yours truly were beating it up, and she expressed a kind of "so what?" attitude toward it all.

Even after admitting, on Monday, that she had mislead the Inquiry, there was no way Boag was going to resign from the TVNZ board of directors. At most, she would settle for a three month leave of absence and resume the position after the election.

Public outrage, the power of a unified news media and the power of the Winebox Inquiry conspired against her.

To my mind, she had to go – there was no other option. If Michelle Boag could admit behaviour that deceived a judicial inquiry – how on earth could she still believe she had a right to sit as a director of a major SOE?

Here was a woman who admitted lying – or, more politely, telling an "untruth" – to a journalist who had asked her directly if she knew who was behind the mysterious film crew videotaping Winston Peters.

Her behaviour is now being investigated by the Public Relations industry's ethics committee.

As the dust settled in the hearing room, Fay Richwhite's QC, Rhys Harrison, attempted to make light of their plight.

"Well, Ian," he cackled, "I can see more conspiracies for you to write about!"

"I don't need to anymore, Rhys, you guys are doing it for me!"

Or, as another wit later put it, I could have offered the Fay Richwhite boys a gun "so they can shoot themselves in the other foot!"

Of course, the Boag jokes are already doing the rounds: Boagus Film Crews, or doing a "Boag" – a brilliant, own, agonising goal!

This week's debacle is further proof, of course, that the Winebox Inquiry will become steadily more controversial and dangerous as it lurches toward a conclusion later this year.

The Boag affair, and its attendant collateral damage on both National and TVNZ, is symptomatic of the hidden pressures that now have the Inquiry and its participants almost bursting at the seams under the strain.

Weak spots that began to show several months ago have now become finger in the dyke material. Fay Richwhite, on this occasion, made the mistake of yanking their finger from the dyke in order to give Winston Peters a rude gesture.

It was a sideshow, in terms of the Inquiry's main focus, but probably important in the way that it illustrated the lengths some people are prepared to go to discredit a politician they see as inimical to their own interests.

Elsewhere at the inquiry this week, we've had a continuation of Brierley Investments "Handy Hints for Harassing The Revenue".

IRD investigators say Brierleys failed to file a tax return for ten years for one of its subsidiaries, after apparently forgetting that it owned the company.

But that gaffe was quickly surpassed when the IRD revealed Brierleys had also failed to file returns for up to thirty tax haven subsidiaries since 1988.

Apparently knowing that it had a legal obligation to file the returns, Brierleys nevertheless sold not only the companies in 1989, but also all their tax records with them.

Whoops, they told the IRD, sorry about that.

The records are now safely ensconced with new owners overseas, and Brierleys can't get them back. So far the tax department hasn't prosecuted Brierleys for failing to file the tax returns, but it claims to be thinking about it.

I wish more of my teachers at high school could have been former IRD tax inspectors. At least they might have believed me when I claimed a goat had eaten my homework.

Chapter 8

Proceed At Your Own Peril

Before he left, Aunt William pressed a sovereign into his hand guiltily, as if it were conscience money. He, on his side, took it as though it were a doctor's fee, and both ignored the transaction.
– Ada Leverson (1862–1933), English novelist. *The Twelfth Hour*

News feature, August 10, 1996

It had been, according to the jungle drums, a long and arduous few weeks in the undergrowth of the Winebox Inquiry.

Tarzan the Taxman adjusted his loin cloth and grimaced as he remembered those pleasurable days in the wake of Winston the Chimp's winebox appearance – a golden goose handed to them if ever there was one!

The Chimp, normally a crafty old operator, had managed to outsmart even himself on that occasion, causing much mirth amongst the other jungle inhabitants as he inadvertently sawed off the tree branch he'd been perched on.

Tarzan the Taxman was still nursing the bruise he'd received – he'd been laughing so hard at Winston that he fell off his vine.

The laughter, unfortunately, hadn't lasted very long.

Jane of the Jungle's appearance at the inquiry late in July had transformed a bagged Chimp into a Boaged Chump – courtesy of Lion King Davison, and Winnie the Chimp had made the most of Jane's predicament to spring to higher ground.

"Never before," muttered Tarzan to himself, "have I seen that Chimp crow so loudly without moving his lips once."

Things, he acknowledged, had gone steadily from bad to worse.

Confident of nailing somebody – hell, anybody – to a tree, Tarzan the

Taxman had asked the Serious Warthog Office to poke its collective snout into a winebox deal involving the Carter Holt Harvey jackals.

Tarzan knew there was tax fraud there, he could smell it to the tune of some $60 million in undeclared income.

Unfortunately, after rooting around it for six months or so, the Serious Warthogs had failed to bring home the bacon on this one. "We can't see any fraud," they said loudly to anyone who would listen.

So for Tarzan, this was the "bad". Then came the "worse".

IRD official Colin Anderson took the witness stand at the inquiry this week, and by the end of it Tarzan's goose had been caught, plucked, and was being slowly roasted over a warm flame.

Anderson had been one of the first IRD investigators to go through the winebox after receiving it from the Serious Fraud Office in February, 1993.

Among the deals he focused on were six transactions worth almost $500 million, involving Fay Richwhite and some corporate clients. Colin Anderson estimated some $50 million could be recovered if the deals were attacked under the IRD's tax avoidance powers.

Unfortunately, his pleas fell on deaf ears at the IRD head office. Repeatedly, senior staff told Anderson they would not support his attempts to use section 99 of the Income Tax Act to claw back that $50 million.

So, quietly, Anderson had to let his plans drop, barring the discovery of significant new evidence.

Imagine his surprise then, when in late 1994 he discovered IRD head office had changed its tune.

During this time, TVNZ's winebox documentary had gone to air, Winston Peters had tabled the winebox and Parliament's Finance and Expenditure Committee had announced plans to investigate the Cook Islands tax deals.

Lo and behold, Head Office had dusted off Colin Anderson's analysis and was now alleging massive tax avoidance in the very same deals they'd earlier effectively cleared.

"The IRD's current view," international audit manager John Nash eventually told the current Winebox Inquiry, "is that the arrangements are simply too contrived for the tax advantages to be considered merely incidental."

In a series of questions to Colin Anderson, the Commission this week established obvious similarities between the investigator's early, and scorned, recommendations, and the new, 'road to Damascus' approach of John Nash.

Anderson added that he couldn't see that any significant new information had emerged that would justify the Head Office u-turn.

He wouldn't be drawn on Commission questions suggesting the change of mind coincided with the setting up of the 1994 parliamentary inquiry.

In other revelations, documents released this week confirm that it took IRD Head Office a year to investigate the tax certificate rorts in the winebox, even though one of their senior inspectors had remarked on them as soon as they received the tax haven documents.

That inspector, John Trezise, had completed an analysis of the papers back in February 1993, which highlighted a "novel" scheme involving Cook Islands tax certificates and a double benefit. The papers were then handed to Tony Loo's Tax Intelligence Unit.

In December of 1993, TVNZ had passed more detailed information to the IRD, during the preparation of its winebox documentary alleging possible tax fraud.

But it wasn't until the TVNZ evidence had been thrashed out publicly in court in early 1994 that the IRD finally appears to have sat up and taken notice.

A memo dated February 18, 1994, was sent by John Nash to senior staff asking them to "urgently" examine how many Cook Islands tax credit certificates had been used and by whom.

Definitely not, in the eyes of this humble scribe, one of the IRD's finest hours.

Up in the treetops, Tarzan the Taxman sighed heavily, watching as the sun went down on his domain, accompanied by a chorus of hysterical hyenas.

"I do wish Sir Ronald would keep those damn journalists quiet," he muttered under his breath.

One of the foundation stones for Sir Ronald Davison's controversial verdict was that there was no fraud in the Winebox. Without this blanket clearance finding, many of his other findings would not stack up.

But before we examine the actual key transactions themselves, it's worthwhile examining what the Court of Appeal and the Privy Council thought of the issues during the turbulent middle portion of the Inquiry.

At this time, Sir Ronald was attempting to force the appearance of former employees of European Pacific, people who had worked on the deals in question.

The first EP staff member to get a tap on the shoulder was a man named David McNair. I had received a tip that he had entered New Zealand, and I in turn passed that information to staff at the Commission of Inquiry.

McNair was duly contacted, but chose to flee the country despite being subpoenaed to appear. His disappearance caused Sir Ronald Davison to apply to the Government for greater powers of contempt.

Sir Ronald, in his report to the Governor-General, wrote:

> *"When a judge of the High Court was a member of the Commission, such Commission had the powers of a judge of the High Court 'in the exercise of his civil jurisdiction under the Judicature Act 1908', but the Act made no provision for the case where a former (retired) judge of the High Court is appointed to a Commission and his powers were limited to those of a District Court.*
>
> *"This situation meant that this Commission had only limited powers to compel attendance of witnesses; it had no power to order the arrest of a witness who failed to attend and it had no adequate power to deal with a witness who refused to give evidence.*
>
> *"A further matter of concern was that there was considerable doubt whether a Commission of Inquiry constituted under the Act had any power to punish for contempt of the Commission."*

On July 29, 1995, Parliament rectified that by giving Davison all the powers of a High Court judge to throw someone in jail for contempt and throw away the key.

The Commission promptly served summonses on a number of key former European Pacific staff that it discovered living in New Zealand. Among them, accountant Peter Brannigan who was then a leading figure in Horwarth, Brannigan McCullagh & Co, and about to become a key player in the Aotearoa Television scandal.

Then there was Brannigan's offsider, Anthony McCullagh, former EP Bank boss Geoff Barry, and David Lilly.

In December 1995 the Court of Appeal heard argument from lawyers representing these men and a group of KPMG accountants, all of whom had refused to testify believing Cook Islands secrecy laws had precedence over New Zealand law.

In February 1996, a full five-judge bench of the Court of Appeal delivered its verdict on their appeal, and four of the judgments were crushing.

In front of a packed public gallery – a rarity in the Court of Appeal – and a big media turnout, the Court found that New Zealand's public interest overrode any laws the Cook Islands could throw at it in this case.

By effectively selling millions of dollars in tax credits for a small fee, the judges said the Cook Islands had descended into commercial transactions and thereby forfeited their right to sovereign immunity. The Court also described the transactions as a blatant abuse of New Zealand's tax system, with one judge going so far as to call them possibly iniquitous.

This, in itself, was a disaster for the Cook Islands Government, because the New Zealand courts effectively ruled that they have no immunity from prosecution if the transactions are later found to be criminal, as alleged in earlier court proceedings.

But the ruling goes deeper, because the New Zealand Court of Appeal appeared to have also kicked out one of the crutches relied on by European Pacific, which is whether the tax credit deals were a commercial transaction or a tax. EP had argued the latter, and used that argument to show that the schemes came in just on the right side of the law.

Sir Ronald Davison, amazingly, would later agree with European Pacific on this legal point, despite the fact that the Court of Appeal had already signalled differently.

If it wasn't a "tax" that was actually paid in the Cook Islands in the first place, so the argument goes, then the parties were certainly never justified in claiming real tax refunds in New Zealand.

News feature, February 24, 1996[13]

It may only be a small winebox, but judging by the 160-page Court of Appeal rulings on its merits last week, the winebox is starting to pack a punch that looks set to make Commonwealth, if not world, legal history.

It's taken lawyers and journalists the best part of a week to fully digest the implications of the Appeal Court judgement, but the judgements appear to be testing the cutting edge of international law on tax havens.

Among the most significant aspects, a warning to users of tax havens that traditional legal rights may no longer apply to them.

Appeal Court president, Lord Cooke, referred to a Canadian report on the use of tax havens.

"According to various US Government studies, the illegal use of tax havens by US taxpayers is increasing significantly. Most of the increase is apparently attributable to organised crime and the illegal drug trade. As indicated at the outset, the illegal use of tax havens is beyond the scope of this book."

Lord Cooke wasted no time picking up on that theme.

"Faced with a serious issue of illegality or iniquity," he wrote in his judgement, "a Court cannot fall back on a bland answer that this sort of thing is beyond its scope.

---

13 Reprinted from Ian Wishart's *Vintage Winebox Guide*.

"A warning seems appropriate that older doctrines such as sovereign immunity, privilege against self-incrimination and the like, will not necessarily be apt when dealing with this sophisticated modern phenomenon.

"The public policy or interest of the country [conducting an inquiry or prosecution] may properly require a different approach and in my view does so in this instance."

A warning like that, coming from New Zealand's highest territorial court, must send shivers down the spines of some. Little could European Pacific and its backers have imagined, when they took out injunctions against the news media three years ago, the scale of the legal destruction they would do to their own cause.

Along the way, we've seen landmark court judgments upholding the right of the media to investigate alleged tax crimes, despite claims that only the IRD could investigate. We've had judgements upholding the media's right to protect secret sources. We've seen the Court of Appeal rule that the long-cherished principle of taxpayer confidentiality comes second to the public interest, and now we're seeing the Court of Appeal talk of stripping participants in tax haven schemes of legal rights that even accused murderers have traditionally enjoyed.

As Justice Ted Thomas put it when ruling that documents held in New Zealand must be handed over:

"The documents are believed to contain evidence of a conspiracy, to which the Cook Islands Government was a party, to make an abusive claim to foreign tax credits in reliance upon tax credit certificates issued by the Cook Islands Government.

"I endorse [Justice Sir Ivor Richardon's] observation that the state has a prime interest in tax enforcement and in the investigation of abuses of its tax system, and that defrauding the public revenue strikes at the heart of government. I agree that it would be indefensible for a friendly state to be party to an attempt to evade or abuse our tax laws."

And in a paragraph likely to horrify all of those financial commentators and regulatory agencies who maintain the tax credit deals were just on the right side of the law, Justice John Henry gave a clear signal of the Appeal Court's view.

"There is evidence presently before [Sir Ronald Davison] to support a contention that some of the transactions may have defrauded the New Zealand revenue or provided a means of evading tax. The foreign State is said to have been instrumental in a significant way in assisting New Zealand taxpayers to that end."

The message from the courts is clear: tax havens, with their attendant financial wizardry and secrecy, appear to be ahead of the law. It's time for the law to catch up, in much the same way that DNA testing has revolutionised investigation of crimes against the person.

A BBC Panorama documentary two years ago estimated that two thirds of the world's money supply is now controlled via tax havens. Their impact is felt by almost every citizen in the western world, although few would realise it.

Over the past decade there have been numerous attempts by investigatory bodies around the world to penetrate tax haven secrecy. Most successful, perhaps, have been the Americans.

In his book *Inside Out – The Dennis Levine Story*, convicted inside-trader Dennis Levine details his own fall from grace courtesy of the Bahamas tax haven.

Levine had been a multi-million earning junk bond dealer with Drexel Burnham Lambert, a colleague of fellow convicts Michael Milken and Ivan Boesky. He'd used secret accounts in the Bahamas for his insider trades, but came unstuck when the US Government heavied the Bahamas – a member of the British Commonwealth.

Unlike the example set by the Cook Islands and its staunch adherence to its secrecy laws, the Bahamas rolled over at the first whiff of trouble from the US. Even more astounding, a major Swiss bank rolled over with it. Between the Bahamas and the Swiss, they coughed up enough banking records on Levine and others to sink several major players.

But despite some successes like these, the eyes of the world's tax and money laundering investigators are now focused firmly on New Zealand and its Winebox Inquiry. The reason? It's thought to be the first time in the world that such a complete set of sophisticated tax haven engineering documents has fallen into the public domain, and according to US academic and tax haven expert Dr Tony van Fossen it's the first time a haven has ever been publicly probed to this extent by an independent inquiry.

With the Court of Appeal examining previous international case law and taking it a giant leap further, the winebox is beginning to make international, not just domestic waves.

In making his verdict of "no fraud", which will be examined later, Davison flew in the face of these rulings from the Court of Appeal. Sadly, there would be signals from the Privy Council itself as to the legality of the deals – signals that the Court of Appeal would later highlight in their critical judgment of the Winebox Inquiry verdict – and Davison would ignore those too in giving his fatally-flawed judgment.

Admittedly, the Court of Appeal verdict forcing European Pacific and KPMG staff to testify was not unanimous. One judge, Ian McKay, dissented.

News feature, March 2, 1996

The ghosts of centuries-dead judges and merchants are likely to be conjured up by lawyers acting for two European Pacific staff in a last ditch legal bid to stop them from being forced to testify at New Zealand's tax-dodge inquisition.

Clasping a sole dissenting judgement from last month's Court of Appeal "grab bag", Auckland barrister Bruce Stewart will next week seek leave for his clients to put their case to the Privy Council in Britain.

His argument, if Justice Ian McKay's dissenting judgement is relied on, will rest on legal precedent set in a case involving the British East India Company way back in 1749, when the lofty and crusty Court of Exchequer, as it was then known, decided that a witness could refuse to testify because by doing so he might break a law in the far away kingdom of Calcutta.

Since that judgement was made, the world has turned nearly 90 thousand times, and in the course of 246 journeys around the sun we have seen the birth of the United States of America and New Zealand, the fall of the British, Turkish and Austro-Hungarian empires, the rise and fall of Napoleonic France, the widespread adoption of democracy, two world wars and the invention of tax havens.

We, the great (x10) grandchildren of these ancient and long-forgotten jurists, have seen and done things they could never have dreamed of in their most hallucenogenic nightmares. Back in 1749 witchcraft was a headline issue, the pursuit of masochists with pyromaniacal leanings, slavery was actively encouraged and suicides were buried at cross-roads with a hawthorne stake through the heart lest, as common wisdom had it, they dug themselves out and roamed the streets at night.

It is not a good period in history, one might argue, from which to rely on legal precedent.

Retiring Appeal Court President, Lord Cooke, also noted the incremental damage to case law from time's passage, saying that modern phenomenon like tax havens may need to be dealt with in a much harsher way than Courts had previously considered appropriate.

More recent legal history, involving prosecutions by the US and Canada against tax haven bankers last decade, has shrugged off the 1749 verdict and a more recent supporting one from 1867, and witnesses have been ordered to testify in those countries despite the fact they'd be in deep trouble if they returned to the haven.

In his dissenting judgement, Justice McKay recognises the tough stand taken by the US, but doesn't agree with it, saying people under threat for opening their mouths should get the same privilege as those who refuse to answer on the grounds that what they're saying may incriminate them.

Alone among his colleagues, the learned Judge McKay also warns that a New Zealand Court may well be prepared to extradite telltale European Pacific witnesses back to the Cook Islands where they can be prosecuted for testifying and jailed for a year.

On that grounds, he says, the European Pacific staff should be excused from testifying in New Zealand.

So far Auckland accountants Peter Brannigan and Anthony McCullagh have clutched the Privy Council appeal straw, while a third witness, former EP Bank boss Geoff Barry, was at press-time still deciding whether to follow suit. Leave to go to the Privy is not automatic in this instance, it must first be approved by the Court of Appeal.

European Pacific lawyers have confirmed, however, that a fourth man, David Lilly, has decided not to fight the Commission of Inquiry any further and will front up as ordered on Tuesday morning for what's expected to be some very tough questioning.

When Lilly did front up, he did so in defiance of his former employer and against the advice of his lawyer, Richard Craddock QC, who also happens to be EP's Counsel. Craddock confirmed that the other three EP staff would be going to the Privy Council. Lilly didn't reveal much, however. There was a lot of "I can't recall", or "I have no recollection of that", although his memory improved when he saw the opportunity to stick the boot into rebel EP employee Witness A, who had testified against the company in exchange for immunity from prosecution.

As I noted in a newspaper column at the time, former EP Financial Controller Lilly was constantly bagging his former colleague.

"Witness A, it turns out," I wrote, "had been 'pretty keen' on doing the JIF deals himself. Witness A would 'normally run' all the transactions. Witness A was essentially a crook and a scumbag. Witness A 'had most of that responsibility'.

"About the only thing Witness A hadn't been involved in, we joked on the media bench, was as one of the assassins on the grassy knoll in the 1963 murder of President John F. Kennedy. Even the assembled lawyers were beginning to smirk at every earnest mention of Witness A's name."

Lilly admitted his own role in the allegedly fraudulent tax credit deals, but told the Inquiry he believed the transactions were above board. He hadn't been told about the opinion from Oslington QC suggesting they were criminal. Lilly was a signatory to many of the documents allowing the transactions to proceed.

The other three European Pacific witnesses had their appeals heard by the Privy Council in the middle of 1996.

News feature, June 29, 1996

It's been out of the headlines in this part of the world for more than a week now, but Pandora's favourite little winebox is about to make waves in London.

The Privy Council will convene this Monday and Tuesday for a special hearing to whether New Zealand or Cook Islands law is supreme in New Zealand.

Not surprisingly, lawyers for former European Pacific staff are strenuously arguing that Cook Islands law was etched by the hand of God on a piece of tapa cloth, and that Cook Islands secrecy and offshore banking laws should be distributed amongst all humanity to be the moral and legal cornerstone of our lives.

Somehow, I personally can't see the Law Lords buying that one.

The issues are relatively clear cut: on the one hand, you have three former European Pacific staff who have been ordered to appear at the Auckland-based Davison Commission and sing like canaries, on pain of being swiftly caged for contempt if they don't.

On the other hand, you have European Pacific lawyers, helped by a dissenting judge on New Zealand's Court of Appeal, arguing that forcing these men to testify, in defiance of Cook Islands secrecy laws, is a breach of natural justice principles regarding self-incrimination.

While some in politics and big business have been quick to criticise our Court of Appeal for its willingness to look not just at the letter but also at the spirit of the law, they may not get any relief from the Privy Council in this case.

For a start, this is an issue of New Zealand sovereignty – of the right of a New Zealand inquiry or Court to subpoena a New Zealand citizen living within its borders to testify. If possession is nine-tenths of the law, and we possess the trio, it's very hard to see the Cook Islands winning this round.

The Cooks' constitutional position may also count against them. In a legal sense they are still an adjunct of New Zealand, permitted limited self-government. The Privy Council may see the Cooks as a tail trying to wag a dog.

In addition, however, with so little British case law on the subject, the Privy Council may follow the lead it's taken in the past and adopt the New Zealand Court of Appeal reasoning as an international trendsetter.

Many observers expect the Commission of Inquiry and Court of Appeal rulings to be upheld and, perhaps reflecting that expectation of certain success, New Zealand's Solicitor-General John McGrath QC is making a personal appearance at the Privy as senior counsel for NZ, with counsel assisting the Commission, Colin Carruthers QC, number two in the lineup.

Also appearing will be Brian Henry, the senior counsel for New Zealand First leader Winston Peters at the Winebox Inquiry, and Peters himself plans to be present as well.

From the European Pacific stable, Richard Craddock QC and barrister Bruce Stewart will be arguing their case on behalf of former executives Geoff Barry, Peter Brannigan and Anthony McCullagh.

The latter two have already illustrated some of the resourcefulness that was so admired as a general trait at European Pacific: when faced with subpoenas to appear, the two Auckland accountants had the good fortune to be offered auditing contracts in the Cook Islands.

Unfortunately, they argued, this meant that not only would testifying put them in breach of Cooks law, but it would also destroy the business they have built up in the Cooks, and as such be unreasonable.

I wasn't sure at the time whether the decision to let Solicitor-General John McGrath QC lead the fight in the Privy. McGrath had come in for criticism during the turbulent 1994 period covered in *The Paradise Conspiracy*. However, it turned out McGrath's appearance was indeed a harbinger of success.

The Solicitor-General and Colin Carruthers appeared to have a strategy: early on in the course of the Privy Council hearing McGrath moved to lay out, chapter and verse, the facts of the allegedly criminal Magnum transaction. The logic was that once the five law lords got a feel for what was involved, then they would realise why the European Pacific staff were so desperate not to testify.

"I remember the look on Lord Lloyd's face," recalls Brian Henry, "and he said to McGrath: 'Mr Solicitor, does this mean that the transaction ran in this way?'."

McGrath looked across at Carruthers, and Henry caught an affirmative nod. "Oh, I see," said Lord Lloyd, and a big broad grin came over his face.

As Carruthers would later tell a legal colleague: "I knew from that moment that we would not lose that appeal."

News feature, July 6, 1996

Lawyers for besieged tax haven company European Pacific found out this week how long the proverbial piece of string is – it ran out as they were holding it.

The company's last chance of halting the Winebox Inquiry juggernaut was crushed on Thursday night as, 20,000 kilometres away in London, five Law Lords from the Privy Council, passed judgement on a bid by three former European Pacific staff to avoid giving evidence at the Winebox Inquiry.

The lords told lawyer Bruce Stewart that his clients' appeal against being forced to testify was being dismissed. Worse, the European Pacific staff would have to pay the costs of the expensive, trans-global legal jaunt.

While the detailed reasoning of the Privy Council probably won't be released for some weeks, the decision announced this week will have an impact around the world.

It drags British and Commonwealth case law into line with United States and Canadian court rulings on tax havens, and further supports the tough new stand on international money-movers that's been signposted by our own Court of Appeal.

It says, in effect, that a nation is master of its own borders and doesn't have to bow and scrape to other nations with conflicting laws – like the Cook Islands for example.

The Court of Appeal went further, and warned that old-fashioned doctrines like the privilege against self-incrimination may not be available to tax haven participants.

Foolishly, in my humble opinion, European Pacific's legal advisors have time and time again refused to accept the obvious, and they've mounted repeated legal challenges. They have lost every single one, according to my recall.

The past four years have been littered with European Pacific's legal failures. In addition, many of those failures have been so spectacular they have made firstly New Zealand and now world legal history.

Remember European Pacific's legal gagging attempt on the media in 1992? Crunched out of existence by TVNZ's court battle to get the Frontline documentary to air in 1994. Along the way, the High Court and Court of Appeal set new precedents allowing the media to investigate tax crimes, and further codifying the media's right to protect whistle-blowing sources.

Remember European Pacific and other corporates and Inland Revenue Department mounting a legal challenge to try and force the Commission of Inquiry to hear all the evidence in secret, based on the idea that the commercial taxpayers had a right to secrecy of their affairs that outweighed the public's right to know?

That, too, was smashed with Court of Appeal rulings that clearly show the public interest in ensuring the tax and law enforcement systems are working far outweighs claims to taxpayer confidentiality. Definitely not a judgement, I would venture, that European Pacific or the other corporates had wanted written firmly into precedent case law.

To its credit, the Serious Fraud Office has consistently argued in favour of a full, open inquiry, but this week SFO director Charles Sturt took his fight against NZ First leader Winston Peters beyond the borders of the inquiry, choosing a parliamentary select committee as his skirmishing venue.

Sturt claimed Peters had tried to hire a private detective to investigate possible links between Sturt and Sir Michael Fay.

It begs the question: with Peters' legal team having opened up at the inquiry a business relationship between Sturt's wife and the Richwhite family, will we now also see the SFO calling the private detective to the witness stand to back up Sturt's claims against Peters?

Just how dirty will the fight get, and who will be left standing at the end of it?

More ammunition will undoubtedly have been added to the grudge match with the revelation yesterday that police armed with search warrants last week raided the home of one of the defendants in the infamous bloodstock and film partnership deals, and took away cartons of documents to the Official Assignee's office.

Winston Peters has already alleged at the inquiry that the SFO cleared the Merry Christmas Mr Lawrence film partnership without investigating the issues at the heart of his complaint, and rebel IRD staff have testified they felt "blackmailed" into backing off prosecution on some of the deals.

Allegations about those deals have been circulating for some years, but the OA's action is believed to be the first move by an investigatory body to seize evidence.

The Serious Fraud Office is understood to have approached the OA's office in Auckland this week seeking to take the documents itself and asking that news of the OA's seizure didn't "leak out".

One thing's for certain: with the Privy Council now forcing European

Pacific executives onto the witness stand, with an election campaign now underway where Winston Peters' credibility on the winebox issues is being challenged, and with SFO and IRD staff yet to face the gruelling cross-examination that everyone else has had to face at the inquiry – it's likely to get very brutal very quickly.

The Privy Council law lords were very brutal indeed. Perhaps most brutal to New Zealand's Justice McKay, the only Court of Appeal judge to take European Pacific's side of the legal argument.

Of McKay's judgment, used by EP in the Privy Council appeal, suggesting that the EP trio shouldn't testify because the Cook Islands could seek their extradition from New Zealand, the lords had this to say:

"The appellants contended that if they give evidence, quite apart from the risk of prosecution in the Cook Islands, they will be at risk of being extradited to the Cook Islands in accordance with New Zealand's own extradition laws.

"Their Lordships are of the opinion that this risk can properly be regarded as fanciful. It is frankly inconceivable that a New Zealand District Court judge would order the return, or even the arrest, of a person whose sole offence was that he had done in New Zealand what New Zealand law had compelled him to do."

News feature, August 23, 1996

A reluctant European Pacific witness has given Winebox Inquiry investigators some major leads this week, despite his apparent inability to remember much.

Former EP staff member Anthony McCullagh has confirmed that members of European Pacific's highly mobile "banking team" had carried out some of the planning for the allegedly fraudulent JIF deals in Auckland.

The deals, worth a total of around $1.9 billion, involved the use of Cook Islands tax certificates to obtain money from the Japanese Revenue.

Commission lawyers have known for a long time that the deals were kickstarted by the Bank of New Zealand and channelled through Citibank in New York, but up until this week it was unclear whether any of the planning had taken place within the New Zealand jurisdiction.

McCullagh confirmed that EP's New Zealand representative office – ironically based only a few floors above where the inquiry is now sitting – had been used by members of the banking team as they worked on the JIFs.

He revealed that European Pacific was plotting raids on the United States and British treasuries using Cook Islands tax credits.

McCullagh said he'd been privy to discussions in European Pacific's New Zealand office.

"There were a number of jurisdictions being thought of at the time," McCullagh confirmed to the Commission.

"One was the US, the other was the UK, Japan."

Other countries on a potential hit-list included Australia, Belgium and the Netherlands.

Two versions of the deals – the Magnum transaction that cost New Zealand taxpayers $2 million, and the JIF deals that cost the Japanese Revenue up to $100 million – have been alleged at the inquiry and in court to be criminal fraud, and an earlier version was also described by an Australian QC as a conspiracy to defraud.

A report commissioned by the Cook Islands Government and carried out by another Australian QC has found the Magnum deal did break Cook Islands law, but the report claims the breach was unintentional and no further action should be taken.

European Pacific denies there was any illegality in the arrangements, and Anthony McCullagh claims he was never aware of the secret details of the transactions in the Cook Islands.

His denial came despite the fact that his name appears on key planning documents for the Magnum deal.

He blamed one of his co-workers, Mark Jones, who has so far escaped the clutches of a Winebox Inquiry subpoena.

"I had no supervision of Mr Jones' work. It was not uncommon for Mr Jones to append my name to documents as a general courtesy ... it did not necessarily mean I was familiar with or even had read the document ... I have no recollection of it."

Can you think," asked counsel assisting the Commission, Colin Carruthers QC, "of any reason why Mr Jones would use your name on this memorandum?"

"No," replied the witness.

Also in the firing line this week was the claim by former European Pacific staff that their tax dodge deals had the blessing of the best lawyers that money could buy.

During cross-examination of McCullagh, Carruthers acknowledged that an early version of the tax credit scheme had received legal scrutiny, but the version eventually put into practice apparently had not.

In particular, Carruthers pointed out that even with the early version one QC had warned it could be criminal.

European Pacific made three major changes to the scheme, including a jurisdictional switch so that "the tax credits are now claimed in New Zealand and not Australia," the party claiming the tax credit was now a member of the group that had devised the transaction and, said Carruthers, "the company claiming the credit is part of the group that knows of the loss-making transaction in the Cook Islands."

"But against all of that background," continued the QC, "no legal advice is obtained to check on how those changes affect the risk or doubt that was identified in the earlier structure – isn't that the position?"

"It would appear so, yes," admitted Anthony McCullagh, who couldn't explain why the lawyers hadn't been consulted on such an important matter.

He'd earlier stridently defended his former employer and colleagues.

"I had full confidence … in the legal advice being obtained and also the calibre of the people who were working with EP. There is nothing to suggest that there would be any countenance of any illegality. These were highly professional people," he'd said.

That answer had come after a hammering from Colin Carruthers over a possible breach of s62 of the Companies Act 1955 in the Magnum deal.

The breach had been signposted by European Pacific staff lawyers, who had concluded that the breach involved a $200 fine and wasn't considered to be a "serious" legal problem.

"Does that reflect the quality of the legal advice that you referred to a moment ago?" asked Carruthers.

"No, it does not," admitted McCullagh, before adding that in his view the staff had acted responsibly by flagging the illegality, and he claimed the problem had been sorted out the following year when the transaction was unwound.

"It may have been a bit late by then though, McCullagh, mightn't it," suggested Carruthers, "entering into a transaction that – at the time it was entered into – envisages illegality."

When the Commission QC challenged the former EP accountant to show where the transaction did not breach s62, McCullagh's lawyer, Richard Craddock QC, objected, saying it was unfair to ask such a question of a layman.

The question was similar to one put to both former Auditor-General Brian Tyler and New Zealand First leader Winston Peters during hostile cross-examination by counsel for various interested parties.

Winebox commissioner Sir Ronald Davison ruled that McCullagh should answer the question, but the witness said he wasn't involved in the unwind of the Magnum deal and couldn't comment on how the s62 problem had been avoided.

After earlier testimony that he wasn't worried about the Magnum transaction being subjected to full scrutiny in its entirety, McCullagh was confronted by statements he'd allegedly made to businessman Stephen Lunn back in 1992 when the winebox was only just starting to make headlines.

McCullagh admitted he probably had met Lunn in the street, outside the Auckland Club, and asked him whether the Magnum documents were in the winebox.

However, the witness couldn't remember what his response had been when Lunn confirmed his suspicions.

"Well," began Colin Carruthers, "I am trying to be polite about it, Mr McCullagh, which is the difficulty. If I put it that you expressed disappointment by using an expletive, does that accord with your recollection of your response to Mr Lunn's disclosure?"

"I can't remember," answered the accountant.

There were other upsets in store, including a statement from McCullagh that he'd resigned his secretarial duties at European Pacific on June 30, 1989. No sooner had the statement been made than a new document appeared on the Commission computer screens, clearly showing McCullagh was still signing official documents as "secretary" on July 31, 1989.

"It must be – have been a mistake," said McCullagh, peering at the computer screen.

With the Carter Holt Harvey transaction firmly back on the agenda following the SFO's investigation and clean bill of health, McCullagh found himself being questioned about documents that he'd apparently signed on March 31, 1988, the day before the CFC tax regime took effect and the deadline that had to be met.

He was confronted with testimony from an earlier witness, who said he hadn't sent drafts of the documents to McCullagh until April 7, 1988.

By far the biggest publicity hit to emerge from the McCullagh evidence, however, was the revelation that European Pacific principal David Lloyd has been funding the legal bills of Anthony McCullagh, Peter Brannigan and Geoff Barry – the three former EP staff who fought against testifying all the way to the Privy Council.

Again, Richard Craddock had objected to questions about who was paying the legal bills, but he was overruled by Sir Ronald, who said "its relevance is that in view of the attitude taken by European Pacific regarding non-disclosure of documents, that if this witness were to have received advantages from EP, that is a matter which goes to credibility, and I direct that it shall be answered."

No figure has been placed on the value of the legal financial assistance.

The Privy Council law lords had certainly tumbled to the Magnum transaction during their consideration of the European Pacific appeals. The IRD and SFO had argued in the Winebox Inquiry that the Magnum deal could not be attacked as tax fraud because of the so-called doctrine of form over substance.

Form over substance is a legal term that up until now has been relied on by tax lawyers and their clients to escape prosecution for questionable tax schemes.

It works on the premise that tax inspectors must give weight to the legal form of a transaction – the way the lawyers have structured it – rather than the substance – the way it actually works.

In Magnum's case, there were a host of separate companies involved which, while they were all owned by European Pacific, had to be regarded as totally independent entities, so the IRD said. There was no fraud because each legal step had been completed properly.

Bollocks, argued lawyers for TVNZ when we went to the Court of Appeal in 1994 to argue the deal was a $2 million fraud. "It has to be treated as one transaction with a deliberate purpose."

This is how the Privy Council described Magnum:

"This involved the payment of withholding tax (in very round figures, $2m) by European Pacific to the Cook Islands Government in respect of interest paid by one European Pacific company to another, the purchase by the Cook Islands Government of a promissory note from a European Pacific company, and the sale of the same note by the Government to another company in the group at a substantial loss ($1.95m).

> "All these dealings were part of a *single, prearranged scheme* [author's emphasis]. Their economic effect was to pay back almost all the tax paid."

This was the same conclusion reached by Auckland tax lawyers, Dr Gary Muir and Dr Anthony Molloy QC way back in 1993. Now the highest court in the Commonwealth was echoing it. How could the Winebox Inquiry verdict have said there was no fraud in the Winebox?

Chapter 9

A Betrayal Of Trust

People of the same trade seldom meet together, even for merriment and diversion, but the conversation ends in a conspiracy against the public, or in some contrivance to raise prices.
– Adam Smith (1723–90), Scottish economist

The time has come in the book to investigate the major transactions at the centre of the Winebox investigation, and to point out to the reader how Sir Ronald Davison got the law so horribly wrong.

I should point out here that nothing in my first book, *The Paradise Conspiracy*, has been superseded by events at the Winebox Inquiry. You should read this book as the logical sequel to *Paradise*, and *Lawyers, Guns & Money* as an adjunct.

As laid out in the first book, the Magnum deal was the best-documented transaction in the Winebox. It was also a criminal fraud.

Briefly, it worked as follows:

The overall idea was to provide a European Pacific client, Magnum Corporation, with an investment that had a high interest rate. To do that, European Pacific had to find a way to cheat the tax system.

They did it by arranging the scheme so that it would appear tax was being paid in the Cook Islands on the investment. Under double taxation rules, New Zealand would accept a Cook Islands tax certificate as proof that the investment had been taxed, and wouldn't question it further.

Because of European Pacific's close relationship with the Cook Islands Government – EP drafted the tax havens laws – European Pacific was able to purchase Cook Islands tax certificates with a face value of $2 million, for only $50,000.

European Pacific then presented those tax certificates in New Zealand to gain a $2 million tax credit at the expense of ordinary New Zealand taxpayers: you and I.

The diagram overleaf illustrates how the tax money was laundered.

In his report, Winebox Commissioner Sir Ronald Davison laid out the facts of the transaction as he saw them.

They included:

1) EPFML (a New Zealand registered company) received income on a debenture. It was required to pay withholding tax on that income to the Cook Islands Government.

2) EPFML paid to the Cook Islands Government in two payments the amount of the tax payable.

3) In return for those payments, it received from the Cook Islands Government what purported to be receipts for that tax.

4) By means of companies in the EPI group entering into transactions, which were quite unreal, for the sale and purchase of promissory notes, with the Cook Islands Property Corporation (a body controlled by the Cook Islands Government) the Cook Islands Government made a loss of sums equal to the two payments of so-called tax (less a sum of $50,000 which was retained on behalf of the Cook Islands Government). Those sums were not paid to the taxpayer, EPFML, but to Harcourts, another company within the EPI group.

5) The receipts obtained by EPFML (the New Zealand taxpayer) were used by that company in New Zealand when it made returns of income to the IRD.

6) Against the tax payable on that income EPFML offset what it claimed were credits for withholding tax already paid in the Cook Islands and produced as evidence of such payments the two receipts for so-called tax paid in the Cook Islands.

7) EPFML in claiming those credits did not disclose to the IRD the sums which had accrued to Harcourts by means of those promissory note transactions, and which effectively amounted to payment of the amount of the tax less a fee of $50,000.

This then is the factual matrix upon which Sir Ronald turned to analyse the deals.

There are several ways in which to attack the Magnum transaction. The first, and perhaps most fundamental, is section 301 of the NZ Income Tax Act, which says:

"A credit for foreign tax shall not be allowed unless ... the taxpayer claim-

STEP 1: HACL pays $881,582 in tax to Cook Islands Inland Revenue.
STEP 2: CI IRD passes $831,582 of that to the CI Government Property Corp.
STEP 3: CI GOVT PROPERTY CORP pays DUNDEE $10,881,582, and gets a promissory note in return.
STEP 4: CI GOVT PROP CORP sells promissory note to EP MERCHANT and gets paid only $10,050,000 in return. A loss to the Cooks Govt of $831,582 – almost the exact amount of tax paid in by HACL earlier.
STEP 5: EP MERCHANT FINANCE sells the promissory note back to DUNDEE, "crystallising" its profit of $831,582 on the transaction.
STEP 6: Not only does the EP Group have its tax money back, but CI IRD also gives it a "tax certificate" to mark the initial tax payment by HACL. That tax certificate is used against the NZ Revenue, without disclosure that the tax had already been refunded.

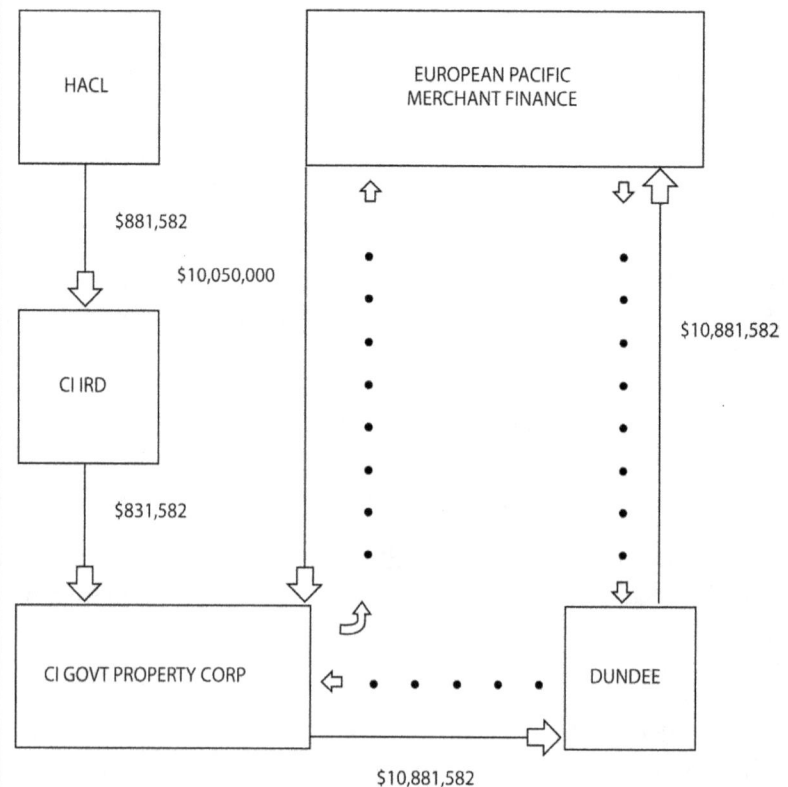

KEY: Solid lines are cash flows. Dotted lines are the transfer of promissory notes in return for the cash payment

ing the credit ... furnishes to the Commissioner all information (including information in relation to any amount to which the taxpayer is entitled in respect of any relief or repayment of the foreign tax) necessary for determining the amount of the credit."

The law says the taxpayer wanting to use a foreign tax credit to get a refund in New Zealand must disclose "all information" about his claim, including "any amount to which the taxpayer is entitled in respect of any relief or repayment of the foreign tax". European Pacific's lawyers argued that EPFML in New Zealand did not have to make a disclosure, because EPFML was not the "taxpayer" that received the refund in the Cooks. It was another company in the group.

Even if it were a legitimate interpretation of the law, and according to the Court of Appeal and the Privy Council it is not, the defence is unsound for another reason: the man responsible for filing EPFML's tax return and presenting the Cook Islands tax certificates, accountant Anthony McCullagh, didn't even know about the requirements of section 301.

The Inquiry discovered he found out about it as a result of the TVNZ documentary.

Nor was European Pacific boss David Lloyd aware of the requirement when I interviewed him in December 1993. If they didn't even know they had a duty to disclose, I don't see how their lawyers can imply that the law was carefully considered and that they reached a considered view that no disclosure was necessary.

On that reading of it, I don't see how European Pacific staff could use one of the other defences that some lawyers trotted out at the inquiry – that by relying on legal advice that the deal was OK the staff formed no criminal intent.

How could you argue "my lawyer told me I didn't have to disclose under section 301" when you never knew about section 301 and there's no evidence your lawyer considered it either?

The European Pacific defence that no disclosure was necessary is based on the so-called doctrine of "form over substance", which we've touched on earlier.

But there's other evidence that European Pacific staff didn't give as much consideration to legal issues as perhaps they should have.

News feature, August 30, 1996

United States law enforcement agents have requested copies of some key winebox transaction documents amid suggestions that a US$200 million dollar tax credit deal may have breached US laws set up to combat money laundering.

The deal in question is the Mitsubishi/JIF transaction, which involved European Pacific, Fay Richwhite and the Cook Islands Government in a joint-venture raid on the Japanese internal revenue to the tune of millions of dollars.

It was one of half a dozen similar so-called JIF deals that have come to light at the inquiry, worth a total of US$1.2 billion, but the Mitsubishi transaction is the best documented.

All the deals were routed through New York, using both Citibank and the Bank of New Zealand's New York branch.

The shock new development was revealed on Wednesday as lawyers for New Zealand First leader Winston Peters questioned former European Pacific executive Geoff Barry.

"Are you aware," asked barrister Brian Henry, "that if the Japanese revenue regards the [Cook Islands] tax receipts being presented to it as being an unlawful activity, that could bring the settlement of this transaction within the laundering of monetary instruments under the United States Federal law?"

"No, I never considered that," admitted Barry.

"Would it surprise you to learn," continued Henry, "that such activity can carry up to 20 years in prison?"

"It would surprise me," said the former European Pacific Banking Corporation manager, although his answer was lost as a frisson of tension rippled through the inquiry hearing room.

Brian Henry continued to up the ante, saying that in fairness to the witness, "I should indicate that we have had discussions with a United States expert in respect of this aspect, and as a consequence of those discussions he took it upon himself to refer the factual situation to the United States District Attorneys in the state of New York.

"They have, at this stage, expressed an interest in looking at the US aspect of the transaction and we have had a request to provide documents which we will shortly do."

Documents released at the inquiry this week show principal and interest flows in the JIF deals were regularly passed through Citibank and the BNZ New York.

They also show that in 1989, income of nearly US$6.5 million had dropped out of the money-go-round in three of the JIF deals alone – Mitsubishi, Sanwa and Fuji – and given the incomplete nature of the documents even more cash could have been involved.

Figures for 1992, again incomplete and covering only three of the Japanese bank deals, amount to almost US$5 million, while papers covering the first three months of 1993 show US$3.7 million dropping out.

The man responsible for controlling the money flows, Geoff Barry, told the inquiry he had never considered whether running the JIF deals through New York would create a United States tax issue, nor was he aware of how the US Internal Revenue Service would treat the income being generated by settling the deals in the US.

Barry's lawyer, Richard Craddock QC, objected to what he implied was the Hollywood nature of the question line.

"He has his television clip for the day with his last few remarks," said Craddock, referring to Brian Henry, "but, with respect, I can't see how this can conceivably be of relevance or conceivably be something that this witness can assist us on."

Henry told the Commission his questions were relevant, and would "result in eventual submission to you in respect of the application of New Zealand law and, given that there are sections in our Crimes Act about planning the commission of actions that are criminal offences overseas within our jurisdiction as part of the Crimes Act, we will make submissions to you in respect of the 'JIFs' at the end of the day."

The US takes the view that it has worldwide jurisdiction on any transaction that passes through its borders. Although I didn't know it when I wrote *The Paradise Conspiracy* in 1995, evidence uncovered by the Inquiry revealed that the massive JIF deals – probably the most politically sensitive of the Winebox transactions – had involved no lesser entity than Citibank, with whom I had been previously acquainted. Citibank's vast banking network was used by Fay Richwhite and European Pacific to move US$1.2 billion in a series of transactions that rorted more than a hundred million dollars from the Japanese Government.

Although documents were examined by the US Internal Revenue Service, they opted not to take action under moneylaundering laws on the grounds that the nil revenue impact on the US didn't necessitate involvement.

Interestingly, several Japanese banks involved in massive tax deals with an undisclosed New Zealand company, and utilising the Cook Islands tax haven, were subsequently accused of either massive tax avoidance or in some cases evasion.

The allegations against the Japanese banks were one of the first signs of financial trouble in the Asian powerhouse. Japan's economy would collapse only a couple of years later in a series of banking and political scandals.

The Magnum transaction can also be attacked under the New Zealand Crimes Act. Section 229a provides for criminal prosecution for using a document to gain pecuniary advantage for yourself or another person So, even if you took a form over substance view that European Pacific didn't need to tell the IRD about the Cooks tax refund under s301 of the Income Tax Act – because the refund was gained by "another person", you may still be committing a crime under the Crimes Act.

The other method of attack is a little more complex, but it provides what I believe are many clues to the issue of criminal intent – mens rea.

This line of inquiry follows the issue of whether the Magnum transaction is in fact legal at each step, or whether the documents drawn up by the parties are a sham made to appear legal, but concealing illegalities.

One of the steps that Counsel Assisting the Commission concentrated on was the issue of whether the "tax" allegedly "paid" in the Cook Islands met international definitions of what a tax was.

Sovereign states, you see, have complete power over their own affairs, and as a rule the actions of a sovereign cannot be called into question, unless the action in question does not come about as an act of Government but as a result of commercial dealing.

To be an act of Government, it must meet certain criteria. The money involved must have been appropriated by Parliament – ie, budgeted for – and it must be accounted for correctly.

If the transactions in the Cook Islands did not amount to paying tax in the proper sense of the word, then the Cook Islands tax certificates would themselves be shonky and the transaction would be a fraud on the New Zealand revenue.

By way of background, the Cook Islands used to have their Government accounts inspected and approved by the Audit Office of New Zealand.

But, just before the tax credit deals were entered into, arrangements were made to get rid of the New Zealand Audit Office from scrutinising Cook Islands affairs. The first step in this move was to ask the Audit Office to appoint a subcontractor who would do the auditing for them. That subcontractor was KPMG Peat Marwick.

News feature, March 23, 1996

It is one of the fundamental obligations of a constitutional auditor, former Auditor-General Brian Tyler told the Winebox Inquiry this week, to report to Parliament on the misconduct of the Executive.

He was talking about the Cook Islands Government's role in alleged fraud, but former New Zealand politicians were this week also sucked into the winebox vortex courtesy of the New Zealand Audit Office. But first, the entree.

It began with former auditor Terry Murphy's testimony about the way the Office used to carry out statutory audits of the Cooks books. Evidence of cooked books apparently wasn't hard to find, although the cause was argued and denied at length.

Murphy said half a million dollars had disappeared from the Cook Islands accounts on one occasion, and he suspected fraud. The Cooks' Financial Controller Alistair Rutherford disagreed, claiming a power surge had "cooked" the accounts computer and caused half a million dollars to drop into cyberspace.

It was Murphy's inquiries about alleged false tax certificate schemes that got him into trouble, however.

After receiving a tip-off from the late Cook Islands internal auditor Richard McDonald in 1987, the Audit Office began serious attempts to get to the bottom of the allegations. The Office also alerted New Zealand's IRD about the possibility of fake tax certificates floating around, but the IRD's man in Rarotonga, Trevor Wallace, blurted the news to the Cook Islands Government, which resulted in Richard McDonald's sacking.

It wasn't the only inadvertent leak about the investigation. Murphy later claimed his own top secret research on the tax credit schemes was accidentally disclosed to Cooks authorities in early 1990. There followed a kind of "please explain" from Sir Geoffrey Henry. The diplomatic furore was a factor in the Audit Office losing the contract to audit the Cook Islands books.

"I was very much persona-non-grata," Murphy said of his status during his final weeks on the Cook Islands audit team. Asked by Commission Counsel Colin Carruthers whether he agreed with suggestions that he was personally to blame for the contract loss, Murphy was blunt:

"Well, I think that's ridiculous quite frankly. I can only speculate that I was possibly getting too close to things.

"The first indication I had was when Mr Ormsby said to me, and inferred, that discussions had even been held by Mr Henry with [NZ Prime Minister David] Lange. I thought 'gee, it has reached that level has it? What have I done wrong?' I have never had a satisfactory explanation as to that."

In fact the Cook Islands Government had been keen to nobble the New Zealand Audit Office for some time. A memorandum in the winebox dated April 1989 showed European Pacific analysing the probability of the Audit Office being booted out, and KPMG Peat Marwick taking over. The memo

also noted how the controversial tax credit deals would be effectively hidden from the auditors eyes.

Terry Murphy had listed more than forty matters that he wanted cleared up before he would sign off on the Cooks accounts, including the tax credit deals. As director of the team he had estimated it would take forty eight person-days to complete. Instead, they were given fifteen.

According to former Auditor-General Brian Tyler, some of the pressure for a quick wrap-up came from the then Minister of External Relations and Trade, Fran Wilde, who had apparently involved herself after meeting Sir Geoffrey Henry.

Tyler also trained his guns on KPMG for what he claimed was a "conflict of interest". KPMG had taken over the Cooks audit as a subcontractor to the Audit Office. While the accounting firm did disclose that it had worked with European Pacific Group in the Cooks, apparently the warning wasn't flagged enough to ring Tyler's alarm bells.

Testifying that in his view the tax credit deals constituted "fraud of a very considerable magnitude", Tyler says KPMG should have brought them to his attention, and added that if he'd known about KPMG's position at the time, "I would not have appointed them as my contractor."

Of particular concern to Tyler was the fact that Peat Marwick appeared to have given European Pacific key advice on how to set the tax credit deals up. Not only that, but the very same staff who had advised European Pacific and the Cook Islands Government on the deals, ended up doing the auditing work that was supposed to discover the deals and report on them.

Don't forget, on the face of it the Magnum deal saw the Cook Islands Government make a $1.95 million loss by buying a promissory note from European Pacific at a high price and selling it back to EP at a lower price.

On the JIF deals, the Cook Islands Government lost hundreds of millions of dollars in such deals. These things were bound to turn up in any competent Government audit.

KMPG's application to become the audit subcontractor without disclosing their own involvement, said Tyler, was like putting Sylvester in charge of Tweetie-Pie.

> *"The conflict of interest that I was concerned with, in terms of the Magnum transaction which I regarded as fraudulent, was that the advice that was central to the decision to proceed appeared to emanate from Peat Marwick. There was a conflict of interest between one's role and responsibilities as the*

Denese Latimer, IRD senior inspector who testified against Head Office.

A Betrayal Of Trust

131

Above: Geoff Clews, Russell McVeagh lawyer who allegedly "blackmailed" the IRD. / *The Independent Business Weekly*

Right: Tony Bouzaid, IRD executive who signed off on non-prosection deal. / *The Independent Business Weekly*

Top: David Henry, Former IRD Commissioner. / *The Independent Business Weekly*

Right: John Nash, IRD Winebox Project Team leader. / *The Independent Business Weekly*

**Right & Below:
SFO director Charles Sturt,
under pressure**

constitutional auditor, and the performance of those advisory activities on behalf of European Pacific."

After all, would KPMG Peat Marwick wish to blow the whistle on themselves?

Under cross-examination he was even tougher, calling it a "basic, fundamental conflict of interest in respect of somebody acting on my behalf as the constitutional auditor."

KPMG's lawyer, David Williams QC, suggested it was the responsibility of the Audit Office to find out what sort of work KPMG had done in the Cooks beforehand, drawing a scathing response from Tyler.

> *"Do you really expect my men to come along and ask you, audit client by audit client, what work you have done, to see whether in fact there is a disqualification. Just asking the question Mr Williams, I think, provides a sensible answer!"*

Then KPMG's other QC, Howard Keyte, tried to have it the other way, suggesting to former Assistant Auditor General Dennis Ormsby that client confidentiality would preclude KPMG from disclosing what work it had done on the deals.

The spectacle of one of the world's largest accounting firms dancing on hot coals and getting badly burnt, was telling.

Commission lawyers interrupted, wanting to know how such an impasse could be resolved.

"In the circumstances where a potential subcontractor is unable to tell you about the work that it is doing for another party like European Pacific, what course would you expect the potential subcontractor to adopt?"

"Not tender," replied Ormsby.

"And why is that, Mr Ormsby?"

"We are talking in hindsight. I think they found themselves in an impossible situation from our point of view. I think it should be stressed too, that the letting of a contract in retrospect is a very unusual situation. Normally, contracts are let for forward work, not back work.

"I think if he [KPMG partner Keith Rushbrook] had said to us: 'I think you should be aware that I have given advice to the Crown Law Office – accounting advice –' we would have been bound to have said 'what was that advice and what was it about? And then, I don't know where we would have gone."

As it turned out, KPMG went on to audit the Cooks books for the very year in which it had earlier provided advice to the Cooks Government, and did not flag the tax credit deals in its audit reports.

Not that the Audit Office had done fantastically well investigating the tax credit deals either. Despite three years spent trying to get to the bottom of them, the Audit Office appears to have forgotten about them in the rush to hand over the contract to KPMG.

Over the following two years, the Audit Office had failed to raise the issue with KPMG's Cook Islands team on a number of occasions.

Keyte gained an admission that Ormsby hadn't placed any "great importance" on investigating the tax credit deals, nor was there any evidence that the Audit Office had asked KPMG to investigate the matter when it took over the contract, although the working papers on the deals would have been handed over amongst other Cook Islands working papers.

"You would accept, therefore, wouldn't you," said Keyte, "that if you looked at it from Peat's point of view, you not having raised it on any of these occasions, you gave no signal, no flag, no indication to them that they should regard it as an important part of their reporting?"

"Well," conceded Ormsby, "I didn't, no."

There was however a massive culture gap between the Audit Office and the private sector legal and accounting advisors.

European Pacific's QC, Richard Craddock, kept trying to suggest that Tyler and the Audit Office had "betrayed" their client, the Cook Islands Government, "which was entitled to have its commercial affairs kept secret".

Tyler kept telling Craddock that his "client" was *not* the Cook Islands Government. Quite the opposite. Under the Cooks Constitution, the Auditor was to keep a watchful eye on the executive arm – Government – and report to Parliament each year on their activities. His clients were, in effect, the citizens of the Cooks through their Parliament, and his report was a public one.

Obviously the Audit Office assumed that KPMG would adopt the culture of exposure that goes with public sector auditing, and it's clear the Audit Office assumed the audit of the Cook Islands Government was in safe hands.

How, asked Tyler, could an auditor doing a public sector watchdog audit, like KPMG, know about transactions where the Cook Islands Government was refunding millions of dollars in tax to European Pacific, but not report it in the accounts?

KPMG's lawyer, again displaying that secretive corporate mentality, tried to claim that even if Audit Office investigators found evidence of tax evasion or fraud involving the Cook Islands Government, the Society of Accountants code of ethics stated they were not allowed to publicise it.

"The burden of that is not that you are entitled to go and talk to other people, but rather that you may have a duty to try to persuade your client to fulfil their legal obligations and, if they don't or won't, to simply withdraw from acting for them," suggested Howard Keyte.

The proposition drew a blunt response from Ormsby, and again illustrated an apparent shallowness in private sector appreciation of the concept of "for the public good".

"How can an Auditor-General withdraw from acting as the constitutional auditor?" snorted Ormsby.

Keyte's response was that the Audit Office should have raised such issues with its "client", namely the Cooks Government.

"The client was the Cook Islands *Parliament*, Mr Keyte, not the Government," explained Ormsby patiently. "When the Audit Office reports to its clients, the documents are public. There is no confidentiality.

Perhaps the most stunning thing about this whole issue is that KPMG and their lawyers apparently have no idea what the role of a public sector auditor actually is. To suggest that public sector auditors should produce secret reports is laughable, in my humble opinion.

Central to Brian Tyler's allegations of fraud were a series of facts about the deal that he regarded as pointers. One of the central issues, he said, was whether the money originally paid to the Cook Islands Government by European Pacific was, in fact, a tax.

According to the former Auditor-General, the transaction documents detail a preplanned scheme to pay the money in and have it paid right back out again.

> *"That document states that 'the Cook Islands Government would refund the amount of the tax, less its cut' – therefore I do not believe we are talking here about a tax.*
>
> *"The Oxford dictionary defines a tax as a legally levied contribution to state revenues. And I don't believe that this was intended to be a contribution to state revenues. The Cook Islands Government was merely intended to be a conduit between one part of European Pacific and another."*

The evidence at the Winebox Inquiry would show a number of serious discrepancies in the way the Cook Islands tax refunds worked.

Chapter 10

It's Worse Than That: He's Dead, Jim

"Practical politics consists in ignoring facts."
– Henry B. Adams (1838–1918), U.S. historian. The Education of Henry Adams

Under Cook Islands law, any expenditure by the Government or Government departments had to be appropriated by Parliament. In other words, a request had to be made and Parliament would have to give its approval to the massive loss-making transactions that the Cook Islands Government Property Corporation was entering into by purchasing promissory notes from European Pacific.

This was never done. There was never any Parliamentary approval for the Property Corporation to take part in the deals. Legally, the tax refunds were misappropriated funds, stolen from the Cook Islands Treasury.

European Pacific's lawyers, and those for the Serious Fraud Office and the IRD, had argued long and hard that investigators must carefully follow the legal steps of the Magnum transaction and not try to take things like tax refunds out of context.

Ironic, then, that those same lawyers would then argue so strenuously that the failure to appropriate the funds in the Cooks was probably a clerical error and of no importance.

Live by the sword, die by the sword.

But then, European Pacific was never the most professional banking company in the world, and the suggestion that tax payments were "deposited" in Cook Islands Government accounts would be sorely tested.

News feature, 25 August, 1996

A tax haven bank described as "highly professional" by its former staff didn't even have its own chequebooks.

Former European Pacific Banking Corporation manager Geoff Barry has told the Winebox Inquiry that he used to create cheques using an office word processor, and give them cheque numbers based on which day of the year it was.

For example, he told the inquiry, a cheque issued by European Pacific Bank on July 27 1988 was numbered 88277.

When asked what happened if European Pacific Bank issued two cheques on the same day, Barry said the bank would add the number "1" on the end.

Questioned about his role in the tax credit deals where European Pacific paid tax to the Cook Islands Government and then got it back, Barry indicated that the transactions were carried out in a very simple way.

He said he would take the tax cheque to Cook Islands Government officials, exchange some documentation, and then they would hand the same cheque back again on the spot.

Barry was also questioned about a memo calling for bank accounts to be opened in 1988, and for bank records to be created documenting transactions that had taken place the previous year.

"Was that a practice that was followed in EPBC," asked counsel assisting the Commission, Colin Carruthers QC, "that is, the creation of bank accounts and entries in those bank accounts some time after the transactions have taken place?"

"Not at all," said Barry.

Another factor that pointed to an intention to deceive or conceal was the fact that the transactions did not take place in the Cook Islands Government's normal bank accounts, but in a series of special accounts set up by European Pacific.

This allowed the Cooks to take in a massive $2 million tax payment, refund $1.95 million of it, and then bank only the net $50,000 in the Public Account. It is this $50,000 that would show up during an audit using this method, not the tax payment and the refund.

And that was the advice given by KPMG partner Keith Rushbrook when he was initially consulted on the deals.

News feature, May 10, 1996

The Audit Office has turned up the heat under one of the most well-known winebox transactions, telling the Commission of Inquiry that the Magnum deal is either an unlawful tax refund, or a commercial transaction that didn't involve the payment of tax in the first place.

Deputy Auditor-General Wayne Cameron testified this week that he'd analysed a Deloittes report on the Magnum deal, carried out at the request of the Cook Islands Government, and reached his own opinion on the controversial deal.

Cameron said problems with the transaction hinged on an alleged tax payment of $881,582 from a European Pacific subsidiary (Harcourt) to the Cook Islands Government, in return for a tax certificate. Most of the money, less a $50,000 fee for the Cooks Government, was refunded later the same day in a promissory note deal.

To be a legitimate tax payment, Cameron said the cheque from European Pacific should have been banked in the Government's Public Account with the Westpac Bank in Rarotonga. It wasn't.

Instead, the cheque went into a different Government account within European Pacific's offshore bank.

"In accordance with commonly accepted principles for accounting and government revenues, unless otherwise permitted by law, all revenues, including taxes, must be paid into the 'Public Account'," Cameron told the inquiry, adding that the Cooks Constitution specifically requires it.

"If the money paid to IRD as withholding tax by Harcourt truly was a tax, it should have been receipted as taxation revenue into the Cook Islands Government accounts and retained there. It could not subsequently be disbursed without appropriate authority; such authority either being annual appropriation or permanent legislative authority as required by Article 70 of the constitution."

The deputy Auditor-General then said he would have expected to see the full tax payment accounted for in the Government's financial statements, and he argues that the money used by the Cook Islands Government Property Corporation to purchase European Pacific's over-priced promissory notes had not been appropriated by Parliament as required by law.

"Section 14 [of the Property Corporation Act] makes it quite clear that expenditure or investment by the Corporation requires annual appropriation."

European Pacific has argued at the inquiry that the Magnum deal involved a legal payment of tax, and then a separate commercial transaction with the Cook Islands Government involving promissory notes. It denies that the tax was refunded via the notes.

Cameron said that if the two legs of the transaction were genuinely unrelated, he would have expected to see the promissory note deals fully set out in the Government accounts, instead of the netting off approach permitted by KPMG auditors which showed only the residual $50,000 fee in the consolidated accounts.

Playing devil's advocate, the deputy Auditor-General then looked at how KPMG had apparently justified accounting for the deals, and said that KPMG's treatment was appropriate only if you accept that the whole deal was a commercial transaction, not a tax payment.

"If it is accepted that the transactions were financial market transactions, then substance over form prevails and the transactions may be netted off for accounting purposes. The transactions have been accounted for properly in the books of the Cook Islands Government, but tax has not been paid by Harcourt.

"My conclusion is that you can't have it both ways. There is validity to the substance over form argument which leads to the net transaction only being reported in the public accounts, but that leads back to the fundamental question of whether tax was paid and the validity of the 'tax receipt'."

Cameron said his KPMG subcontractors doing the audit of the Cooks books should have either reported the Property Corporation's massive losses on the tax credit deals, or alternatively noted the use of tax money to prop up those losses and flagged it to the Auditor-General by saying "Hey, that's a funny way to apply tax, isn't it?".

"Basically," said Cameron, "it sure is, and it would have given rise to some further action on our part."

Under cross examination from European Pacific's Richard Craddock QC, Cameron agreed that if the bank accounts used by the Cooks Government had all been set up by law and with the appropriate legislative authority, then payments to and from those accounts would be "kosher".

To a question from the Serious Fraud Office's Nick Davidson, Cameron also agreed that Harcourt could have paid a legitimate tax in the Cooks, but the payment was misrepresented and wrongly accounted for in the Government's books.

Meanwhile, KPMG senior partner Keith Rushbrook got his first chance yesterday to clear his name after being accused of being a possible party to a prima facie fraud, and failing to declare a conflict of interest.

Rushbrook came out punching, saying he had never had any "involvement with European Pacific in any capacity."

He said he was unaware of the detail of KPMG's relationship with European Pacific, and told the Commission he had "not been involved in the development of the so-called tax credit product."

Rushbrook said his sole involvement was on the fringes of the issue when he was asked to advise the Cook Islands Government in 1989 on how a tax credit transaction might be accounted for in the consolidated public accounts.

"No one at the meeting told me what they thought the answer to the question should be. Nothing was said to suggest they might wish to 'hide' anything concerning the transactions."

After listening to a briefing that covered the principle but not the full detail of such a transaction, Keith Rushbrook says he concluded that the only benefit to the Cook Islands Government was the $50,000 fee, and accordingly suggested adopting the "netting off" approach for the public accounts. However, he also warned the Cooks officials to check with their auditors.

A winebox memorandum naming Keith Rushbrook and suggesting he was also advising European Pacific on the issue has been labelled incorrect by the KPMG partner, who said he cannot remember providing a briefing to European Pacific, nor can he find such a briefing on KPMG's files.

On the failing to declare a conflict of interest issue, Rushbrook admits he didn't raise his earlier advice with the Audit Office when applying for the Government contract, but says he still doesn't believe "there was any conflict arising out of the accounting advice which I gave on that occasion. I believe the advice which I gave to have been correct and I cannot see why it raised any conflict.

"The suggestion made by Mr Tyler that by giving this advice I became a party to fraud is absurd.

"I do not believe Mr Tyler can be genuine in his continual assertions against me. I am angry about them, especially in view of the apparent failure of his office to pursue the foreign tax credit scheme.

"I believe he has been extremely irresponsible and unprofessional. The impressions he has created have been most damaging. I am firmly of the view that I acted professionally and completely reject all the allegations made against me."

Rushbrook's strident denials had been, as most of us on the media bench agreed, an Oscar-winning performance, right up until the moment that Counsel Assisting the Commission, Colin Carruthers QC, asked his first questions.

Rushbrook has claimed that he only advised on the tax credit deals once, in April 1989. He says he was accompanied on that trip to the Cook Islands by Gordon Price, a man helping European Pacific design the tax credit system.

Counsel assisting the Commission, Colin Carruthers QC, suggested Rushbrook had attended more tax credit meetings than just the one he's testified to, but the KPMG partner says he can't recall any others.

"Was the only meeting that you had with Gordon Price in the Cook Islands the one described in your brief?"

"As far as I can recall, yes," replied the accountant. Snap, went the Carruthers trap. Waving a passport, the QC asked one of those dreaded questions that lawyers are so good at: the kind that they already know the answers to.

"Well," said Carruthers, "what I put to you about Mr Price was if his last visit to the Cook Islands was in May 1988, how do you suggest he had a meeting with you in the Cook Islands in April 1989?"

Scotty looked as though he'd just seen a Klingon.

"I – I simply can't explain it, except for the entries on my passport," answered the accountant, throwing what I mischievously interpreted as one of those "I cannae hold her much longer Jim, she's breaking up!" looks at KPMG's legal counsel, Howard Keyte.

It transpired that Gordon Price had given evidence last year of a tax credit planning meeting as early as February 1988 involving Keith Rushbrook, a meeting that Rushbrook insists happened in April 1989. It's what they call a conflict of evidence. One of the protagonists must be mistaken.

Keith Rushbrook says he never helped plan the deals, and only flew up to Rarotonga in April 1989 with Gordon Price for one half hour meeting with the Cooks Government, but he could not get away from the fundamental problem that Price's last visit to the Cooks was a year earlier.

Gordon Price had claimed his first meeting with Keith Rushbrook on the tax credit deals had taken place between the 6th and 9th of February 1988 in Rarotonga during a flying visit. When Colin Carruthers asked Rushbrook to read his own passport dates for February 1988, an apparently confused accountant read out a set of dates that didn't match.

"No," said the QC, "I think you gave me the February 89 visit. I put it to you that the February 88 dates were 6 February, entry, and 13 February, exit."

"Sorry," apologised the KPMG partner, looking as if he desperately wished he could have been beamed up and away.

Rushbrook has now been asked to produce his passport as evidence and also his timesheets for all of his Cook Islands visits in 1988.

After denying any involvement with European Pacific or briefing EP executive Peter Brannigan on the meeting with the Cook Islands Government, Keith Rushbrook found himself having to explain why he'd sent the bill for that advice to European Pacific "as agreed with Mr Brannigan".

"I think how it happened was simply me tidying up affairs and having a conversation with Peter who said 'send the bill to me'."

"Well," pushed the QC, "why did that suggestion ever arise if the client was the Cook Islands Government?"

"I can't answer that now," said Rushbrook.

So far, there's been no indication that the Enterprise is willing to beam down a support crew. Scotty's just going to have to hang in there.

But if Rushbrook had had a bad week, it was about to get worse for his colleagues.

Chapter 11

Acquitted On A Technicality

"The first step towards vice is to shroud innocent actions in mystery, and whoever likes to conceal something sooner or later has reason to conceal it."
— Jean-Jacques Rousseau (1712–78), French philosopher

News feature, May 17, 1996
Top accounting firm KPMG has admitted it's withholding documents from the winebox Commission of Inquiry, despite orders to produce them as exhibits of evidence.

In a shock revelation yesterday afternoon, KPMG partner Jan Dawson admitted under cross-examination that KPMG audit files on the Cook Islands Government are still being held at KPMG's Rarotonga office, files prepared while KPMG was an Audit Office subcontractor.

"You have been asked to return those," stated Counsel assisting the Commission, Colin Carruthers QC, "and they are the subject of a notice from the Commission. Why haven't they been provided?"

"Because our legal advice was that they had to stay in the Cook Islands," replied Dawson.

She confirmed that KPMG had not told the Audit Office about the existence of the files.

"Why weren't they told?" asked Carruthers.

"I don't know."

The QC demanded to know why their existence hadn't been spelt out to the Commission either, but Jan Dawson said a letter to the inquiry in March disclosed that there were still some working papers in Rarotonga.

That letter has itself been the centre of another shock development, with Dawson admitting that the KPMG letter mislead the Commission of Inquiry about her role auditing the tax credit transactions.

"Who is taking responsibility for it?" demanded Carruthers, "your firm, or is it the responsibility of your counsel?"

"I would imagine it is joint responsibility," said the accountant.

Earlier in the week, the KPMG audit partner made some startling admissions in the context of why the Cook Islands Government's involvement in the tax credit deals wasn't flagged to the New Zealand Audit Office. They included evidence that, when it tendered for and won the sub-contract to audit the books of the Cook Islands Government, KPMG didn't understand what Carruthers described as one of the "fundamental" principles of public sector auditing.

"What I am asking you," said Carruthers, "is whether you understand that it's fundamental, in Government sector accounting, that expenditure by the Government is by way of appropriation in some form?"

"It was not understood at the time," conceded Dawson.

"So," continued the QC, "is the position that your firm tendered for a Government auditing position on the basis that there wasn't an understanding that Government expenditure had to be authorised by appropriation in some form?"

"It was not my understanding, no," she replied.

The Cook Islands Government Property Corporation had been instrumental in the tax credit deals, spending and losing millions of dollars in pre-arranged promissory note deals with European Pacific. Dawson, a senior accountant and the partner responsible for the Government audit, admitted that she was not aware until very recently that expenditure by the Property Corporation should have been approved by Parliament under Cook Islands law.

She claimed to have seen a Cabinet minute authorising the tax credit deals, but admitted not making a copy or even a note of it, despite the fact that it was usual practice for KPMG audit staff to make notes in such cases.

"I didn't," she stated bluntly, in response to a question from Colin Carruthers.

"Why not?" asked the QC.

"Because partners sometimes don't document things as adequately as staff do," she replied.

Carruthers was openly staggered.

"Mrs Dawson, this is the – this is the fundamental document that gives – that you say gives approval to multi-million dollar transactions, and you say that it wasn't necessary for you to have it on record?"

"Yes."

As this issue went to press, Dawson was being cross-examined on a KPMG document missing a section that had been torn off, followed by subsequent renumbering in her handwriting.

Dawson said she might have torn off the section, but couldn't remember what it related to. The document had then been passed to the New Zealand Audit Office for review.

"How," asked Carruthers, "was the Audit Office to understand what had been done if there was no note or explanation to why the file was in this state?"

"Well, I don't know," said Jan Dawson. "I assume that they would just see it as a piece of paper that was partly there."

It's been a rough week for KPMG.

Earlier this week senior partner Keith Rushbrook was forced to retract some of his evidence at the Winebox Inquiry after apparently getting it wrong.

Rushbrook had earlier come out swinging against former Auditor-General Brian Tyler over the latter's allegations that Rushbrook's advice on the tax credit deals could make him a party to a prima facie fraud.

Rushbrook had strenuously denied being involved in the planning stages of the deals, and said he'd only ever given one piece of advice, at the request of the Cook Islands Crown Law Office, which set out how the deals should be treated in the public accounts.

That advice, he insisted, was given in April 1989, and he remembered that one of those attending was Euronational Corporation executive Gordon Price. Euronational had been exploring the possibility of a joint venture with European Pacific on the tax credit deals.

Rushbrook described as "absurd" the suggestion that giving routine, and what he considered correct, accounting advice to the Cook Islands Government could make him a "party to fraud", especially as the deals had already taken place when he became involved.

"I have not been involved in the development of the so-called tax credit product, either through discussions with the Cook Islands Government, European Pacific, Euronational or any other entity," Keith Rushbrook had insisted previously.

"I have never dealt with Gordon Price in relation to Euronational matters," he had added.

Both answers were wrong, and this week the situation changed dramatically.

In a shock reversal of his earlier testimony, a sombre Keith Rushbrook read a prepared statement on Tuesday admitting that he may have taken part in a tax credit planning meeting as early as August 1987.

The backdown followed evidence that Gordon Price couldn't possibly have been in the Cook Islands with Keith Rushbrook in April 1989. Price's passport showed his last visit to the Cook Islands was May 1988. The only occasions the two men had been together in the Cooks were in August 1987 and February 1988, while the tax credit deals were still in their planning stages.

Price gave evidence that by April 1989 he was self-employed, and involved in the export of live deer to Australia. He definitely was not in the Cooks.

Which had left the KPMG partner between a rock and a hard place. After going through his own worksheets, Rushbrook discovered that he had indeed met Gordon Price, but in August 1987, not April 1989.

A KPMG billing record shows Euronational Corporation was billed for work in Rarotonga involving Keith Rushbrook, although Rushbrook can't remember what the work was.

"I have not been able to locate time sheets for the period including 9-11 August 1987," Rushbrook explained. "It appears that all of KPMG's time sheets prior to 20 November 1987 have been destroyed. I have, however, located a fee note."

Gordon Price told the inquiry it was a planning meeting for the tax credit deals, which involved briefing the Cook Islands Government on how they would be accounted for. For his part, Rushbrook could not recall.

"My recollection," admitted Keith Rushbrook under cross-examination on Tuesday, "and I am struggling here because I have obviously rolled two meetings together into one, is that I did not know very much [about the tax credit deals].

"Clearly, evidence shows that I was there earlier, so potentially I would have known something about them in 1989."

Although KPMG took a hammering for withholding the documents, the Privy Council ruled that it was unreasonable to expect KPMG to provide documents that were still in the Cook Islands and subject to Cook Islands Government prohibitions on their movement.

Again, what was stunning was that senior accountants in one of the world's leading accounting firms appeared to have no idea about what public sector auditing involved. Jan Dawson's admission that she had only recently become aware that Government money movements had to be appropriated by Parliament is staggering.

News feature, May 25, 1996

There's a new refrain emerging from witnesses at the Winebox Inquiry.

US President Ronald Reagan has a lot to answer for, but uttering the line

"I don't rightly recall" during the Iran/Contra scandal is the cardinal sin that I will hold him personally responsible for as long as I draw breath. The really frightening thing is that when the old B-grade movie star said it, we put it down to his age and the special Ronald Reagan brand of senility that permeated his entire Presidency.

Over recent months the illness has taken a wicked toll of some of our top business leaders and advisers as they paraded before Sir Ronald Davison's Winebox Inquiry, but now there's a refreshing new twist, which goes something along the lines of "yeah, I was there, I saw it all, but I was just too dumb to realise what it was."

You've gotta admit, this new line has some charm.

KPMG partner Russell Florence put it to good use this week when he told how he gave advice on and later audited the US$1.2 *billion* JIF tax credit deals. Take this exchange that began with a question from Commission counsel Colin Carruthers QC.

"Did they raise any question in your mind as to the propriety of the claim for a tax credit for a full amount of the tax?"

"No"

A pause as Carruthers stared at the accountant.

"Why?"

"It didn't occur to me," said Russell Florence.

The accountant then admitted that he didn't regard it as a normal transaction, but then said he didn't regard it as being unusual for a tax haven. OK, said Carruthers, so how much experience of tax havens do you have?

"I don't have any experience in tax havens other than the Cook Islands," replied the accountant. He later conceded that he now believes the transactions were striking and unusual, and would make further inquiries if he came across them again.

"What sort of inquiries would you make?" asked the QC.

"I don't know."

Entertaining as this and other cross-examination proved to be for the assembled media, they are however only an entree to the main course this week, the release of the long awaited and bitterly disputed issues paper.

It's easy to see why they were fighting so long and hard behind closed doors to prevent or modify its publication, because it reveals the inquiry is investigating areas that, by law, it is not allowed to mention in its final report to the Government.

This investigation includes finding out whether the Serious Fraud Office gave adequate consideration to "whether or not an offence of conspiracy to defraud all or any of the revenue authorities of New Zealand, Australia, Japan and elsewhere or the offence of conspiracy to commit an offence has been committed in New Zealand and elsewhere by any person including all or any of the directors and/or so-called alternate directors or employees of [European Pacific], directors or employees of Fay Richwhite, Capital Markets Ltd and their advisers (Crimes Act s257, s229A, s310)."

Big paragraph, big ramifications. This was just one of a number of issues in relation to a number of winebox deals, but before you gasp in horror I must inform you that you may never know the answer to the question.

Lawyers for some of the corporates had argued the Commission was stepping beyond its terms of reference in deciding to investigate the possible criminality involved, but Sir Ronald Davison makes several important points.

Firstly, he's required to report on whether the IRD and SFO acted lawfully and competently in their handling of the winebox. How can he do that, he argues, if he doesn't first work out whether the transactions broke the law or not?

Secondly, he's also required to report on whether existing laws are tough enough, or whether the winebox deals exploited legal loopholes that need to be closed. How can he do that, he asks, without working out whether the deals broke existing law or not?

Thirdly, however, Sir Ronald is specifically forbidden from publicly disclosing whether or not he has found criminality, and instead must secretly refer such matters to law enforcement agencies for further investigation. So whatever the answers are, you probably won't hear them.

There is another very important aspect to this. The issues paper was drawn up by Colin Carruthers, and merely sets out areas that he wants to further investigate. The "issues" are questions, not answers, and affected parties haven't yet had the chance to call their own evidence. The moral in this? Do not prejudge the issues. As the Commission itself noted: "It is not to be taken as signifying in any way a view or conclusion, tentative or otherwise, by the Commission."

ISSUES PAPER HIGHLIGHTS:
1) Were the tax credit deals evasion?
2) Did the IRD and SFO properly analyse all the evidence?
3) Was the money paid in the Cooks really a "tax"?
4) Should $7.48 million received by Fay Richwhite from the JIF deals have been returned as income?
5) Should IRD and SFO have liased more closely?

6) Did the SFO make the right call in originally deciding not to investigate the winebox?

7) Was the SFO investigation of the Magnum deal competent?

8) Did the SFO consider whether profits from the deals were properly reported by Fay Richwhite and Capital Markets?

9) Did the allocation of those profits between those two companies have an effect on the price to shareholders of the Fay Richwhite/Capital Markets merger in 1990?

10) And have SFO/IRD investigations been hampered by inappropriate claims for legal professional privilege, destruction of documents and the protection of tax haven secrecy laws?

Despite the mountains of evidence suggesting the tax credit deals did not involve the payment of a real tax, Sir Ronald Davison later ruled thus:

"The real problem the Commission faced in determining whether the so-called payments of tax were in fact such arose because of the circumstances under which the moneys were paid over to the Cook Islands Government. The evidence of Mr Barry and other evidence showed that:

1) The moneys were paid over and repayments made to Harcourt on the same day and within the same banking period.

2) The usual Government receipt book was not used, but receipts for the tax credits were issued out of a separate book.

3) The payments were not recorded in the usual Government book of account and only the net 'fee' ($50,000 in the case of Magnum) was recorded.

4) The payments were not deposited in the usual Government bank account but in another account opened with the EPBC for the purpose.

"In those circumstances the issue for the Commission was whether a tax had genuinely been paid, or whether the actions of the Cook Islands Government were simply part of a device entered into by European Pacific with the cooperation of the Cook Islands Government to create false tax certificates.

"The evidence created suspicions that such was the case. That meant that the Commission would have to look closely at the question of whether or not the so-called tax was levied under the exercise of its sovereign power, for public purposes.

"Whilst the Commission has been concerned as to whether or not the payments amounted to a tax, there arose a more fundamental issue as to whether any New Zealand Tribunal has any power at all to enter upon an inquiry into such a matter."

The conclusion of the retired Chief Justice was that he had no power to question Cook Islands sovereignty, and therefore had to ignore the evidence on that subject before him. The basis for making his decision appears mainly to have been some legal opinions contained in submissions provided by lawyers acting for Fay Richwhite.

Fay Richwhite's legal team, in their final submissions, wrote:

> *"The contents of the Cabinet Minutes of the Cook Islands Government, the existence or otherwise of a Parliamentary appropriation to acquire the promissory notes, the choice of a bank for processing the foreign tax credit transactions, the identity of the person who drafted the banking transactions for the Cook Islands Government, the treatment of receipts and expenditure on foreign tax credit transactions and the account for the Cook Islands Government etc are the acts of a foreign sovereign state exercised in its own jurisdiction.*
>
> *"Furthermore, they are not justiciable by a New Zealand Court when considering a charge of conspiracy to defraud the IRD by those who participated in lodging EPFML's tax return."*

Frustrating as it may be to the reader, Fay Richwhite's lawyers may have been legally correct. Quoting eminent QC's and previous New Zealand Court of Appeal judgments, they pointed out that no matter how Mickey Mouse the "tax" payment and documentation were in the Cook Islands, none of that could be used as the basis for criminal charges.

This didn't mean that the evidence of what took place in the Cooks could not be presented at a criminal trial, but it did mean that no charge could be laid solely on the basis that the tax certificates were false. The Cook Islands was a sovereign state. If it wanted to tax corporates in bananas instead of dollars, it was allowed to do so and New Zealand tax investigators couldn't quibble.

Because the partner in crime was the Cook Islands Government, a cloak of state immunity descends upon that portion of the evidence.

There is a contrary view. The Court of Appeal has ruled that although the Magnum transaction does involve the payment of a "tax", the promissory note arrangements to refund the money "lends the transaction as a whole a commercial character, with the element of tax collection becoming largely illusory.

> *"A Government which descends to this extent into the marketplace cannot fairly expect total immunity. Its auditors and financial advisors can be in no better position."*

Nevertheless, Sir Ronald concluded that:

> *"For the reasons which have been earlier discussed the tax credit certificates must be regarded as valid receipts for tax."*

All of which made European Pacific "special" in the tax haven world, because most tax haven companies did not "own" Governments, in the way that European Pacific effectively did.

Indeed, the Winebox scandal was a cover story in the November 1994 issue of *Offshore Investment*, one of the world's leading journals for users of tax havens.

Editor Charles Cain remarked:

> *"From time to time, however, reminders of the old ways creep in. In a programme on Television New Zealand recently there was a sustained examination of the activities of a financial institution in the Cook Islands.*
>
> *"What emerged, for an offshore European, was very reminiscent of some of the less reputable activities of 25 years ago.*
>
> *"A minute new sovereign country has allowed itself to be manipulated by certain unscrupulous financial interests to permit activities which, if not actually criminal, are certainly unacceptable.*
>
> *"What is worse is that the parties to the scandal are not merely the 'businessmen', but the Government itself, who were certainly treated as being in the pocket of the financial institution concerned.*
>
> *"Indeed, the scam analysed in the Television New Zealand programme could not have happened without active and knowing Government collusion. (I recall, quite recently, a professional from the Cook Islands protesting that a particularly aggressive piece of legislation, which invited activity on the part of citizens of another country which could have been construed as fraudulent according to the law of that country, was the 'will of the people'!)*
>
> *"The scandal now breaking in New Zealand relating to the Cook Islands, its former protectorate, is inevitably going to grow. It is a scandal that affects every one of us in the offshore world. We shall all be tarnished."*

When you look at the precedent-setting Court of Appeal and Privy Council rulings, you get some idea of how prophetic those words were back in 1994.

Chapter 12

Blind Justice

"Law grinds the poor, and rich men rule the law."
— Oliver Goldsmith (1728–74), Anglo-Irish poet, essayist, playwright. The Traveller

When the IRD returned to the witness stand at the Winebox Inquiry at the end of 1996 to face cross examination, there were some pretty heavy issues on the agenda.

Firstly, there was the question of basic competence, as we touched on earlier in the book.

Back in 1990 the IRD had let not one but two tax credit certificates slip through its goalposts, both certificates indicating that a New Zealand company had paid *two million dollars in tax* – in a tax haven!

In 1993 the department had waited three months before finally asking the SFO if tax inspectors could examine the Winebox papers that Stephen Lunn had dropped off.

For a few months the documents were examined by the Tax Intelligence Unit, whose staff did not understand the Magnum deal at the time, and the papers were fed into routine company audits, rather than centralised as the focus of a specialised investigation.

In early 1994, the IRD's John Nash signed off as having completed the department's analysis of the deals, and there is not a single document that shows he understood the Magnum or JIF deals at that time either.

It wasn't until media publicity about the tax credit deals broke that the IRD suddenly went into a frenzy.

As readers of *The Paradise Conspiracy* will already be aware, the IRD and SFO downplayed the significance of the Winebox and the deals at every opportunity, and took public positions that no fraud existed – before proper investigation or legal analysis had even been carried out.

News feature, October 6, 1996

The Inland Revenue Department is coming under heavy fire at the Winebox Inquiry, as lawyers for the Davison Commission attempt to find out just how well the tax department investigated the winebox deals.

Senior IRD audit manager John Nash was forced to admit on Friday that he'd misread a key document that could have alerted him to possible fraud in the Magnum tax credit deal.

The IRD went public in early 1994 with a statement that the Magnum deal was within the law, and it has maintained that stance ever since. However, the IRD's position began to look even shakier this week with the release of more documents on the transaction.

One was a diplomatic cable from the New Zealand Government Representative in the Cook Islands in March 1994. The cable alerted the Ministry of Foreign Affairs and Trade in Wellington that documents on the Magnum deal were circulating in business circles in the Cooks.

"The documents," wrote the diplomat, "indicate that a tax scam involving EPBC and CIGov has been operating, probably to the detriment of New Zealand tax revenue. We find it difficult to believe that such a scam could not be illegal in the Cook Islands – it would be our understanding, for example, that tax revenue must be appropriated by parliament and cannot be passed by the tax agency direct to another agency of government.

"We note in passing that on two recent occasions CIGov has been caught out over procedures or legislation that are unconstitutional.

"The documents," concluded the diplomat, "show that CIGov intentionally assisted in defrauding foreign governments, including New Zealand, of large amounts of tax revenue. The implications for the Cook Islands' relations with those governments must be considered to be very severe."

Despite being given the cable to read in March 1994, the IRD's John Nash failed to grasp what was described as the true sting of the document, and consequently didn't act on it. Nash told the inquiry he must have misread the cable.

Another document released this week also hit the IRD amidships. It was a legal opinion on the Magnum and JIF tax credit deals from leading tax lawyer Peter Jenkin QC, the IRD's most senior outside tax consultant.

Jenkin says if "it can be established that refund of tax credits claimed for the 'taxation' imposed by the Cook Islands was an essential part of either transaction, then in my view 'tax evasion' would be established."

He went on to say that "it would be naïve to regard the withholding tax certificates issued by the Cook Islands as genuine."

The inquiry heard last week that when the IRD told the public and Parliament there was no fraud in the Magnum deal, it had not sought a legal opinion on the deal at that stage. When it did finally seek legal advice, the department went to Grant Pearson, a more junior barrister, not Peter Jenkin QC.

Indeed, the IRD did not seek a second opinion, despite the fact that several of the country's top tax lawyers were calling Magnum a fraud, along with IRD Auckland solicitor Michael Scott.

John Nash was asked why the department had stuck with Grant Pearson's legal advice, and not sought a second opinion, in the face of such overwhelming legal argument to the contrary.

"Did it ever occur to the department," suggested Colin Carruthers, "that the views of Dr Prebble, Dr Molloy, the Court of Appeal and, indeed, Mr Scott, indicated that it was possible there was another view of these transactions?"

"You can go on forever looking for other views," said Nash, who added that the Solicitor General appeared happy with the department's legal advice.

John Nash was forced to concede that Grant Pearson had failed to get his facts right, however.

When sending his opinion to the Solicitor-General, Pearson had written that "there is no material suggesting that officers of EPFML [the NZ company using the Cooks tax certificate] knew of the promissory note transaction."

Carruthers showed John Nash a list of the directors of EPFML, most of whom appeared to have been involved in the planning of the secret tax refund scheme.

Nash admitted the IRD lawyer was wrong, and that there was evidence that officers of the company may indeed have known, an issue which goes to whether there was any criminal intent when the tax certificates were used in New Zealand.

News feature, October 11, 1996

The Inland Revenue Department's view that there's no fraud within the Magnum tax credit deal is being sorely tested as lawyers for the Davison Commission continue a relentless cross examination of IRD audit manager John Nash.

Now at the end of his second week in the hotseat, Nash has revealed that the "no fraud" call was essentially his, after a review of the transaction in early 1994.

When NZ First leader Winston Peters raised the Magnum deal in Parliament in March 1994, the IRD's position on the deal became public without the benefit, at that stage, of a legal opinion supporting its stand.

That "shoot first, ask questions later" decision has left Commission counsel Colin Carruthers QC testing the IRD's weak spots, particularly on whether the Magnum deal may have been a sham.

It was a question addressed by John Nash at the time but, by his own admission, not in great detail.

A sham can be determined where parties enter into formal agreements that do not reflect their true intentions. Carruthers pointed out that the formal promissory note deals set out interest coupons and redemption dates for the promissory notes, that were never used or intended to be used in the Magnum transaction.

Instead, he argued, the promissory notes were being used just as a capital item to be bought and sold as a mechanism to refund tax.

The IRD has attacked the Carter Holt Harvey deal, where $37 million worth of AHI notes were allegedly overvalued to around a hundred million, as a sham. But at least, argued the QC, the AHI notes in the Carter Holt deal had a real intrinsic value.

"As far as the [Magnum] promissory notes are concerned," he suggested to Nash, "we finally get to the position that they are just words on a page, don't we?"

Nash went on to concede that you could equally have substituted an old domestic refrigerator for the promissory notes in the Magnum deal and achieved the same result.

"Well, that's really a very good point, isn't it?" said Colin Carruthers. "It could have been the domestic refrigerator that you used in another context, even a secondhand one, or I suppose – to pick up another example – it could have been one of [Russell McVeagh tax partner] Richard Green's socks, couldn't it?"

"I'd rather not comment on Richard Green's socks," replied John Nash diplomatically.

Still arguing the issue of sham, Carruthers pointed out that formal documents in the transaction required the interest payments to the New Zealand taxpayer in the deal to be in one lump sum payable on day one. Instead, despite the formalities, the interest payments were split in two over a period of a year, creating two Cook Island tax certificates a year apart. Nash told the inquiry that the discrepancy may be a "company law" issue, but it didn't affect the tax consequences of the deal. He disagreed with Carruthers that it went to the issue of "sham".

Another element of the deal under attack was the fact that the Cook Islands Government had broken the law in the Cook Islands by not obtaining parliamentary appropriation to refund the tax.

John Nash told the inquiry that while this might be a factor in arguing tax avoidance, they weren't determinant of an illegal deal.

"Those features do not determine the issue of sham, because for sham you must look at what was done, and you look at the documents which represent what was done, and not the accounting entries for a lack of an appropriation."

After spending several days this week defending the Magnum transaction's legality, Nash felt compelled to explain why he was playing Devil's advocate.

"I stop at saying that the arrangements are shams. I stop at saying that they are tax evasion. But I do agree with a lot of the points you are putting to me, and they are points that the department would argue, given the opportunity to disallow the tax credit claims and collect the tax.

"I really don't want to leave an impression that I am a friend of the taxpayer, when I thought from day one that it was a blatant tax avoidance arrangement."

The past fortnight has been devoted almost exclusively to the Magnum deal.

So before leaving the IRD for awhile, let's examine the chronology and what was done:

1992. Winebox documents surface, and claims are made in Parliament of massive tax evasion.

November 1992. Documents handed to Serious Fraud Office.

November 1992. SFO seeks to immediately return the original documents to European Pacific. SFO staff spend around 33 hours examining the more than 3,000 documents before deciding no further investigation will be done.

February 1993. IRD team inspects them. Documents sent to Tax Intelligence Unit for analysis. John Nash supervises their work.

February 1994. Nash signs off on the last of the 59 deal analyses completed by his team. The analysis of Magnum did not indicate that the tax credit issue had been detected. Special Project Team disbanded. Their work is later described as a "complete review".

February 1994. Media publicity over Magnum and JIF tax credit deals. SFO launches investigation into TVNZ's *Frontline* programme, seeking to seize the network's files. The SFO does not make any attempt to get files from European Pacific.

February 1994. IRD panics, Nash orders staff to immediately "review all tax credit claims made by EPNZ Group companies". IRD discovers EPFML has been liquidated.

March 16, 1994. Peters tables Winebox in Parliament, further publicises Magnum deal.

March 18, 1994. IRD boss David Henry says department's Winebox investigations found no fraud.

March 18, 1994. SFO boss Charles Sturt says he cannot investigate tax matters. Says there is no fraud in the Winebox.

March 21, 1994. IRD asks barrister Grant Pearson to provide legal opinion backing up previous "no fraud" statement.

March 22, 1994. David Henry tells Parliament there is "no fraud" in the Winebox. He does not yet have Pearson's legal opinion.

March 22, 1994. Attorney General Paul East tells Parliament "The Commissioner of Inland Revenue has quite clearly placed on public record the fact that he has investigated a number of claims with regard to tax fraud in the Cook Islands and he is satisfied that these investigations have been resolved satisfactorily."

March 23, 1994. Pearson's opinion arrives. He says "no fraud".

April 1994. European Pacific uses IRD and SFO blanket clearances as evidence of "no wrongdoing" in legal attempt to stop *Frontline* from going to air.

May 16, 1994. Court of Appeal rules there is evidence of possible tax fraud, throws out European Pacific's legal challenge.

May 23, 1994. European Pacific pulls out of legal fight with TVNZ.

May 29, 1994. *Frontline* TV programme on Magnum and JIF deals goes to air, watched by more than 800,000 people.

May 29, 1994. Tony Loo, the Tax Intelligence Unit boss who analysed the Magnum deal for the IRD, finds out for the first time how the deal worked by watching TV.

May 29, 1994. Anthony McCullagh, the accountant who helped craft the European Pacific tax schemes, is also watching TV and finds out for the first time that section 301 of the NZ Income Tax Act required him to declare the refund when he filed the Cooks tax certificates in New Zealand.

June 1, 1994. Public uproar. Winston Peters calls for inquiry in Parliament and talks of conspiracy.

June 4, 1994. Government announces that Parliament's Finance and Expenditure Select Committee will investigate, under the Chairmanship of Ruth Richardson. Peters is offered one of Labour's seats on the Committee.

June 4, 1994. SFO decides it had better examine the Magnum deal in detail.

June 8, 1994. Large corporates and legal firms tell the Government behind closed doors that they will mount a legal fight challenging Parliament's jurisdiction to investigate.

June 21, 1994. IRD investigators meet former European Pacific staff in New Zealand to discuss Magnum transaction. IRD also begins questioning lawfirm Russell McVeagh over its role in a Winebox deal for Carter Holt Harvey.

July, 1994. National MP Max Bradford, a member of the Select Committee investigation, sides with Peters, saying Winebox documents appear to evidence possible evasion. This potentially tips balance of power on the Committee away from the Government.

July, 1994. Ruth Richardson announces resignation from Parliament. Max Bradford aims for Committee Chairmanship. IRD begins investigating various Brierley Investments deals.

July 17, 1994. Prime Minister Jim Bolger, Finance Minister Bill Birch and Revenue Minister Wyatt Creech summon Bradford to a meeting. He is told to withdraw his bid for the Chairmanship in favour of a more junior MP, Tony Ryall. Ryall has been consistently loyal to the Government, and was one of those who previously prevented Peters' attempts to table the Winebox. Bradford tells the Prime Minister to get lost.

August 23, 1994. Government prevents Select Committee from investigating Winebox by handing the task over to Sir Ronald Davison. Davison gets paid $3,000 a day, telling the Government he can get it wrapped up for them by March 31st, 1995.

November 1994. Winebox Inquiry begins in Auckland. IRD reveals it has begun a number of investigations into Winebox deals in the latter half of 1994.

November 1994. Serious Fraud Office staff testify that there was no need to investigate Winebox because there was no evidence of dishonesty in the transactions.

August 1995. Nash undergoes what critics labelled a "Road to Damascus" conversion. IRD accuses Carter Holt Harvey of massive tax evasion, and gets tough on other corporates as a result of new investigations into Winebox deals.

August 1995. SFO immediately announces it will investigate the Carter Holt deal on IRD's behalf. SFO has previously said "no fraud". SFO will again say "no fraud".

The rest, as they say, is history. It is indicative of the fact that my first book is still up-to-date that the questions I raised in *The Paradise Conspiracy* still haven't been answered by Davison's "no fraud, no incompetence" verdict.

Why did the SFO and the IRD rush so quickly to the public aid of European Pacific and its shareholders by declaring that there was categorically "no fraud" in the Winebox, when neither department had done enough investigative work to know? Is it any wonder to the reasonable person that Peters, who in March 1994 was essentially accusing the two departments of incompetence, went a bridge too far in June 1994 and came to believe that there must be some sort of active collusion going on between the departments and the corporates?

He had told Parliament during one of the infamous speeches that "if it looks like a duck, if it waddles like a duck, and if it quacks like a duck, then I suggest to the House that it is a duck!"

Winston's single biggest problem was his inability to prove that the feathery creature making quacking noises outside his window was, in fact, *Mallardus Duckus* or, more correctly, *Anas Platyrhynchos*.

And don't forget the role of the National Government. At every step of the way the politicians were attempting to stop details of the Winebox transactions from becoming public.

Why?

Why should senior National Government ministers care whether possible tax fraud is exposed?

What message, explicit or implicit, was given or taken between the Government and its departments?

There was no hard evidence before the Winebox Inquiry of political influence on any investigations, purely and simply because Sir Ronald Davison did not call any politicians to the witness stand.

It is very easy to find no evidence of fraud if you don't actually look for it. Likewise, it is very easy to find no evidence of corruption if you don't actually look for it.

None of the political events that I revealed in *The Paradise Conspiracy* were investigated by the Davison Commission, and yet they all took place.

Peters' lawyer Brian Henry may have stumbled across a possible motive during his cross-examination of John Nash, when he discovered that New Zealand Cabinet Ministers might have been implicated in massive rorts against foreign governments, via the trading divisions of the State-Owned Enterprises.

In June 1993, John Nash had discovered evidence of Telecom – during the time it had been an SOE – and Electricorp being involved in massive financing operations through Japan that effectively enriched the New Zealand tax base at the expense of the Japanese.

"It is, in economic terms," said Nash, "a type of subsidy from the Japanese to a New Zealand corporate in relation to its borrowings."

When Henry pointed out that SOE's would need the "approval of the Minister of Finance and the Minister of State Owned Enterprises, which would be Messrs Douglas and Prebble", John Nash said he didn't know.

"Mr Nash," continued the NZ First lawyer, "doesn't this matter have a very major political dimension, because really what we have here is the New Zealand Government running a scheme that obtains a subsidy from the Japanese Revenue … and you have got, and must have, Government ministers signing it off?"

The NZ IRD initially chose not to alert the Japanese Revenue to apparently similar tax absorption deals it found in the Winebox, such as the Mitsubishi JIF transaction.

"Was a potential consequence of reporting Mitsubishi to the Japanese Revenue," asked Henry, "that it could lead the Japanese Revenue to investigate Electricorp and Telecom's facilities?"

"No, that doesn't follow, Mr Henry," claimed Nash.

And yet, the Japanese Embassy in Wellington *was* ordered to investigate by Tokyo once publicity about the Winebox deals broke and, of course, a number of Japanese banks involved in the JIF and other Cook Islands tax deals would later be accused of tax avoidance and in some cases fraud by the Japanese Revenue.

Politically, approval for the Bank of New Zealand to get involved in European Pacific came from no less a figure than ACT Party founder, Sir Roger Douglas.

But even if the political dimension went largely unexplored, there was still plenty for Sir Ronald Davison to consider when it came time to write his report. His Counsel Assisting, Colin Carruthers QC, wrote a very hard-hitting submission that left observers in little doubt what the Commission's lawyers thought.

But somehow, the Winebox Inquiry was about to go seriously off the rails. In doing so it sealed the fate of the Deputy Prime Minister, and gave the Government the verdict it so desperately wanted.

Chapter 13

A Change In The Wind

A government which robs Peter to pay Paul can always depend on the support of Paul.
— *George Bernard Shaw (1856–1950), Anglo-Irish playwright, critic.*

There was clear evidence that, despite earning $3,000 a day on top of his Government pension as a retired Chief Justice, Sir Ronald Davison was getting sick of the Winebox Inquiry by Christmas, 1996.

"Mr Nash," the Commissioner had interrupted one afternoon, "let's not have the long speeches. We have had them hour after hour. You haven't got to justify everything by a long speech. I would prefer you to answer the question."

Davison's testiness surfaced on a number of occasions, although it was a condition affecting all of us at the hearings. We had, after all, been cooped up in the same room together over four calendar years.

News feature, January 25, 1997

It could have been a morning like any other. But it wasn't.

No, the faces may have been familiar, and the Winebox Inquiry hearing room still looked the same, but there was definitely a sense of anticipation present that hadn't been there before Christmas.

Like Melbourne Cup racehorses thundering down the home straight, the lawyers, journalists, members of the public and assorted hangers-on who gathered for the inquiry's 1997 resumption last Tuesday could sense the winning post was finally in sight.

Not that Commissioner Sir Ronald Davison exactly galloped down the aisle to his desk, but the sentiment was clearly there in his opening words.

"Let me wish you all a happy New Year. One thing that will make it happy for us all is to complete this inquiry as soon as possible."

The snorts and grunts from the legal beagles, and the whinnies of delight from the media bench, made it clear Sir Ronald spoke for us all.

Cracking the whip as if to reinforce the point, Sir Ronald wasted no time in telling lawyers for the various corporates that if any of them wished to call their own witnesses before the inquiry ended, Sir Ronald wanted an indication that very afternoon and briefs of evidence from those witnesses in his hands by this coming Monday.

Lawyers for Fay Richwhite stood up to tell the inquiry that they planned to call three witnesses but then, in perhaps an example of why Fay Richwhite's arithmetic works such wonders in tax transactions, they reeled off not three but five witnesses they were planning to call. Perhaps Rhys Harrison QC was adding them up on the hoof, so to speak.

Included in their list were several expert witnesses, who will undoubtedly offer expert opinion supporting Fay Richwhite's interpretation of tax laws, but also, intriguingly, a "witness of fact" who is currently outside New Zealand's borders and reluctant to come back.

Harrison indicated that Fay Richwhite was still trying to offer a large enough carrot to persuade this person to testify.

"His availability or, should I say, his willingness to give evidence has not yet been resolved. He is outside of the jurisdiction. Negotiations are continuing to obtain a written brief of his evidence. As soon as it is obtained, Commissioner, and I can assure you it will be relevant, a brief will be provided to you."

European Pacific, the tax haven company at the centre of the winebox storm, managed to raise a few eyebrows by announcing it hoped to call an expert witness called Lindsay McKay.

McKay is a specialist tax lawyer who had previously been assisting European Pacific in its gagging action against TVNZ in the High Court in 1994. From there, he was appointed as an independent tax expert to help advise Ruth Richardson's short-lived parliamentary select committee inquiry into the winebox deals.

So, with the entree out of the way, it was down to the main course at the inquiry this week as the Serious Fraud Office was wheeled in to face the questions.

Significantly, the most useful aspect of the SFO opening submissions was a recognition that the New Zealand public find aggressive tax deals, like the Magnum transaction with its dodgy Cook Islands tax certificates, unacceptable.

SFO counsel, Dr Willie Young QC, insisted that many tax schemes can't be prosecuted because unlike simpler commercial frauds, tax law contains too many grey areas, making it easy for taxpayers to claim that they honestly thought their scams were effective tax minimisation, rather than fraud.

"The willingness of [legal and accounting] advisers to sign-off on aggressive tax schemes means that few if any schemes can ever later be categorised as having been known to be ineffective. Against that background the ability to conceal doubtful schemes from the IRD without incurring a real risk of criminal liability is legitimately a matter of public concern.

"If there is to be a serious criminal law approach to sophisticated tax schemes, where knowledge of ineffectiveness will seldom be able to be proved, a new offence would have to be created."

He suggested drafting a new law so that "where a taxpayer adopts a questionable tax position against the Revenue (perhaps defined along the lines of the existing definition of 'unacceptable tax position') it is a criminal offence not to disclose to the IRD all information which the IRD might reasonably consider to be material."

As for the first of the SFO's star witnesses – assistant director Gib Beattie – by week's end he was taking a hammering from Counsel Assisting the Commission, Colin Carruthers QC, over whether his view that Magnum is not a fraud is sustainable.

Carruthers read out seven points in the Magnum transaction, including
- The "tax" allegedly paid in the Cooks was never recorded as a tax payment in the Government's books
- The only payment recorded was described as a "fee"
- The tax receipt given to European Pacific "was not a normal receipt for tax payments but [came] from a separately numbered receipt book"
- The tax money was not paid into the Cooks Government's normal bank account
- The money was given back to European Pacific in a series of promissory note transactions "that were never reported to or appropriated by Parliament
- There appears to have been no intent to honour the promissory notes in accordance with their terms
- Official documents executed in the deal stated a different series of events to what actually happened.
- And the cheques to pay the tax didn't come from a chequebook, they were made up on a word processor

The Commission lawyer asked the SFO witness if, after all that, he still stood by his contention that there was no evidence that the Magnum deal might be a $2 million sham?

"I am content that tax was paid," said Beattie. "I don't see how the accounting for that treatment impacts that fact at all. I was satisfied that this transaction was not a sham."

At least Gib Beattie still had his sense of humour, however. As he scanned the inquiry room, perhaps looking for an emergency exit as the relentless cross examination dragged on, his eyes settled on a man wearing a t-shirt featuring the TV programme "The X-Files". Emblazoned across the top were the words "DENY EVERYTHING" and underneath was written "The Truth Is Out There … "

Gib Beattie smiled, and settled in for a grilling that will probably continue into next week.

So it is against the background of a desire to get the Inquiry completed sooner, rather than later, that the next portion of our story is set.

The seeds for Sir Ronald Davison's controversial verdict may have been sown in February and March 1997 – the final weeks of hearings. It was during this time that the Serious Fraud Office was being crucified by Colin Carruthers QC.

The corporates like Fay Richwhite and European Pacific had been expecting Sturt to crush Carruthers and ensure a Winebox Inquiry verdict that cleared everybody. When Sturt's performance didn't measure up, there was panic. [inserted text follows]They were saved by a magazine article.

Metro magazine commissioned an "exposé", written by Keith Davies, a journalist who'd originally worked alongside me on the Winebox investigation but who also gave the Serious Fraud Office PR advice. The article rubbished the Commission of Inquiry and attempted to play down all the allegations as nothing more than conspiracy theory.

News feature, March 1, 1997

I've discovered, over the past five years or so, that you can always get an accurate reading on the temperature of the winebox and related matters by measuring the paranoia and dirty tricks levels in the surrounding atmosphere.

Judging by the latest readings, one gets the impression that the Winebox Inquiry is once again going into Ruapehu mode.

Metro magazine managed to light the fuse on Monday with a curiously-timed article firing bullets at the Commission of Inquiry, the witnesses, and journalists who broke the winebox story – yours truly included.

Because of the personal conflict of interest – my lawyers are doing lunch with *Metro's* lawyers – I won't touch on the issues in the article that I have problems with, but I will take you through the errors that Metro has admitted in regard to some of the other players, because this article has captured the spotlight at the inquiry in the absence of Charles Sturt.

Firstly, to the article itself. It is written by Keith Davies, once a journalist but more latterly a public relations consultant who's given "specialist" advice to the Serious Fraud Office in relation to the Winebox Inquiry. The SFO has so far not released the amount that it paid to Davies.

The central premise of the article, entitled "Oops, wrong Winebox", is that the Davison Commission has spent the past two and a half years looking at the wrong winebox, instead of a more comprehensive one held by the SFO.

"Of one thing we can be certain," says the article: "the Winebox Inquiry is not investigating the documents handed to the SFO by Stephen Lunn. It is not even investigating the documents tabled in Parliament by Winston Peters.

"How do we know this?" continued writer Keith Davies, "simply because the SFO's winbox contained 3149 pages. The documents tabled in Parliament by Winston Peters comprised 1927 pages, of which 422 were duplicates. The IRD had 1865 pages, of which 422 were duplicates. And it is the IRD's documents which were scanned into the Commission's computers to form the basis for the inquiry.

"So what happened? Why have more than two years been spent delving into the wrong box?"

If this were a game of snakes and ladders, Keith Davies could be said to have landed on a snake.

In a hard-hitting three page media release, the Commission fired back saying "there is no factual foundation whatever for these claims."

Commission executive Susan Evans pointed out that the Commission had used its powers to obtain documents from a number of sources. "This included a request of the SFO that it provide all documents in its possession. As part of this process the Commission received a copy of the set of documents originally delivered to that office by Lunn."

The Commission also attacked inaccurate claims elsewhere in the article, and concluded "it is unfortunate that no check was made with the Commission concerning the allegations made in the article prior to publication. The Commission is considering whether any further steps are required to be taken in relation to the position of *Metro* and the author, Mr Davies, regarding publication of this article."

By yesterday the business media were claiming representatives from *Metro's* publishers had been summoned to meet the Commission. Commission staff won't confirm the reports, but say the matter is being investigated at Sir Ronald Davison's request.

The reason it has become such a hot potato behind the scenes is because of the timing. The article bags the Commission before the Commission has even finished hearings. Except that when the article went to press, it had been anticipated that the hearings would be over by now. In addition, there had been an expectation in some corporate winebox circles that the SFO would emerge triumphant from cross-examination.

If that had happened, maybe a different climate would have greeted the *Metro* piece. Instead, it's been overtaken and dumped on by events.

The only person to wade in publicly in support of Keith Davies has been radio host Paul Holmes who, on Tuesday morning, waxed lyrical about "a very long, and very acceptable, very praiseworthy article by Keith Davies" before launching into ridicule of Sir Ron Davison, Colin Carruthers QC, conspiracy theorists, newspaper columnists, former SFO senior prosecutor Susan Pilgrim and the media in general, contrasted with effusive praise for the Serious Fraud Office and Charles Sturt.

But what of the other problems with the article? On Friday *Metro* was forced to eat humble pie in the country's daily newspapers. In a large advertisement headed "Retraction and Apology", *Metro's* editor Paul Little unreservedly apologised to businessman Stephen Lunn for accusing him of trying to sell the winebox papers, and to Jenni McManus and Warren Berryman of the *Independent* newspaper for suggesting that they "may have committed perjury and contempt of court in their handling of the leaked Serious Fraud Office timesheets in March 1996."

The woman identified in the article as "Mary" claims she never gave the magazine an interview, and that the journalist published details of an "off-the-record" explanation that she had given. She was furious at the baseless sexual innuendo that the article contained about her (yes, sex in the Winebox Inquiry. Now I've seen everything!).

As the heat builds, there remains a chance that people could be called before the Commission to explain their motives in preparing the article and publishing it. If that happens, I for one will take my knitting along.

Charles Sturt, meanwhile, is also scheduled to reappear on Tuesday morning after a week and a half's sick leave.

In his book, Sturt writes:

> "*While I was at home, resting in preparation for my return to the witness*

box I received a telephone call from Paul Holmes, New Zealand's best-known radio broadcaster and television presenter. He was putting together something for his radio programme and wanted a few details on the prosecution success rate of the Office.

"That I could help with, but I explained that I had yet to complete my evidence and could only give him information that was already public knowledge. He fully understood, commented on aspects of the Inquiry and particular people involved, wished me well and the call ended.

"Holmes then told his nationwide radio audience:

"Some thoughts on this Winebox Inquiry – the stuff going around in the head and perhaps in other people's heads as well, and I see Metro magazine this month has a very long and very acceptable ... very praiseworthy article by Keith Davies who's been watching the 'whinebox' for a long time as well. So perhaps some thinking going on about the Inquiry.

Question no. 1: *Why has it gone on so long?*
Answer: *Good question. Now Sir Ronald wants a further extension.*
Question no. 2: *Is this acceptable?*
Answer: *Hardly. Millions of dollars. Enough is enough. It could go on for ever. It could spawn a civilisation of its own. The Winebox Inquiry called 'The Conspiracists'. In future years archaeologists could well be digging for its beginnings, for the civilisation of 'The Conspiracists'. Under the piles of earth they'll find Sir Ronald, still sitting there.*
Question no. 3: *Has Sir Ronald lost control of the Inquiry?*
Answer: *You'll meet competent legal opinion that will say so and that he relies increasingly on Mr Carruthers.*
Question no. 4: *Does he understand it all, Sir Ronald?*
Answer: *How can he? Nobody else can.*
Question no. 5: *Who is Colin Carruthers?*
Answer: *Now Mr Carruthers is the appointed friend of the court. He's Counsel for the Inquiry.*
Question no. 6: *So is he the neutral counsel for the Inquiry?*
Answer: *Yes. What about it?*
Question no. 7: *Why therefore is he perceived as being the prosecutor?*
Answer: *Exactly. Good question.*
Question no. 8: *What's the other big concern about the Inquiry? Indeed, the whole issue?*
Answer: *The number of conspiracists it attracts. It attracts some wacky people who have come up with some preposterous theories, some of which have been published, some of which have just been passed around. There*

was an allegation that Chas Sturt had been seen on a yacht in Monaco with Fay and Richwhite. Do me a favour!

Question no. 9: *Have the news media fallen into the trap of identifying goodies and baddies?*

Answer: *Oh yes.*

Question no. 10: *Are the news media frightened to disagree with those general perceptions?*

Answer: *Oh yes. It's uncool to do that. Who's going to put their neck up on this one?*

Question no. 11: *What's the worry about the way the Winebox has been reported all the way through?*

Answer: *Each day's testimony seems to be reported or regarded as a verdict. Guilt has been encouraged. Much of the reporting has been done with an almost malicious glee. Much has been written about the Winebox by people from outer space, planted there as columnists, perhaps.*

Question no. 12: *Can anybody understand what Fran O'Sullivan writes?*

Answer: *There may be such people. I regret I've not met them.*

Question no. 13: *There's the aspect of the politics between so many of the names we associate with the Inquiry. For example has it slipped everyone's mind that it's ... that Susan Pilgrim might be wrong or might simply be a self-promoter, or might have an axe to grind?*

Answer: *Apparently.*

Question no. 14: *What is the record of the New Zealand Serious Fraud Office?*

Answer: *I understand it's a very good one. I understand the SFO of New Zealand's got a record of over 90 percent prosecution success over months totaling around $800 million.*

Question no. 15: *Does that represent therefore ... does that show us a demoralised, incompetent Serious Fraud Office?*

Answer: *Hardly.*

Question no. 16: *What's happened to Chas Sturt this week?*

Answer: *Who knows? But the conspiracists of course are in a lather of almost sexual excitement. He may simply be exhausted.*

Question no. 17: *What is the worry about the way Chas Sturt gets results?*

Answer: *Well on the odd occasion in the past I've spoken to Mr Sturt ... for what it's worth I've found the man to be intelligent, informed, genuine, knowledgeable, extremely courteous.*

Question no. 18: *Yes, but there are those who'll tell you he can be a difficult sod.*

Answer: *So? Can't we all be difficult sods on a bad day, under pressure, stuff coming at us from everywhere?*
Question no. 19: *Was he obsessed with Winston Peters, Mr Sturt?*
Answer: *Might have been. There was evidence of that I'm told. But he was under severe attack. Anybody can develop an obsession with an attacker if they're suddenly in the public eye and being constantly dumped on. It could happen to everybody.*
Question no. 20: *So what are you saying?*
Answer: *I'm saying this: that we should all be careful. Beware the conspiracists and remember the testimony is just that. It's testimony. No corruption or incompetence has yet been established at the SFO.*
In the end, Mr Peters' testimony was lacking. Remember that. Somebody knew somebody's nanny appeared to be the central plank of the Peters evidence."

I had no problem with his warning not to rush to premature judgment, but the claim "It's just testimony" was either a demonstration of Holmes' ignorance when it comes to complex issues like the Winebox, or an attempt to pull the wool over the eyes of the more sheep-like members of his fan-club.

Testimony is called evidence. In most cases it was accompanied by damning documentary evidence that further confirmed what had happened.

In addition, the nature of an inquiry is to reveal information. The whole country had long ago heard the Government and the two departments insist that everything was above board and had been investigated properly. Consequently, of course every revelation that showed that wasn't true was going to make headlines.

The only creature from another planet that was anywhere near the Winebox that day was the one in the studio hotseat at Newstalk ZB.

People like Holmes tell the world they don't subscribe to "conspiracy theories, I subscribe to the cock-up theory". Well, for his benefit and others, let me remind him that a cock-up is the result of a conspiracy that's gone wrong. For something to be "cocked-up", someone had to plan it first.

Who put Holmes up to it? That's the question I never got an answer to. And I'll lay bets now: Paul Holmes won't have the courage to interview me about this book, and in that lies a clue to Holmes' own weakness.

John Banks, his breakfast-time radio rival on the Radio Pacific network, has crossed swords with me on many occasions. Like Holmes, Banks has made no secret of his views of the Winebox allegations.

Unlike Holmes, however, John Banks has always had the guts to debate the issues with me. I believe the former National Government cabinet minister has shown more journalistic integrity than I have ever seen in Holmes. I no longer listen to, nor watch Holmes, except on rare occasions.

But, getting back to the Inquiry, the fun and games over the *Metro* article were only just beginning. Up until this point, Sir Ron's Inquiry had been one that pushed the boundaries without fear, and at times even the Commissioner himself played a proactive role, as evidenced by the following:

News feature, August 17, 1996

Never before have so few gone so far to fight so hard to avoid being forced to say so little!

Yes folks, the boys from European Pacific are back from the Privy Council, back on the Winebox Inquiry witness stand, and telling me less about the winebox documents than my pet budgie.

Perhaps the EP boys are at a disadvantage. Admittedly, my budgie's had to sit through my own winebox investigation for four years now, and can recite the Magnum tax credit deal to the letter.

"Polly want a promissory note!" he squawked only the other day, which is a lot more than former European Pacific banker Peter Brannigan could manage.

"Did [EP executive Anthony] McCullagh know about the promissory note transactions in the foreign tax credit scheme?" asked counsel assisting the Commission, Colin Carruthers QC.

"I don't know," replied Brannigan.

Those three words, and variations on them like "I don't recall" or "My recollection – and this is again regrettably hazy ... ", proved to be the dominant theme of the Brannigan testimony, prompting more than one observer on the media bench to wonder why he'd bothered going all the way to the Privy Council, when he could have saved everyone a lot of time and trouble months ago by giving his "I regret I don't, I don't recall" speech back then.

"What is it about tax havens," queried one scribe, "and the savage struggle to get to the top of the corporate palm tree, that turns the memories of people to mush?"

Brannigan confirmed his involvement in the Magnum tax credit deal but said he was never involved in the massive $1.9 billion JIF schemes, nor was he aware that one Australian QC had described the tax credit deals as a conspiracy to defraud.

The senior accountant was also unaware of section 301 of the New Zealand tax act, which requires people claiming foreign tax credits in New Zealand to also disclose whether any of the foreign tax they paid has already been refunded.

It was a disappointing start, given the sense of occasion surrounding Peter Brannigan's appearance on the orders of the Privy Council.

Even Richard Craddock QC was there, leading his European Pacific legal team, after an absence of almost a month.

"What brings you here?" said a lawyer as he teased one of the EP barristers, Chris Allan, a man who bears a striking resemblance to "Grandpa Munster" from TV's *The Munsters*.

"We're here for some purposes," joked Allan, referring to last year's classic quote from 'Craddock, the Friendly Ghost' about haunting the inquiry for some purposes but not for others.

By far the biggest issue to arise from Peter Brannigan, however, was the allegation that he may have been keeping his mouth shut for some purposes and not for others.

Had he, questioned Colin Carruthers, received in May 1995, a month after being subpoenaed to give evidence at the inquiry, "a substantial sum of money from [European Pacific owner David] Lloyd or his interests?"

There is a word to describe both the look on Peter Brannigan's face and on the faces of the journalists: gobsmacked.

A sense of silence and expectation pervaded the inquiry room like a baited mousetrap awaiting a dinner guest.

"In May 1995?" asked Brannigan doubtfully, appearing to place an emphasis on the date, "I don't think so."

The inevitable follow-up question of "when" had to be asked, and was.

"Many years ago," replied the tax accountant, "when I left EP, Mr Lloyd lent me some money and that loan was recycled, I thought, in December of 1995."

"How much was it?" asked Carruthers.

"The recycled amount was, I believe, US$125,000. There was a further advance of NZ$70,000."

The original loan amount, said Brannigan, had been up to NZ$600,000, given to him back in late 1990 by David Lloyd so that he could refinance a housing loan he'd taken out during his employment at European Pacific.

Generously, David Lloyd's loan to Brannigan was interest free and with "no firm arrangements for repayment," as far as the latter was concerned.

"Are you aware that that sum has been described as hush money?" inquired Colin Carruthers.

"Not to me it hasn't," retorted the accountant.

"Has it been described to you as an amount paid in order to keep you silent before the Commission of Inquiry about certain dealings with European Pacific?"

"No it hasn't," stated Brannigan.

For the record, while no interest is accruing on the US$125,000 still outstanding, the second advance of NZ$70,000 from David Lloyd to Peter Brannigan is attracting interest.

The QC representing both European Pacific and Peter Brannigan – Richard Craddock – was outraged.

Within a minute of the inquiry adjourning for the day, had approached the media warning them that the question and answer session "may not be covered by privilege", and to be "very careful" how they handled the issue.

By the resumption on Wednesday morning, Craddock was in full flight and gunning for counsel assisting, lashing out at what he called "an unfounded attack on the witness" and claiming the Commission had not told him in advance that this might be one of the topics for questioning.

"Indeed, it seems actively to have been concealed!", he complained, perhaps forgetting for a moment that it was European Pacific's concealment of dodgy tax deals that had brought everyone to this juncture in the first place.

He demanded that the Commission produce its evidence to back up the "unfounded attack" on his client's reputation and integrity.

"Now, sir, it was perhaps one of the most seriously damaging allegations that could conceivably have been made – the damage arising from the fact that is made, not from the fact that the witness may have dealt with it with dignity and, indeed, disdain.

"It was made, sir, in my submission to a witness whose answers have been frank -"

"When he gave answers!," interjected Sir Ronald.

"Who in no case prevaricated," continued Craddock, "who in no case declined to answer and in no case had an answer challenged by my learned friend."

The European Pacific QC spared no ammunition in his criticism of Colin Carruthers QC.

"As far as my friend's professional conduct is concerned," added Craddock, "if there is an issue there that is a matter for the New Zealand Law Society."

Closing his submissions, Craddock called for Carruthers to front up with the evidence on which he'd based the hush money allegation. Inquiry observers were about to be treated to an even bigger shock.

"Mr Craddock," began Sir Ronald Davison, "the information on which

Mr Carruthers cross-examined was information which was conveyed to me which I was aware of.

"It came from a reliable source, which I am not prepared to disclose, and having discussed the matter with Mr Carruthers I indicated that he should examine upon it and that is what has happened."

A clearly surprised Richard Craddock was left with little immediate choice but to accept Sir Ronald's ruling against disclosure of source and his reasons.

The incident served to overshadow the rest of Peter Brannigan's evidence, patchy as it was because of an apparently failing memory when it came to the detail of some of the tax haven dealings.

Brannigan could not remember writing a winebox memorandum on the controversial tax credit transactions and how they could be accounted for in the books of the Cook Islands Government.

"My recollection, and this is again regrettably hazy, is that the concern that was expressed about reporting the transaction was a political concern, and the concern was – broadly – not that any impropriety had to be covered up, but – put bluntly – it was going to be hard to explain to Cook Islands politicians why these payments [out of the Treasury] were being made.

"It wasn't the income side that was a worry, it was why the payments were being made when they needed new schools."

The top accountant told the inquiry he didn't think "accounting entries are very important" when it came to the way the deals were being presented in the Cooks accounts, until you came to the actual accounts being presented to Parliament.

He later also revealed he'd been unaware of a requirement under section 301 of the New Zealand Income Tax Act governing foreign tax credits.

The section states that taxpayers claiming a credit for foreign tax paid must first furnish details of any refund of the foreign tax they may already have received.

"Regrettably, I had never dealt with 301 and didn't know its existence," confirmed Brannigan.

So, in this instance, Sir Ronald himself had come across a scandalous tit-bit and was personally responsible for flinging it at Peter Brannigan.

But the infamous *Metro* article hit the newstands six months later in March 1997, and it contained a poison arrow that went straight for the Commission's Achille's Heel. In a small section of the article, it quoted Stephen Lunn saying he'd been privately interviewed by Sir Ronald Davison.

What did this mean, the corporates wondered? It transpired that the

Davison Commission had carried out a number of secret interviews with potential witnesses. This included the secret interview with lawyer Paul Darvell, referred to earlier.

Although the Commissions of Inquiry Act 1908 gives Commissioners power to interview witnesses privately, the aggrieved corporates felt they could make a go of it.

The admission was enough for Fay Richwhite, European Pacific and lawyers for the IRD and SFO to mount a legal challenge to the Winebox Inquiry in its final weeks.

Having heard from the SFO witnesses, from Lindsay McKay and from the written submissions from Fay Richwhite's international law experts, Sir Ronald Davison suddenly found himself being attacked in *Metro* magazine and by establishment wanna-be's like Paul Holmes.

Then he found himself facing the biggest legal challenge to the Inquiry to that point: the judicial review proceedings over his secret interviews. There was even a suggestion that the challengers would apply for an injunction to stop Davison's final report from being published until the end of the judicial review – a point that could have been two or three years away!

Someone, or something, certainly seemed to be playing on Sir Ronald Davison's mind. Staff noticed the change over the last month of the Inquiry. Sir Ron became "more withdrawn, less communicative." He would no longer look some of them in the eye.

"There was a definite change in the atmosphere. We felt something was going down," said one.

The Winebox Inquiry was in recess while lawyers for the various parties, and the Commission's own lawyers, wrote their closing submissions, and Davison appeared to be wrestling with his conscience. A lawyer passed on to me the following conversation.

"I have a problem," Davison had allegedly confided in July 1997. "No matter how I look at it, I think I'm going to have to classify several sets of Winebox transactions as fraud! I can't see any way around it."

But only a matter of days later, Sir Ronald Davison's mind appeared made up, and he was tearing down allegations of fraud, not reinforcing them.

Sir Ronald, during final submissions that July, turned on Winston Peters' barrister, Brian Henry, and tried to make him prove why he thought the Magnum deal was fraud.

"Do you say that the fraud is the way in which the tax credit was presented to the IRD and a credit obtained against tax?"

"Yes Sir," answered Henry.

"If the tax credit was a valid tax credit certificate, what say you then?"

"Even if it is a valid tax certificate ... when you go to section 301 it talks of a requirement that they provide all information and then, in brackets, including refunds."

The Winebox Commissioner then asked about the alleged conspiracy to defraud.

"Briefly identify for me what was the nature of the conspiracy."

"The conspiracy, Sir, was to defraud the Inland Revenue by the obtaining of the $2 million tax credit in the company EPFML."

"Next question," pushed Sir Ronald. "When was the conspiracy entered into?"

Henry explained that the conspiracy began with the agreements between various European Pacific staff and directors to enter into tax credit deals.

"Who were the parties to the conspiracy?" continued the Commissioner, pausing to add, "Let me remind you of this: Mr Peters' allegation in the House was – he named the guilty as Mr Lloyd, Richwhite, Collins, Travers; they are all directors of EPI aren't they? All right, just a minute. Now he also named employees at EP, Peter Brannigan, Anthony McCullagh, David Barry [sic], Robert Hay, Mark Jones, Witness A, Trevor Clarke, didn't he?"

"Yes Sir."

After establishing that Peters had also named a number of accountants and lawyers, Sir Ronald went for the jugular.

"Well, now. I want to know from you, when – what was the conspiracy between all of those people?"

"There is the earlier agreements reached by the directors where they are obtaining legal advice and accountancy advice as they put together the plan to run a system they call the foreign tax credits. These are transactions that are planned quite deliberately."

"I am very well aware of those allegations," snapped Davison, but a conspiracy involves an agreement. Clearly, knowing of something doesn't amount to a conspiracy, there must be an agreement to effect a dishonest purpose."

Henry hit back, arguing again that the conspiracy to defraud began with the directors' decision to go ahead with the deals despite knowing that they may be illegal. The lawyers and accountants, he said, became part of the conspiracy by giving advice, helping implement the deals and helping conceal them.

"Well, tell me how did the employees who are not decision-makers agree to a conspiracy?"

The "employees" named by Peters in Parliament had all been listed performing key roles in the documents that planned the Magnum transaction, or they were actual signatories to key transaction documents. Anthony McCullagh, for example, was listed in the winebox documents as one of the authors of the transaction blueprint.

Henry told Davison that no criminal intent could attach to staff who didn't know the full picture, but he claimed those who did know had become part of the conspiracy to defraud by carrying out their actions instead of walking away from it.

The Nuremberg Defence – "I was just following orders" doesn't wash.

Broadly, there were four categories of transactions that the Peters legal team believed involved fraud. The Magnum deal speaks for itself. The JIF deals, argued Henry, ripped off the Japanese Government to the tune of around $100 million.

He believed that those involved in the JIF transactions could be prosecuted for conspiring to commit an offence under section 310 of the New Zealand Crimes Act, which says:

> "Every one who conspires with any person to commit any offence, or to do or omit, in any part of the world, anything of which the doing or omission in New Zealand would be an offence, is liable to imprisonment for a term not exceeding seven years ... "

A similar clause is section 69(3) of the Crimes Act, which says:

> "Everyone who, in New Zealand, aids, incites, counsels, or procures the doing or omission outside New Zealand of any act ... "

That section also carries a seven year jail term. In both cases, it is a defence to the charge if the defendant can prove the act involved was not an offence in the overseas jurisdiction.

Another set of transactions under the Peters blowtorch were the so-called MCN/RPS deals, a series of massive loans, including $400 million dollars' worth to Fay Richwhite, which the Peters legal team alleged involved tax avoidance being illegally concealed. The files are allegedly still up in the Cook Islands, in a tax haven bank vault.

> "The wiring diagrams (and no doubt other documents) which are evidence of transactions being Capital Markets Ltd deals, ie, part of their records,

are concealed in the Cook Islands master files," wrote Brian Henry.

"That they continue to deny their existence, in the face of [CML chief executive] Simon Tompkins' own handwritten notes and the evidence of Witness A, one of the European Pacific Trust officers who looked after the transactions and the master files, is of grave concern.

"The IRD is unable to do its job ... Where a taxpayer goes to the length of creating or 'styling' false payment descriptions and the holding of records properly inspectable by the New Zealand Revenue in another country so they can simply not be inspected, the Commissioner of Inland Revenue is defeated by fraud and the conduct is dishonest in terms of s257 of the Crimes Act and is a concealment for fraudulent purposes under s231 of the Crimes Act 1961 which states:

" 'Everyone who destroys, cancels, conceals or obliterates any document for any fraudulent purpose is liable to the same punishment as if he had stolen the document, or to imprisonment for a term not exceeding three years, whichever is the greater.' "

The fourth transaction under Peters' scrutiny was the BNZ Captive Insurance scheme.

During my own investigations while researching *The Paradise Conspiracy*, one of *the* top BNZ executives of the relevant period advised me of what he believed was a multi-million dollar falsification of the BNZ accounts. He should have known: it was his area. He explained that the captive insurance deal was peanuts in comparison.

Nonetheless, similar allegations were already in the ring over the captive insurance deal, which effectively covered up the full extent of the BNZ's losses, as Brian Henry made clear in his submissions.

"The 'insurance' policy and all who were involved in its establishment were involved in a dishonest transaction which had the intent of causing financial detriment to anybody who relied on any accounts of the Bank of New Zealand prepared using the 'balance sheet enhancement' effect of the scheme.

"The Securities Commission accepted that there was a material effect on the accounts in the year 1990 by the use of this policy. As a consequence anybody who relied on the accounts without disclosure that such a device was in operation, in particular the shareholders of the Bank of New Zealand and the shareholders of Capital Markets who owned some 30 percent of the shareholding in the Bank of New Zealand, were the victims of this conspiracy to defraud."

Henry alleged that the purpose of feathering the 1990 accounts by hiding losses was to placate the market in the lead-up to the 1990 buy-in by Capital Markets. The BNZ later required a billion dollar bail-out at the taxpayer's expense.

Despite finding that the bank's accounts had been fudged, the Securities Commission did not attempt to join the dots and ask whether the fudging – which would have influenced the decisions of small investors to buy or sell BNZ or Capital Markets stock – was done with dishonest intent.

And if you look at the law, there's plenty of precedent to suggest Brian Henry was dead right. So why did he get such a pasting from Sir Ronald Davison?

News feature, July 6, 1997

The Winebox Inquiry has come to an end, with an unexpected twist.

Spanning four calendar years, hearing 73 witnesses, swallowing five tonnes of drinking water and a further eight thousand cups of coffee, and creating 13 thousand pages of evidence, the inquiry closed its doors this week with a savage attack on Deputy Prime Minister Winston Peters.

It began when commissioner Sir Ronald Davison prevented Peters' counsel, Brian Henry, from delivering his closing oral submissions.

All the other lawyers representing the corporates, the IRD and the SFO, were permitted to address the inquiry for an hour, but Henry was instead grilled for more than three hours on questions of Sir Ron Davison's design.

Sir Ronald told Henry it was time to end the "shadow-boxing", and he wanted to know what evidence Peters had to support allegations he'd made in parliament in 1994.

Although some media reports suggested the Winston Peters team had withdrawn allegations of fraud in the winebox, this was not the case.

Under heavy questioning from Sir Ronald, Brian Henry continued to assert that the Magnum tax credit deal, the JIF deals, the BNZ captive insurance scheme and $400 million worth of share deals involving the BNZ, Fay Richwhite and other parties were fraudulent.

Henry conceded that his client had no evidence of corruption involving the SFO and the IRD that fell within the inquiry's terms of reference, but this was not a new revelation. Winston Peters admitted the same under cross-examination last year.

After arguing that Peters should have got his facts right, SFO counsel Willie Young QC this week excused the performance of former SFO director Charles Sturt on the witness stand.

"So what," asked Young, if Sturt had made "infelicitous" comments and media statements? Loose phrasing, he said, shouldn't be used to hang Sturt out to dry.

The SFO legal team said the Peters allegations were "vile and unsubstantiated", a claim repeated by Fay Richwhite's QC, Rhys Harrison.

In a wide-ranging attack on Peters, some journalists and the Commission's own lawyers, Harrison claimed "Fay Richwhite have been subject to nearly three years of constant attack. They have been subject to unfounded allegations of fraud. They say that they have faced the unrelenting efforts of counsel assisting to find criminality.

"No fraud or criminality was found for the simple reason that none exists."

Harrison called Winston Peters a "liar", and said he should be held accountable for his "corrupt actions". He echoed the view of other counsel who demanded that Peters be made to pay costs to the inquiry.

Brian Henry said the Peters corruption allegations related to a range of issues, including film and bloodstock partnerships and the Bank of New Zealand issue, that had been ruled outside the inquiry's terms of reference, but lawyers for European Pacific, Fay Richwhite and the Serious Fraud Office hit back by claiming that European Pacific had no involvement in the film or bloodstock partnerships.

Henry scored the Winebox Inquiry's final point, telling the commission at the end of the final day that the Ministry of Commerce's Commercial Affairs Investigation Unit had just delivered eight Eastlight folders of documents to the Commission, relating to a Cook Islands company set up by European Pacific called Investment Management Services, which was allegedly involved in fraudulent film partnership deals.

Henry also quoted from a letter where the Serious Fraud Office had decided not to prosecute over the Investment Management Services file, partly because it would be too difficult to bring witnesses back from overseas.

Sir Ronald Davison is now considering his final report, which is due to be handed to the Government by the end of August, barring any legal action to prevent its publication.

The other lawyers in the Winebox Inquiry hearing room were shocked. Sir Ronald Davison had prevented Winston Peters' barrister from making his final closing address. Was this an issue of fairness that could potentially derail the Inquiry?

Even European Pacific's blunt legal sword, Richard Craddock QC, stood up at the end of Sir Ronald's three hour grilling of Henry, and asked whether Henry would be getting the chance to speak further.

Sir Ronald brushed it aside, saying he'd heard enough.

But if Davison seriously believed he could knock aside years of evidence with a few theatrical gestures against Peters' legal team, he was in for a big surprise.

Chapter 14

The Real Inquiry

"Secrecy is the badge of fraud."
– Sir John Chadwick (b. 1941), British judge.

For a start, Colin Carruthers had made a pretty good case in his submissions for the fact that the Magnum deal was, as alleged, fraudulent.

This chapter will set out what Carruthers believed Davison needed to consider.

Under the heading, "The Consideration of Illegality", Counsel Assisting the Commission laid out three broad areas for Davison.

First was the issue of Concealment.

"In addressing the factual material held by the IRD and SFO, and the conclusions reached on the transactions, the IRD and SFO witnesses were asked what consideration was given to whether elements of the transactions were concealed by dishonest means in order to protect a financial advantage claimed by the transaction.

"A consideration of concealment may involved the following questions:
1) Was the 'refunding' nature of the transactions concealed?
2) If so, how was it concealed?
3) What evidence of such concealment was held by IRD and SFO?
4) Was the evidence held by IRD and SFO in relation to any concealment sufficient for IRD and SFO to reach conclusions on illegality without further inquiry?

"Factors relating to concealment were raised with IRD and SFO in cross-examination. Each one of those factors is the subject of debate and dispute. The factors raised in relation to 'concealment' (meaning the taking of steps designed to prevent discovery and legitimate inquiry into the transactions) were:

1) Whether the mechanism designed to effectively return the value of the tax, (involving private promissory note transactions as opposed to customary public/governmental mechanisms for tax refunds) was designed to give the appearance of being unrelated to the tax payments.

2) Whether the tax payment and promissory note transactions were recorded in the general ledger accounts of the Cook Islands Government, and if not, whether this was done to hide the transactions.

3) Whether the tax payments and promissory note transactions were reported in the audited accounts presented to the Cook Islands Legislative Assembly, and if not, whether this was to hide the transactions.

4) Whether separate receipt books were used by the Inland Revenue Department and Treasury of the Cook Islands Government for the transactions and whether special purpose bank accounts were opened for the transaction at the International Bank, EPBC, (the taxpayer's parent) in order to hide the transactions.

5) Whether parliamentary appropriations were required by Cook Islands law for the promissory note transactions, whether the Cook Islands Government made appropriations, and if required but not obtained, whether they were not obtained in order to hide the transactions.

6) Whether a decision was made by the EPI Board not to mass market the foreign tax credit product but to market in particular case situations was made to prevent discovery and inquiry into the transactions.

7) Whether there was an agreement between the Cook Islands Government and a EP/ENC joint venture to grant 'exclusivity' to the joint venture, and whether this was to prevent discovery and inquiry into the transactions.

8) Whether the change of auditor for the accounts of the Cook Islands Government (from the New Zealand Audit Office to KPMG Peat Marwick), was done in order to further the hiding of the transactions, and whether there was any illegitimate non-disclosure of the transactions by KPMG to the Audit Office.

9) Whether there were any other techniques used to limit the information available concerning the transactions such as:
- Limiting disclosure to advisors.
- Removing documents from New Zealand concerning the transactions.
- Restricting knowledge as to the availability of those transactions to those who strictly needed to know within European Pacific.
- A lack of frankness about the transactions when inquiries were made?"

Counsel Assisting then moved to the second issue: Honesty.

"Concealment alone does not amount to criminal conduct. If there was concealment, the next question for consideration might be whether any of the concealment steps were taken dishonestly.

"This may involved consideration of the following questions:

a) What information did the IRD and SFO hold in relation to the honesty of the persons involved in the transactions?

b) What additional information in relation to honesty was available to the IRD and SFO?; and

c) Was the information held by IRD and SFO sufficient for them to conclude that there was no dishonesty in relation to the transactions, without further inquiry?

"Once again, the factors possibly relevant to honesty are subject to dispute and debate. The factors raised with IRD and SFO were:

1) Whether aspects of the transactions were 'concealed' because the designers knew that if the full facts were known to the Inland Revenue Department, the Department would deny the benefit of a tax credit claimed.

2) Whether in taking any steps to conceal the transactions, the designers not only knew that the Department were likely to deny the benefit of the tax credit claim, but also that should the full facts be known a Court might regard the deal as fraudulent.

3) Whether any concealment steps, if taken, were illegitimate and reflective of dishonest intent.

4) Whether following the taking of legal advice the designers concluded that there was a risk that if the full facts were known a Court may regard the transaction as fraudulent, whether the structure of the transaction was then changed so that the company making the claim for the tax credit knew of the promissory note transactions in the Cook Islands, and the 'refund' of the tax was to a member of its own group, and whether legal or accounting advice approving of the final form of the transaction was then taken either at the time of the transaction, or at the time the tax returns were filed in New Zealand.

5) Whether the transaction involved a knowing likely breach of Section 62 of the Companies Act.

6) Whether the nature of the tax credit transactions, and particularly the Magnum transaction was such that irrespective of the primacy of the form over substance rules, any person involved in the transaction would have realised that there was an issue of legitimacy involved because of the contrived nature of the transactions."

It is worth noting that the answers to most, if not all of the above questions in both categories, were "yes", if you looked at the evidence. Readers who have access to *The Paradise Conspiracy*, which deals with the transactions in minute detail, will probably have picked this up by now. But Carruthers wasn't finished. Under a third issue, he tackled "Sham".

> "A further related aspect is the consideration given by IRD and SFO to the sham concept. The relevant transactions where it has been alleged sham might have been considered are the internal European Pacific transactions between EPFML, Harcourt, EP Merchant Finance, Dundee and the Cook Islands entities (the Cook Islands IRD and the Cook Islands Government Property Corporation).
>
> "The relevant questions may be:
> a) What consideration did IRD and SFO give to the question of sham?
> b) What conclusions did each of IRD and SFO reach in relation to sham?
> c) What tests did IRD and SFO apply in relation to sham?
> d) What facts did IRD and SFO have when considering sham?
> e) What further facts were available to IRD and SFO in relation to sham?
> f) Was it possible to reach the conclusions that there was no illegality in relation to the transactions without making further inquiries on the issue of sham?
>
> "Whether the sham concept could have had any ramifications for consideration of the tax credit transactions by IRD and SFO depends on what the 'real deal' was if sham is established."

Carruthers then quoted from previous Court of Appeal judgments on the Winebox transactions. Such as this comment from Justice Sir Ivor Richardson:

> "To put it bluntly ... the Cook Islands Government was, in effect, selling tax credit certificates for a fee which was only a fraction of the amount showing as withholding tax."

Or Justice Ted Thomas:

> "The commission or fee charged by the Government cannot be categorised as tax; it represents a profit on the deal the Cook Islands Government entered into with its 'taxpayer'. Whether too loose or not, the blunt description of the deal as selling tax payment certificates for a fee, adopted by Richardson J in this judgment is not inappropriate."

As a result of the Court of Appeal's views, Colin Carruthers continued, "the relevant questions may be what consideration was given to the issue of whether the documents executed in the transactions were shams, and that the 'real deal' involved the sale of tax credit certificates?

"The factors put to the IRD and SFO witnesses in cross-examination as to a consideration of sham are similar to those relevant to the consideration of concealment. They were:

1) Whether it could be argued that the significance of the economic substance of the transactions undertaken and the artificiality of the steps evidenced by the formal documentation were such that the substance of the transactions effectively nullified the form.

2) Whether there was evidence of an over-arching agreement or arrangement between the Cook Islands Government and the European Pacific Group for the sale of foreign tax credits, and if so, whether this over-arching agreement or arrangement represented the real transaction.

3) Whether the Cook Islands Government Cabinet Minutes authorising tax credit transactions spoke of entering into tax credit arrangements under which it received 'fees' and if so, whether this was evidence of sham.

4) Whether the only accounting entries made in the Cook Islands Government General Ledger were for the receipt of fees, and if so, whether this was evidence of sham.

5) Whether the receipts issued by the Cook Islands Government Inland Revenue Department (and the Treasury in respect of the transfer from IRD to the Treasury) were issued from a separate receipt book kept for the purposes of the transactions and if so, whether this was evidence of sham.

6) Whether there was any reference to or account of the tax payments or of the promissory note transactions in the audited financial statements presented to the Cook Islands Government Legislative Assembly, and if not, whether this was evidence of sham.

7) Whether the Cook Islands Government executive required parliamentary appropriation for the purposes of the Cook Islands Government Property Corporation acquiring the promissory notes, whether such appropriations were obtained, and if not, whether this was evidence of sham.

8) Whether the bank accounts used for the transactions were separately opened bank accounts at the international bank, EPBC, and if so, whether this was evidence of sham.

9) Whether the banking instructions for the transactions, including the internal Cook Islands Government banking instructions, were all drafted by European Pacific, and whether in the case of some of the banking instructions, the instructions were properly authorised and signed as

required by European Pacific procedures, and whether such factors were evidence of sham.

10) Whether there was any intention to honour or deal with the promissory notes in accordance with their terms."

Question 10 was a good question: The Cook Islands Government had purchased promissory notes from EP which, if they'd hung onto them until the day they matured, would have paid them millions of dollars. But instead, the Government Property Corporation ignored this potential windfall and sold the notes at a two million dollar *loss*.

Question 11, the final one in relation to sham, asked whether the fact that the transaction differed in reality from its official documents was "intentional, to enable European Pacific to give the appearance that EPFML had accounting profits allowing payment of the up-front dividend, and whether such factors were relevant to sham."

In case anyone still doubted the seriousness of the Winebox transactions, Carruthers then used the "F" word when he listed "three main motives for any concealment":

1) To cover up a fraud.
2) To prevent IRD assessing additional tax.
3) To prevent IRD promoting the closure of 'legislative loopholes'.

> *"These are not the only motives addressed in evidence, however. Others included:*
>
> *1) The 'reputation risk' associated with an allegation of fraud, even if the allegation was erroneous; and*
>
> *2) A desire to avoid IRD attention being directed at schemes and so avoiding time-wasting investigations."*

There is a fundamental rule in tax law, which the New Zealand IRD and SFO appear to have forgotten: A tax avoidance scheme is honest, and not criminal, if no attempt is made to hide it from the IRD. This doesn't mean that a taxpayer is required to shout what they're doing from the rooftops, but the rule is that you do have to cough up relevant information.

On the other hand, a legal tax avoidance scheme can become criminal overnight, if an attempt is made to conceal it from the Revenue, in the knowledge that the Revenue might attack it. What was legal becomes illegal, merely with the introduction of concealment, and knowledge.

To borrow a Biblical analogy, human nakedness was not an issue until Adam and Eve ate the forbidden fruit and then attempted to conceal themselves.

On a more practical level, imagine you find $10,000 lying outside your front door one morning. You pick it up and put it in your bedside drawer. It may be immoral, but so far you've done nothing illegal.

Suppose, however, you become aware that the money dropped out of a pensioner's pocket while they were taking their lifesavings to a bank. There is publicity. The police come around. You tell them you've seen nothing.

Have you crossed the line? Have you now stolen the money, in effect? You didn't tell the police because you knew you'd have to hand the cash back.

European Pacific didn't tell the IRD about the tax refund, because it knew the IRD would attack the deal, and that would cost European Pacific two million dollars.

Isn't that a fraudulent motive for concealment?

Apparently the concept was too difficult for Gib Beattie, one of the SFO's golden boys, to grasp.

Beattie's comments were reprinted in Carruthers' submissions:

"I asked you whether you agreed that the critical question is whether a concern about fraud and protecting the financial advantage from challenge by IRD were material motives for concealment?" the QC had asked during cross-examination.

"They could be motives for concealment," fudged Beattie. "It didn't appear to me that way on these documents."

> "I asked you whether that is the critical question. Do you agree that it is, or not?"
>
> "The critical question is the apparent reason for the concealment. That may be answering your question yes. The question is whether the concealment is to protect a fraud or to protect an income stream."

During the questioning, Carruthers showed Beattie six documents indicating that European Pacific wanted to keep the tax credit schemes hidden from the Inland Revenue because of the potential threat to income, and also documents that referred to possible fraud.

Beattie, and the SFO, appeared to have reached a decision not to investigate further and not to examine any possible dishonest motives, purely because Beattie looked at *one* document that referred to a possible "change in tax laws", which he interpreted as meaning that the tax scheme designers were attempting to stay inside the law.

Both the SFO and the IRD, on the evidence before the Inquiry, bent over backwards to give European Pacific and Fay Richwhite the benefit of the doubt every step of the way, and the rich, white merchants involved must have been laughing all the way to their banks.

It isn't the duty of prosecution agencies to run the defence as well. The job of the IRD and SFO is to collect points of evidence that could form a potential prosecution, and consider whether the points in favour of prosecution are plausible enough that a jury will believe them over the defence argument.

I personally have little doubt that a prosecution on the Magnum deal would be simple, based on the weak defences raised to date.

The transactional facts of the deals have been laid out before you in three books:
The Paradise Conspiracy
Lawyers, Guns & Money
The Paradise Conspiracy II

The test of whether the deals were criminal lies in motive and intent. What were the participants wanting to do and why?

From the Winebox documents on their own, TVNZ's high powered legal team had garnered enough information to indicate to us a criminal intent, based on concealment in order to obtain money.

The SFO and the IRD had these same documents, but looked for references suggesting the opposite.

Why?

Both the IRD's John Nash and the SFO's Beattie were crucified by Carruthers when asked to put up good reasons why the deal planners were honest.

Beattie had relied on four words in one document, "change in tax laws".

Colin Carruthers pointed out that tax transactions have numerous strands that can run afoul of one regulation or another, and how did Beattie know that the reference referred to the scheme as a whole?

Under pressure, the SFO "top gun" admitted "I didn't turn my mind to what particular change in the tax law might impact [the scheme]. It's not within my field of expertise."

So much for SFO competence. He judged the four words to mean that the scheme was within the existing tax laws, but he had no idea really.

Likewise for John Nash. The IRD had access not only to the memo Beattie referred to, but also a letter from David Richwhite to the Cook Islands Government discussing the issue of fraud, and the legal opinion from Brian Oslington QC suggesting the deals were criminal, and the memo from EP's Mark Jones warning that a judge may well side with Oslington. Despite all of that, Nash didn't believe there was evidence of dishonest intent, or EP being prepared to break the law and take the risk.

Nash began by saying that he believed EP staff would identify a risk of criminality by putting it in writing in the transaction documents, and then five minutes later told Colin Carruthers "I agree with you, it would be one of the last risks to record in writing."

SFO boss Charles Sturt also expected criminals to dob themselves in.

"Are you suggesting," probed Carruthers, "that if they were doing this transaction dishonestly they would commit that statement to writing?"

"I would have thought if they were doing this dishonestly, they would have been alluding to problems that were in breach of – about breach of the law," mumbled Sturt.

Which is ironic, given that another transaction stated there was a possibility of illegality and "Russell McVeagh may go to gaol". The SFO told the Inquiry this was *not* evidence of dishonest behaviour.

The Oslington legal opinion, which only surfaced *after* the Inquiry had been announced and the IRD went to see the BNZ and asked for any other Winebox-related documents, is in my view damning.

It is also a document that could have been obtained by the SFO under its vast powers back in 1992, if the Office had understood the significance of the Winebox and made even the *slightest* effort to investigate the transactions.

But I believe the Serious Fraud Office, under the leadership of Charles Sturt, should be remembered as the investigation agency that lets the big ones get away.

Oslington's original opinion was never made available to the Commission, but his views are contained in a memorandum to the EP Board from executive Mark Jones. It is this memorandum that the IRD discovered in papers held by former BNZ executive Peter Travers.

"In Mr Oslington's view," writes Jones, "as the premium paid for the purchase of a note by the Property Corporation is essentially for a smart business dealing by the Government, it is not for public purposes.

"Therefore, the Cook Islands withholding tax is not a 'tax' for Australian purposes[14]; and if it is not a 'tax', promotion of a note constitutes a criminal offence by company officers and those knowingly involved in a conspiracy to defraud the Australian Revenue."

---

14 Oslington was referring to Australia because the original plans for tax credit schemes in late 1987 were aimed at the Australian market. It may be significant that following this advice European Pacific did not pursue its plans to market the deals in Australia, despite advice from two other Australian lawyers that sovereignty rules meant the scheme couldn't be attacked.

Further on in the memo, Jones reports that a Sydney lawfirm, Mallesons, and two other Australian QC's took a less harsh view of the transaction.

"Mallesons have advised EPBCL to proceed with the issue. Nonetheless there remains the chance that if the matter ever went to Court it may well be that a judge could side with the view taken by Mr Oslington."

Under the heading "Recommendation", Jones concludes:

"I suggest we proceed with a note issue notwithstanding the small risk that the Cook Islands 'tax' may not be levied for a public purpose.

"This is a commercial question. There is a small legal doubt. I recommend we continue to fulfill the original commercial objective, and generate the significant revenue that can flow from this project."

Now, does that sound to the ordinary reader like a company fearful of committing fraud, or does it sound like a company that wants to make a lot of money and is content to play the odds when it comes to legal risk?

Nash took the view that the memo shows the EP Group acted responsibly, and pointed to the involvement of two other Australian QC's and also a line in the Jones memorandum that reads: "I have talked over the New Zealand taxation implications of the note issue over with both Geoff Harley and Paul Darvell of Rudd, Watts & Stone and they are of the opinion that the tax is a proper tax for New Zealand purposes."

"Instead of looking at it by numbers and reputation," challenged Colin Carruthers, "let's take the fact that one silk [QC], chosen by EP, advises that what is proposed is a criminal offence. Do you think a group is acting conservatively if it goes ahead with a transaction despite that advice?"

"Well, we can break it right down like that but I didn't read it like that," said Nash, who then tried to justify it by talking of the "sheer weight, the authority" in the other lawyers who disagreed with Oslington.

In clutching at this straw Nash, and the SFO investigators, missed the point: European Pacific's board of directors were put on notice that the deals may be criminal. Directors like David Richwhite are, or should be, bright enough to know that simply having contradictory opinions from other lawyers doesn't remove the risk. At the end of the day, it could be a call for a judge and jury to decide.

Therefore, pushing ahead on the basis that the deals will make buckets of money, despite the risk of committing fraud, displays in my view sufficient criminal intent to at least mount a prosecution.

Is it all that different from somebody who robs a bank despite knowing there's a chance of getting caught?

Perhaps even more significantly, the scheme that Oslington and the other two QC's advised on was known as the RIBUN scheme – an early prototype of the Magnum-style tax credit deals.

Under the RIBUN, the party claiming the tax credit would be the end user – one of European Pacific's clients. In Magnum, the party claiming the tax credit was European Pacific itself.

Counsel Assisting the Commission wanted to know if Nash and the SFO had considered the "honesty" implications of the change in the scheme.

"Just going back to the RIBUNs structure, do you agree that one feature that distinguishes RIBUNs from 'Magnum' is that the party claiming the tax credit in its tax return is the ultimate investor in RIBUNS, rather than a member of the EP Group in 'Magnum'?"

"Yes," admitted Nash, "that is a difference."

"And in the RIBUNs case," continued Carruthers, "do you agree that it would be unlikely that the investor – the ultimate investor – would have any knowledge of the transactions with the Property Corporation?"

"Yes."

The point Carruthers was making was that if Oslington thought that the RIBUN tax credit deal was criminal – where the party presenting the tax certificate had no knowledge of the tax refund mechanism – then what would that mean to the Magnum transaction where the company claiming the credit had intimate knowledge of what had taken place?

Both the IRD and the SFO made much of the fact that European Pacific often consulted lawyers, which must illustrate honest intent. However, it may also be significant that after Oslington's warning about the RIBUN deals, the scheme was arguably made even more criminal but no further legal opinion appears to have been sought.

The SFO and IRD ignored this.

Geoff Harley, who was one of European Pacific's key external legal advisors, told the Winebox Inquiry "I had never heard of 'Magnum' or anything about it until all of this became public."

Questioned again by Carruthers, Harley insisted he had never been asked to provide legal advice on Magnum.

"I am sure about that."

"Did you have any role at all in giving advice on the 'JIF' transactions?" asked Carruthers.

"No."

"Was it any part of the advice that you gave," continued Carruthers, "the point that was raised by Mr Oslington, that is, the law concerning conspiracy to defraud?"

Harley – an engaging and refreshingly straight-talking lawyer – told the simple truth.

"I would have treated myself as being completely unable to express any opinion on a subject like that," replied the tax lawyer, "and I would have gone to someone else who did know about the law in that area.

"I also think that it is likely that I probably would have run a mile if I had known that there was anything like that in issue. I can certainly say that with the benefit of hindsight."

Nor had Geoff Harley given European Pacific any advice about the consequences of conspiring to deliberately breach section 62 of the Companies Act in the Magnum deal.

"I wouldn't have been quite as reactionary to it as the earlier point," he told the Inquiry, "but section 62 is a very serious issue and I would have gone for expert advice on it because it is not my area."

Harley was one legal advisor. Paul Darvell was the other, and Darvell had told Winston Peters, Brian Henry and lawyer Chris Dickie that the deals were fraudulent. So who were the illustrious lawyers that the IRD and SFO claimed had advised European Pacific that the Magnum deal was kosher?

They didn't exist.

The fact that the SFO and IRD used these mythical people and their mythical opinions as a reason not to prosecute or investigate further, should be contrasted against Sir Ronald Davison's finding in regard to each department:

"There can be no substance to an allegation that it was incompetent."

Nor had anyone given European Pacific expert outside accounting advice about the Magnum deal or the implications of section 301 of the Income Tax Act, which requires people claiming credits to disclose the existence of refunds.

Nash told the inquiry that he simply *assumed* that EP must have taken accounting advice on section 301.

Charles Sturt, in true 'buffoon' mode, was asked more key questions on these matters but was either being deliberately obtuse or he genuinely didn't understand the issues. If it is the latter then it has frightening implications for the Serious Fraud Office, even post-Sturt.

Asked about the non-disclosure of the promissory note deals in the Cook Islands Government accounts, Sturt was asked whether this might illustrate dishonest concealment.

"Well, I suppose that comes down to how they do things in the Cook Islands."

"Do you appreciate that this was on advice from New Zealand accountants?" asked Carruthers.

"I suppose for tax purposes, it could be frowned upon in that context," opined Sturt, puffing his chest out slightly and taking on the air of someone who believed he had some expertise in the subject.

"Did you understand," edged Carruthers, obviously convinced that Sturt didn't, "that the consequence is that the relevant entries concerning the promissory note transactions would not appear in the Cook Islands Government accounts?"

"I understand that, yes."

"Do you regard that step as being relevant to concealment?"

"Yes."

"And as relevant to whether the concealment was proper or improper?"

"Improper, certainly," replied Sturt, "but in terms of criminality, that is another matter … you are really getting beyond my area of, shall I say, expertise. These are all, again, all tax matters that you are referring to."

"No," sighed Carruthers. "I am not referring to a single tax matter, Mr Sturt."

"Yes, but the motivation behind it is."

"Whatever the motivation," growled an exasperated Carruthers, "what we are looking at is factors that go to dishonesty."

Pinning Sturt to the wall, Carruthers then forced a series of admissions:

Yes, the absence of the transactions in the Audit reports is relevant to illegitimate concealment.

Yes, the absence of appropriation is relevant as well.

Yes, the moves to get European Pacific's accountants – KPMG – appointed as Government auditors were relevant too.

"Would you regard as relevant the maintaining of separate receipt books by the Commissioner of Inland Revenue and Financial Secretary for the purposes of the transaction as relevant?"

"Yes, I can't understand the reason for that but –"

"And using separately opened bank accounts at a bank other than the usual Government bank?" thundered the QC.

"That – wasn't the other bank certainly one that was within the group – that is used by the Government – wasn't there a Government bank as well?" asked a confused SFO Director.

"Is that your understanding of it?"

"No, I am not now sure, but I know they used another bank rather than the ordinary bank that they would normally use."

Yes, Sturt eventually conceded, the use of separate accounts was relevant to dishonest concealment as well. In Carruthers' final submissions he questioned whether the two Government law enforcement agencies had any real understanding at all of what they were dealing with.

"The question for the Commission may be whether SFO's conclusion that any 'concealment' steps taken in relation to the transactions was not a matter requiring further investigation was based on adequate analysis and information. Relevant questions may include:

"What things, if any, did the participants do that prevented or impeded IRD from discovering any inquiry into the transactions?

"Were the participants entitled to do those things?

"Did the IRD and SFO discover those things had been done?

"Did IRD and SFO analyse whether the things done were legitimate and did they analyse whether any of those steps evidenced dishonesty?

"What were the IRD and SFO conclusions?"

"Could the IRD and SFO have reached a conclusion on the legality of the tax credit transactions without undertaking further analysis or inquiries into the 'concealment' steps?"

Another factor in the issue of the Magnum deal's criminality is, of course, section 301.

We now know European Pacific didn't even realise the provision existed, so the argument that they took legal advice on the point is plainly untrue.

Nor did the Inland Revenue Department appear to realise its significance. The first reference to s301 by the IRD comes in a legal opinion from Grant Pearson in March 1994, and he only tumbled to it because it had been handed to him gift-wrapped, in a TVNZ affidavit.

"The element which Mr Wishart adds to the legal analysis is a reference to s301 of the Income Tax Act 1976," Pearson told IRD boss David Henry, "which obliges a taxpayer to disclose 'any relief or repayment' on foreign tax on which a tax credit is based."

As you will see later, the Court of Appeal takes a particularly strong view of section 301.

John Hicks, SFO officer / *The Independent Business Weekly*

Left: Susan Pilgrim,
SFO senior prosecutor:
testified against Sturt /
The Independent Business Weekly

Right: Gib Beattie,
SFO accountant /
The Independent Business Weekly

Left: Brian Henry,
Counsel for Winston Peters
/ *Ian Wishart*

Right: Richard Craddock
QC, European Pacific
Counsel / *The Independent
Business Weekly*

Winston Peters / *The Independent Business Weekly*

Above: Colin Carruthers QC Counsel. Assisting the Commission / *The Independent Business Weekly*

Right: Stephen Lunn, Winebox "whistle blower" / *Ian Wishart*

Sir Ronald Davison, Commission of Inquiry / *Ian Wishart*

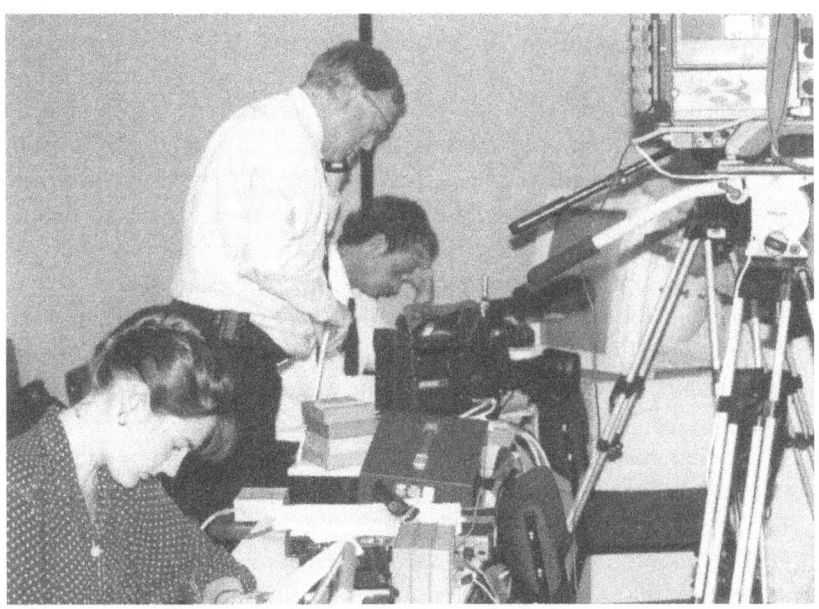

Media bench. Left to right: Maria Slade, RNZ; John Stewart, One Network News; Graham Skellern, New Zealand Herald / *Ian Wishart*

Chapter 15

Criminal Intent

"We don't pay taxes. Only the little people pay taxes."
– *Leona Helmsley (b. 1920), U.S. businesswoman*

Commission investigators set out 17 possible points of sham or concealment in the Magnum deal alone – sham being areas where the parties prepare documentation suggesting they will do one thing, but actually do something different in reality. A sham, for example, can be a false paper trail.

Under IRD rules, a finding of sham can allow an entire transaction to be struck down and examined for avoidance or fraud.

"In short, it would appear," wrote Carruthers in his final submissions, "the Department's decision not to undertake a greater analysis of sham arose from a 'judgment call' made by Mr Nash, and possibly Mr Pearson.

"In considering whether any greater analysis should have been performed, it may be relevant that, at the time the Department had concluded that no further audit action was called for, there was unlikely to be any ability to recover any tax from the transaction should sham be established."

But perhaps one of the biggest impediments to an investigation was a belief by the SFO and IRD that mounting a criminal case would depend on being able to prove that the defendants were "actively and deliberately" dishonest. The inherent dishonesty of the scheme wasn't enough.

In tackling this myth, Colin Carruthers dug out leading court rulings on the issue. One of those was the case of *O'Donovan* v *Vereker and Forsyth*, a 1987 judgment of the full Australian Federal Court.

In *Vereker*, the court examined a scheme where a company purchased a painting for $500, and then sold it to an Art Gallery for $10 million. Why would the gallery pay $10 million for a $500 painting? Because the company involved had "loaned" the gallery $10 million with which to purchase it. It was, in effect, a money-go-round for tax minimisation purposes.

The court found that the participants genuinely believed their cunning plan fell on the right side of the law, and they had even consulted a barrister, Forsyth, on the point.

One judge ruled "that in a case of this sort, the degree of risk of failure of the scheme, as seen by the participants, bears upon proof of fraud."

Which is a line worth remembering in light of Oslington's opinion and the fact that the directors and some executives of European Pacific knew there was a risk of going to jail. This is a much greater risk than the *Vereker* risk – which was that the scheme might be mere tax avoidance.

Another judge in the case noted "it appears that the inflated price was charged as a means of passing back to the promoters the monies constituting the gifts to [the Art Gallery].

"That by itself does not constitute and unlawful means but, as part of a larger scheme, could constitute part of *unlawful means to achieve a lawful object*. [author's emphasis]

The case had come before the Federal Court judge on appeal, after a lower court judge ruled that there could be no conspiracy to defraud unless and until it had been determined that the scheme was not effective. But the higher court saw it differently.

"Any opinion by the Courts as to the probability of the [Art Gallery] scheme being effective of necessity is irrelevant in conspiracy charges."

Colin Carruthers summarised the main points of *Vereker* for Sir Ronald Davison.

1) It is not necessary in conspiracy charges relating to a tax scheme that it be proved that the scheme is ineffective.

2) Neither is it necessary to prove that the defendants believed it was ineffective.

3) It was sufficient to prove a dishonest intent to deprive the Commissioner of tax that *might* be payable.

4) That such intent might exist where the scheme involved an effective asset strip, so that there were no assets to pay any tax assessed.

"The case is different from wine-box transactions such as the tax credit scheme," wrote Carruthers, because of the allegation that the scheme involved an 'asset strip' of any companies that might be assessed."

Another judgment brought to Davison's attention was Equiticorp, where senior executives were convicted of defrauding – among others – the Inland Revenue Department.

Justice Tompkins ruled:

> "When consideration is given to all of the circumstances to which I have referred relating to the setting up and use of the Yeoman Loop for each of the five transactions, the purpose of it all becomes apparent beyond any reasonable doubt.
> "It was set up and used in order to conceal the payments that were intended to be, and were, made, and to make it difficult for any person who had cause to enquire, to find out what they were, and their source.
> "The cumulative effect of all the evidence to which I have referred leads to the clear conclusion that the only reasonable inference that can be drawn is that the concealment was dishonest –that is, with intent to defraud. Concealment for innocent reasons is not a reasonably possible inference.
> "Was anyone defrauded?
> "If the purpose of the structure were dishonest concealment, the question answers itself. The persons the conspirators intended to defraud were those from whom it was intended to conceal.
> " ... It is easy to see that they would embrace the directors of EHL (other than the conspirators), other employees of Equiticorp who may talk about these exceptional transactions, the auditors, who would be intensely interested in any of those transactions that did or may have involved an Equiticorp company, the Revenue, and enforcement agencies on both sides of the Tasman."

The comparisons between Equiticorp, which the SFO successfully prosecuted, and European Pacific, which the SFO refused to prosecute, scream out for recognition. Another case quoted by Carruthers is pertinent not just to intent on the Magnum deal, but also on the $400 million dollars of secret BNZ loans to shareholder Fay Richwhite which were concealed from the Reserve Bank and which exceeded the BNZ's lending limits.

> "In Wai-Yu-Tsang, the chief accountant of a bank agreed with the bank manager not to record dishonoured cheques in the bank's accounts, but to make entries giving a false impression of the state of the bank's finances whilst keeping secret accounts disclosing the true position.
> "They were charged with conspiring to defraud the bank and its customers and creditors. The trial judge directed the jury that the defendant could be convicted even if no loss had actually been suffered, and even if the defendant had not desired to cause loss, provided that he had agreed to imperil the economic or property rights of a person.

"The Privy Council concluded that it was sufficient to establish an intent to defraud, to prove an intention to act to the prejudice of another person's right, and that it was not necessary to prove an intention to cause economic loss to another."

Applying that principle to Magnum, the SFO would not need to prove that European Pacific intended to cause the Inland Revenue a $2 million loss, the SFO would only need to prove that the defendants intended to carry out a scheme that put the Inland Revenue at risk of losing tax money.

Applying the *Vereker* principles, the SFO wouldn't even need to prove that European Pacific [inserted text follows]believed that its Magnum scheme would not be effective for tax purposes.

"In the case of the tax credit transactions," wrote Carruthers, "it might be argued that the Commissioner [of Inland Revenue] had a potential financial interest at stake. He gave credit against payment of New Zealand tax where he says he would not have done so if the full facts were known. On this view the Privy Council held that a right of recovery need not be established."

Carruthers also informed Davison of precedents in United States law, including cases where people were found not guilty in the end of *tax evasion*, but guilty none the less of *conspiring to defraud*.

An article in the April 1990 issue of *The Tax Magazine* highlights the issues.

"As part of the Government's intensifying war on tax evasion, the IRS and the US Department of Justice with increasing frequency have selected the 'conspiracy to defraud' statute as their prosecution vehicle.

"From the Government's viewpoint, prosecuting tax fraud and tax-related crimes under the conspiracy to defraud statute had substantial legal, evidentiary and tactical advantage.

"For example, evidence of crimes which are barred by the statute of limitations is routinely admitted in conspiracy to defraud prosecutions.

"Also, the Government need not prove a tax deficiency in a conspiracy to defraud case [author's emphasis], whereas proof beyond a reasonable doubt of a tax deficiency is an essential element in a tax evasion prosecution."

Carruthers asked Sir Ronald Davison to consider whether this was the case in New Zealand law and, if not, to consider recommending a law change making it so.

Despite all these leading court rulings from around the world, the Director of the Serious Fraud Office, Charles Sturt, told the Inquiry:

"The concealment of a suspicious transaction, or in fact put another way a doubtful transaction, by dishonest means, is not fraudulent."

But the man Sir Ronald Davison later ruled was "competent" was then taken by Carruthers to the Equiticorp verdict – the very case upon which Sturt had staked the SFO's reputation – and read the passage quoted earlier in this chapter.

"Do you recall the judge analysing the matter in that way?" asked Carruthers after a moment.

"I recall that. Yes."

"And I take it you will have read the reasons for verdict at the time that they were delivered?"

"Yes."

"And is your position that despite this judgment, in the very month you were looking at the Winebox documents, you have proceeded on the basis that you needed to show a knowing lack of entitlement before dishonesty could be shown?"

"Yes."

I don't care what anybody says: in my view Sturt must be corrupt – nobody could possibly be that incompetent! This was a court case his own office had just won. A landmark ruling. And he didn't apply that ruling to the Winebox.

Why not?

Bombarded with all these court cases that the SFO should have been aware of at the time of examining the Winebox, the SFO's lawyers at the Inquiry went into overdrive to try and play down their significance vis a vis SFO inaction.

"Looking at the matter as it is being presented to the Commission now," queried Carruthers, "do you agree that a number of quite sophisticated legal arguments are being advanced by [lawyer] Mr Young for the Serious Fraud Office, to justify the Serious Fraud Office's position?"

"To explain his position, yes," said Sturt.

"Do you agree that the Serious Fraud Office did not approach the Winebox transactions with that sophistication at the time they were under consideration?"

"Not with that sophistication, no," admitted Sturt.

But then, no one had ever called it "The Sophisticated Fraud Office".

Interestingly, the SFO and the IRD both maintained to the bitter end that the transaction was legal because a "real tax" was paid in the Cook Islands, entitling European Pacific to a "real credit" in New Zealand.

This was the public position, even though the IRD lawyer Grant Pearson had nevertheless put up a strong argument that the tax was not genuine, regardless of issues of sovereignty.

Pearson, in the opinion he had provided to IRD boss David Henry in March 1994, examined the rules governing tax credit claims. A credit, he said, could only be allowed if the overseas tax paid is "in the opinion of the Commissioner ... substantially of the same nature as income tax imposed" in New Zealand.

The key words here are "opinion of the Commissioner".

This rule, under section 293 of the Income Tax Act, means the NZ IRD can disallow any credit claim regardless of the authenticity of the foreign tax if, in their opinion, the foreign tax paid is not comparable to NZ tax.

Pearson wrote:

> "I have reached the view that it is very likely that the tax benefits claimed for the transaction are illusory.
>
> "I consider that the tax credit did not comply with s293 of the Income Tax Act and was not able to be off-set against New Zealand income, as you are to allow a tax credit only if you hold the 'opinion' that tax 'substantially of the same nature as income tax' under the New Zealand Act has been paid.
>
> "If a payment of tax triggers a refund or partial refund simply by reason of the payment, I think that you would be likely to hold the opinion that the payment was not of the same nature as income tax under the New Zealand Act – which results in a real economic cost to the taxpayer."

In Pearson's view the transaction was tax avoidance, and this became the IRD's view as well. On the witness stand, John Nash said that in the Department's view European Pacific were only entitled to claim a $50,000 tax credit, which was the amount that hadn't been refunded.

And this brings us to yet another lie, or possibly another example of incompetence, from former SFO boss Charles Sturt.

In his book, Sturt states that "the IRD and its counsel ... expressed the opinion that there was neither evasion nor avoidance. They gave the transactions a clean bill of health."

You've seen the IRD opinion. They may have a run a million miles at suggestions of evasion in Magnum, but they certainly felt it was tax avoidance. And, as we now know, the concealment of a doubtful transaction can indeed amount to a conspiracy to defraud.

So how could Sturt truthfully[15] make the statement that the IRD did not find any tax avoidance in Magnum?

---

15 Sturt's 'competence' is such that he couldn't even get the facts straight in his own autobiography. In the book he makes a number of sweeping allegations completely without evidence or foundation. If the research into his own life story was that sloppy, one can only wonder what skills he brought to his criminal work. In pulling his publishing company up on a number of untrue statements Sturt makes about me, he was forced to back away from an earlier claim that he could prove it, to a point where it became plain that he had no evidence and had relied on inaccurate hearsay. Ironically, exactly the same sort of complaint that he was making about Peters.

Chapter 16

The Devil's Advocate

"Where God hath a temple, the Devil will have a chapel."
— *Robert Burton* — *The Anatomy of Melancholy (1621)*

Before looking at Sir Ronald's verdict, it's worth perusing the submissions from the other main parties: the IRD, the SFO, European Pacific and Fay Richwhite.

IRD counsel Bruce Squire told the Inquiry that it would be unfair to call the IRD incompetent, given the huge amount of work required to examine the transactions.

> *"The reality is that tax investigations of large corporates require thousands of hours of effort by IRD investigators.*
>
> *"This Commission's own processes demonstrate the need for substantial investigative effort rather than a superficial reaction. This Commission, at least in the hearings, has scarcely touched on 49 of the 60 transactions in the winebox.*
>
> *"The relatively limited number of transactions that remain have taken some 3 years for this Commission to investigate, and the cost of doing so is a matter of public record.*
>
> *"The advice Mr Molloy gave to Mr Peters that a conclusion could be reached on the basis of an examination of papers found in the winebox simply cannot be reconciled with the detailed work this Commission has found necessary to report on the winebox transactions."*

Squire's pleas for mercy because of the IRD workload may strike some sympathetic cords, but they shouldn't.

The reality is that eight weeks after discovering the key to the tax credit deals, a TVNZ investigative team had prepared a legally watertight documentary alleging serious fraud had taken place.

The IRD, with a similar aggressive approach and proper legal advice, could have reached the same conclusion just as fast.

Once you read the Court of Appeal judgments later in this book, I believe it will become blatantly obvious that the IRD have misunderstood the law and their own powers, and millions of dollars have probably been wasted by the department in time spent doing lengthy investigations that were not necessary.

The Magnum deal, of course, was very well documented and not too difficult to understand.

Another key to the IRD's closing submissions was the issue of whether investigating the Magnum deal was pointless, as no tax could be recovered from the liquidated European Pacific company involved.

There is certainly some validity to this, but there is another responsibility held by the IRD, and that is to enforce the law and set examples and boundaries.

> *"When five separate official examinations of the Magnum transaction have reached the view that the Magnum transaction was not fraudulent, this Commission cannot possibly say that was an unreasonable conclusion. Indeed, for this Commission to reach a contrary view, it must be conscious that its view becomes a minority of one among the six separate official examinations of the transaction."*

Unless of course, the law enforcement agencies were playing a game of pass the parcel and didn't understand the law.

If you make 100 children sit a maths test, and 70 get the answers wrong, does that mean that they should be declared "winners" because they are in the majority?

Since when was the truth ever decided by a majority vote? Yet this was the logic employed by IRD lawyers in their submissions, and it was logic echoed by Ron Davison when he reprinted the above quote in full in his report.

Not that the IRD's closing submissions conveyed "the whole truth and nothing but the truth" either.

> *"Before entering the Magnum transaction the European Pacific Group had the advice of the late Mr Darvell and Dr Harley who have told the Commission that they did not consider the transaction was fraudulent."*

As you have seen earlier, Geoff Harley told the Inquiry he was "never asked" to give legal advice on the Magnum deal, and was not qualified to express an opinion as to fraud. So who was the IRD trying to kid by slipping that one in?

Another claim by the IRD was that by failing to challenge the evidence of European Pacific's tax expert, Lindsay McKay, the Commission was forced to accept his views on the Magnum deal as gospel. This, on the basis that evidence not challenged must stand as fact. One can only speculate on why Sir Ronald Davison chose to allow experts like McKay to testify on the tax efficacy of the deals, but not Dr Molloy.

> "It is a familiar role for a Judge to evaluate and assess the evidence of competing experts," noted Squire, "but it is outside that judicial expertise and beyond the lawful powers of a Judge to reject uncontradicted expert evidence because the Judge thinks he or she knows more about the subject than the expert."

On the issue of competence, Squire called for the IRD to be judged in this context:

> "The Commission must look at the overall investigative process, standing back from the minutiae to have a perspective of the overall process. IRD is a department which had more than 5,000 employees when the winebox papers were received. Individuals will make errors. Dealing with the whole range of human frailty exhibited by employees is, and always will be, a feature of administering the department.
>
> "Organisational competence does not require processes to be error-free, only reasonable safeguards in place to detect and correct errors. Inevitably there will be irretrievable errors."

If only the IRD were so forgiving when they deal with ordinary taxpayers; instead the department is more than willing to chuck the book at everyone else.

And, as you shall see by the end of this book, the IRD incompetence transcends anything, in my view, that the department could throw up in its defence. The ultimate IRD incompetence, uncovered by the Court of Appeal, may have cost taxpayers *billions*.

The reader, meanwhile, can be the judge as to whether the incompetence outlined so far is "forgivable" in an organisation supposed to be at the cutting edge of tax law enforcement.

IRD lawyers claimed that Peters had taken a simplistic view that Sturt and David Henry must be corrupt because they disagreed with Winston.

"Mr Henry and the Department's officers have never wavered in carrying out their duty to exercise their judgment independently of political influence. They have not buckled under political pressure, nor will they," wrote Squire.

> *"In order to maintain a submission that IRD officials have been either incompetent or corrupt, counsel for Mr Peters must overcome a number of factual obstacles, including:*
> *"The fact that the IRD had sorted, examined and fed the papers into the appropriate audits more than a year before they were tabled by Mr Peters [and] the fact that, independently of the efforts of Mr Peters or this Commission, IRD has identified $140 million in assessable taxes."*

Squire poked more borax at Peters, quoting a parliamentary exchange where National MP John Luxton had accused Peters of peddling "conspiracy theory", saying "when we get evidence, that is the time to call for a Commission of Inquiry. When he can actually give evidence of corruption by the Commissioner of Inland Revenue or by the chief of the Serious Fraud Office, then this House will sit up and listen."[16]

To which Peters had replied: "I can do that and I will."

The IRD claimed Peters had failed to meet that challenge. But one could easily argue that the terms of reference were too narrow. The IRD could not be judged on the film settlement deal *that its own staff* said was illegal, because it was outside the terms of reference. Nor could the SFO be judged for lying about having investigated Peters' claim about the settlement and found nothing, despite having not investigated.

Nor could the SFO be judged for a similar stunt over the Paul White case. None of these events have ever been adequately explained. Nor do I believe that they can be. In my view a law enforcement organisation that dispels public or political concerns about an issue by saying it has investigated, *when it has not done a credible investigation that would stand up in court*, must be corrupt, for there can be no honest intent in telling such a lie.

The IRD, incidentally, held that its Commissioner was entitled to settle the

---

16 Conveniently overlooking the fact that National Government MP's like Tony Ryall and Bill English had repeatedly prevented Peters from tabling his winebox on 17 occasions. Incidentally, my political sources tell me that English and Wyatt Creech are both vying to topple Jenny Shipley if National loses the election. If National must change leaders, then in my view either Max Bradford or Clem Simich would be better alternatives, as both have shown a willingness to investigate the winebox deals in defiance of the "party line". Simich, for example, welcomed the Court of Appeal verdicts.

film deal in a way favourable to Russell McVeagh and not to other taxpayers in the same film investment deal, under his general powers.

In regard to Magnum, the IRD repeated its claim that the deal avoided tax, but disputed that European Pacific had any duty to disclose the tax refunds under section 301. Nor, they said, was the deal a fraud. The form over substance rules precluded an attack on the Magnum deal, except under the anti-avoidance provisions of s99.

Fay Richwhite, for their part, reserved most of their venom for Colin Carruthers QC, over his claims that fraud existed within the Winebox deals. Rhys Harrison QC reminded the Inquiry that his client was *not* a party to the Magnum deal.

> "Fay Richwhite accepts, as it always has, that Mr David Richwhite in his capacity as EPI Chairman knew of the company's planning for tax credit transactions and participated in negotiations with the Cook Islands Government in 1987 and in a board discussion in February 1988 about an issue of promissory notes in Australia. Fay Richwhite subsequently participated in the JIF transactions in late 1988 and early 1989.
>
> "Its directors and officers did not have prior knowledge or participate in Magnum. Even Fay Richwhite's most vociferous critics have not attempted to implicate Mr Richwhite or other Fay Richwhite employees in it."

This, too, is a fair point and worth bearing in mind in relation to the warning in the introduction about criminal intent. David Richwhite and his fellow board members gave approval to tax credit transactions which they were advised could be criminal.

This is an issue that I have previously suggested may indicate some criminal intent, that the directors have been put on notice. But, as I said at the start, is it *sufficient* evidence of criminal intent?

A Court might also note that the Magnum deal was a new variation on the tax credit scheme, and that legal advice was not obtained, nor was the board advised about Magnum.

On the other hand, prosecutors might be able to argue that without board approval of the tax credit deals in principle, despite potential criminality, the Magnum deal would never have gone ahead.

How much criminal intent in regard to the directors would flow on from the original decision to proceed? I don't know. Maybe some, maybe none.

An analogy might be a parent who lets their underage child borrow the car for the evening, only to have the youngster arrive on the doorstep accompanied by Mr Plod, having been arrested for drinking and driving.

The parent is liable for letting an unlicensed driver use the car, but do they carry the can criminally for the child's flow-on stupidity? Interesting debate.

As for European Pacific's closing submissions, Richard Craddock QC spent much of his time attacking Brian Henry and Colin Carruthers for taking the Inquiry on "a wild goose chase" looking for fraud "where none existed".

Craddock relied on Lindsay McKay, EP's tax expert, for his contention that the deals were not fraudulent and that there was no requirement to disclose the secret refunds.

The Serious Fraud Office rejected allegations of incompetence or corruption, saying that as the deals were tax related they left them to the IRD to investigate. Again, the SFO pushed the difficulty of mounting a prosecution in a tax case, saying they would need to prove that the participants knew their scheme was ineffective in order to secure a conviction.

And so the stage was set for Sir Ronald Davison's Magnum Opus.

Chapter 17

The Verdict

*"Power tends to corrupt, and absolute power corrupts absolutely.
Great men are almost always bad men."*
— *Lord Acton (1834–1902), English historian*

One of the strange things about Davison's defective Winebox verdict was that Sir Ronald appeared to narrow down his terms of reference even further when it came time to rule on the competence of the IRD and the SFO.

I have quoted the rulings on competence several times so far, but I have deliberately left out the qualification on the end of them. Until now.

The reason I quoted the findings of "no incompetence" in a universal sense is because the actual terms of reference were universal in that regard. Davison was required to examine whether the IRD and the SFO had acted "in a lawful, proper and competent manner in dealing with the transactions referred to in the [Winebox] papers."

The instruction is pretty simple, one would have thought.

So why did Sir Ronald's findings of no incompetence read in this much narrower fashion:

> "There can be no substance to an allegation that [the IRD] was incompetent ***in that it failed to detect fraud or tax evasion*** [author's emphasis] when there was in fact no evidence at all to indicate that such occurred in relation to any of the wine-box transactions."

Or, in the case of the SFO:

> "The SFO cannot be held to have been incompetent for not detecting fraud [ditto] in transactions where no fraud existed."

The Government, in setting the terms of reference, did not restrict the issue of incompetence merely to detecting fraud. It asked Sir Ronald to find out whether the two departments acted competently, in a general sense, in their handling of the Winebox.

As the reader has seen, I believe there is ample evidence that the two departments acted thoroughly incompetently in their investigation or non-investigation of the deals. But Sir Ronald appears to have ignored the terms of reference and invented one of his own choosing.

Even so, Davison may have been too clever for himself, as the Court of Appeal is now strongly indicating that the deals are fraudulent, in which case the main finding of the Winebox Inquiry can be overturned.

So how did Davison come to the conclusion that there was no fraud in the Winebox, especially after all the revelations so painstakingly unearthed by the Commission's legal team? Especially after Sir Ron Davison's comment to Brian Henry that the deals were straight-out criminal fraud?

While the news media happily reported Davison's final verdict as though it was the truth from on high, and politicians called for Winston Peters head on a plate, there were things happening behind the scenes that the public didn't get to hear.

Legal circles were abuzz: Counsel Assisting the Commission, Colin Carruthers QC, was sickened at what had taken place and for a while contemplated giving up law. His second chair, Suzanne Clark, they whispered, was so traumatised she left the country and no longer works in New Zealand.

But perhaps the most disturbing beat on the legal tom-tom drums was a report that neither of the Commission lawyers believed Davison's verdict was an honest reflection of the evidence. This was serious, and it echoed the views of a large number of their colleagues in the legal profession and the judiciary.

As one lawyer later remarked:

> *"I think what probably happened was that somebody made it plain that the only way Sir Ronald Davison was going to enjoy a peaceful retirement without ongoing legal hassles was to bring down a 'safe' verdict. I have no direct evidence of this, I hasten to add, but as a lawyer I know how the system works, and I think it's a matter of public interest."*

Whatever the reasons, the judgment – when it came – was already known to me: complete exoneration of the two Government departments and the corporates involved.

For the record, his decisions follow:
On Magnum:
"The Magnum transaction was a 'smart' transaction designed to take advantage of loopholes in income tax law. It did not exhibit any elements of illegality or fraud nor could it be claimed that it resulted in any evasion of tax. The proper returns of income were made and the IRD assessed tax on that income.

"There are some who have suggested that EPFML was guilty of tax avoidance. However, such could not be the case when it had disclosed and returned all of the income received. The payment of the tax on that income was made by a tax credit. It has not avoided any tax at all."
On the IRD's investigation of Magnum:
"The evidence that IRD's processes and conclusion were competent is overwhelming. The evidence before this Commission simply does not support the view that the Magnum transaction was illegal, and that became patently clear when Mr McKay gave his evidence to that effect."[17]
On the SFO investigation of Magnum:
"The SFO was entitled to expect the IRD to analyse for tax evasion/fraud.

"Although various issues in respect of the IRD analysis and investigation of Magnum are set out in the IRD evidence, what is quite obvious is that Magnum was assessed within the IRD who examined and reached views on the issue of fraud. The SFO was not required to be a backstop for the IRD in these circumstances."[18]
On SFO's failure to investigate:
"Section 49 of the Serious Fraud Office Act 1990 makes it clear that the director of the SFO is never under a duty to investigate any particular matter. Furthermore s20 of that ACT provides that the power of the director to make his decision as to whether a matter may involve serious or complex fraud is clearly his alone and such decision shall not be challenged, reviewed, quashed or called into question in any court.

"The right of the director to make his own judgment as to whether or not to investigate any particular matter is highlighted by the way in which he dealt with the four winebox transactions discussed.

"They were being investigated by the IRD; he would not conduct his own investigation."

---

17 McKay was European Pacific's hired tax expert. Significantly, the only tax experts allowed to testify at Sir Ronald's Inquiry were those who supported the European Pacific position. Sir Ronald Davison refused permission for Winston Peters to call expert evidence from Dr Tony Molloy QC. Nor did the Commission hear from Dr John Prebble or other leading tax practitioners who believed the deal was fraud
18 See *The Paradise Conspiracy*, Ch. 27 "The Piggy Bank", and also *Lawyers, Guns & Money*, Ch. 29 "Charlie's Angels".

On improper conduct by lawyers for corporates:
"Attempts by the Commission to obtain documents from various corporates were delayed by claims of legal professional privilege ... Many of such claims were found to be totally unsupportable."

On Alzheimer's:
"There were difficulties experienced by witnesses who on occasions could not remember matters upon which they were questioned. This was perhaps understandable to some extent because many of those matters occurred in many instances more than six years ago.

"However, some failures of recall arose perhaps more by reason of convenience rather than loss of memory."

On Winston Peters:
"In the course of his evidence, W.P. made reference to a number of matters which the Commission ruled were outside its Terms of Reference and could not be inquired into.

"He was pressed by Counsel on numerous occasions to say where there was evidence to support his allegations. At the end of his evidence, it was apparent that there was little he could contribute.

"Throughout its Inquiry the Commission was most conscious of the impact its decision might have on W.P. if it decided either that any of his allegations were untrue or that there was no evidence to support them.

"It was also conscious of the fact that W.P.'s aallegations against the IRD, the SFO and the corporates and individuals named having been made under circumstances of absolute privilege, they would have no redress against him or opportunity to prove these allegations false except through te decision of this Commission.

"In those circumstances it went to great lengths to probe the issues, particularly the allegations of fraud which W.P. had scattered so widely in the course of his speeches.

"The questioning of Mr Brian Henry was like chasing a will-o-the-wisp, in that no proper foundation for or evidence in support of any of W.P.'s allegations could be identified."

On Corruption:
"There was no evidence of corruption on the part of the Commissioner of Inland Revenue, Mr David Henry, or the Director of the Serious Fraud Office, Mr Charles Sturt."

On Conspiracy to Pervert the Course of Justice:
"This allegation was made against Mr David Henry and Mr Charles Sturt. There was no evidence of such a conspiracy."

On Conspiracy Not To Prosecute:
"This allegation was made against Mr David Henry and Mr Charles Sturt. There was no evidence of such a conspiracy.

On Conspiracy to Defraud:
"This allegation was made against the corporates and individuals as evidenced in this report. The Commission dealt with this allegation in relation to the four types of transactions specifically identified by Mr Brian Henry:
a) The Magnum transaction – this transaction was not fraudulent.
b) The JIF transactions – there was no evidence of fraud.
c) MCN/RPS transactions – these transactions were not fraudulent.[19]
d) The BNZ Captive Insurance scheme – there was no evidence of fraud.
"The Commission's examinations of the Winebox transactions generally indicated clearly that they were implemented by corporates intent on escaping the impact of the heavy taxes imposed on their activities at that time.

"In making his allegations of fraud W.P. grossly overplayed his hand and elevated the four types of transactions which he specifically identified to a level of fraudulent conduct which in fact none has been proved to have possessed.

"There is simply no evidence at all of the existence of such fraud as he alleged in any of the winebox transactions."

On the IRD in general:
"No evidence of any unlawful conduct on the part of the IRD was detected.
"No evidence of any impropriety on the part of the IRD was detected.
"There can be no substance to an allegation that it was incompetent in that it failed to detect fraud or tax evasion when there was in fact no evidence at all to indicate that such occurred in relation to any of the Winebox transactions."

Sir Ronald Davison had the chance to give the Serious Fraud Office a sting, but chose not to do so.

> "*During the course of its examination of Mr Sturt the Commission referred him to a passage contained in a press statement made by him on 18 March 1994.*
>
> "*Having considered that evidence the Commission formed the opinion*

---

19 The SFO's "excuse" for failing to investigate the Winebox was the much vilified "we don't do tax" claim. During cross-examination Sturt was asked why, if the claim was accurate, he hadn't told journalists this back in early 1994. At that time he told reporters he was waiting for Court action to finish before taking action. "Well, do we take from that that the SFO does, in fact, do tax fraud?" asked Carruthers. "You can take from that that the SFO does do tax fraud in particular situations, as I have just explained. Yes," Sturt admitted.

that for whatever reason the word 'investigation' was used, it was clearly misleading for Mr Sturt to have said that an investigation had been carried out when such had not been the case. In SFO terminology, an examination is clearly a different thing from an investigation.

"Whether its use was unintentional and had 'slipped in on the odd occasion' as he said seems an unreal explanation when the statement was not made orally but in a written statement prepared (it would be thought) with care for publication.

"The use of the word 'investigation' would likely have conveyed to the reader a far more extensive inquiry than an 'examination'.

"The Commission considered whether or not it should regard this incident as one where the SFO did not act in a 'proper' manner in dealing with the Winebox transactions, but concluded that it should not be elevated to such a level."

Having reached that view, Davison found:

On the SFO in general:

"No evidence of any unlawful conduct on the part of the SFO was detected.

"No impropriety on the part of the SFO was detected.

"The SFO cannot be held to have been incompetent for not detecting fraud in transactions where no fraud existed."

As you're about to discover, Sir Ronald Davison was putting his neck on the line. His entire finding of no incompetence, and his subsequent savaging of Winston Peters and Brian Henry, rests on his conclusion that the deals were not fraudulent.

Davison had said, only a few days before attacking Henry on the Inquiry's last day, that he believed the deals *were* criminal. He should have trusted his hunch.

Chapter 18

Methinks They Doth Protest Too Much

"Agitators are a set of interfering, meddling people, who come down to some perfectly contented class of the community and sow the seeds of discontent amongst them. That is the reason why agitators are so absolutely necessary. Without them, in our incomplete state, there would be no advance towards civilisation."
– *Oscar Wilde (1854–1900), Anglo-Irish playwright, author.*

Let's get one thing straight: this book is not out to make apologies for Winston Peters. He is a man who lives by the political sword, and who may die by the political sword.

On the other hand, I will not stand idly by and be a party to his murder.

Peters, and/or his party, have committed many sins in the eyes of the voters, the biggest of which was probably jumping into the National Party's electoral bed.

Brian Henry phoned me up when Peters was still wavering, and asked my opinion.

"If you really want to know, stay independent. Forget the trappings of power, let a Government form between the rest of them and hold the balance of power responsibly. The MPs need time to learn about politics."

Only a few months later the media caught Tuku Morgan with his pants down, and the rest is history.

Despite the disappointment New Zealanders shared in the performance of the so-called "watchdog" party, New Zealand still needs Winston Peters, or someone like him.

In a Parliament dominated by major parties and internal discipline to make sure everyone toes the party line, we need politicians who are not afraid to rock the boat and speak out on issues that may be important to the public, but detrimental to their own parties.

Sometimes those allegations will be wrong. Sometimes. But is that an excuse to shoot people like Peters?

Sometimes the Police or the Serious Fraud Office arrest people. They turn their lives upside down, sometimes breaking up their families in the process.

And then, further down the track, a Court and a jury discover the accused person is innocent.

People are declared innocent in our Courts every single day, but do we sack our Police Chiefs or SFO Directors because they got their facts wrong on one occasion? Or two? Or a thousand over a three year period?

The answer is no. Allegations are made. The issues are eventually tested in Court. Right or wrong, that is the price we pay in our efforts to be democratic.

But even if they didn't deserve all the public odium that has been heaped upon them (and as the astute reader has probably already guessed I believe they deserve it by the cart-load!), the SFO and IRD offices and the corporate players have had less harm done to them than the David Dougherty's or the 'Gisborne Five' police officers of this world.

And then, of course, there are the victims of Government agencies like Social Welfare and the Inland Revenue Department – the ordinary New Zealanders like 35-year-old Ian Mutton who took his own life under pressure from the IRD, and whose 13-year-old son also killed himself as a result.

They are the tip of the iceberg, and they are victims of a systemically corrupt system in which political parties reward their large corporate constituencies with financial windfalls and lucrative Government contracts, and where Government agencies are prepared to get tough with ordinary New Zealanders but not the rich and well-connected.

When Sir Ronald Davison's Winebox verdict came out, the rich and well-connected were dancing on Winston Peters' political grave. Prematurely, as it turned out.

But the *Listener's* Jane Clifton identified it succinctly enough at the time.

> *"Last year, it would have been Jim Bolger telling us that the Winebox [Inquiry] was a McCarthyist outrage, designed to slander some of our finest citizens, at ridiculous cost, for the advancement of Winston Peters' shabby little career.*
>
> *"It would have been [Labour's] Michael Cullen telling us that the inquiry was necessary to protect investors from the immoral dealings of the unscrupulous friends of the Tory government, which had the handy spinoff effect of advancing Peters' shabby little career so his party would be nice and plump*

for Labour to coalesce with after the election.

"*The two men and their parties have now undergone a mystical transference of belief. Bolger has developed a zen-like serenity about the inquiry, its cost and its victims, while Cullen is decrying Peters' hounding of now apparently innocent businessmen.*

"*In Parliament, Labour passes many happy hours taunting Peters with his own favourite sayings: 'baseless allegations', 'innuendo and rumour', 'complete lack of evidence' and 'quisling'.*[20]

"*National MPs sit clench-mouthed, pretending to be hopelessly absorbed in upside-down copies of the Evening Post when this happens.*

"*The urge to join in with Labour is almost primal. Most spent their formative early and middle years in politics learning to hate Peters as the enemy. He may be a baseless allegator, but he's now their baseless allegator, and they have to share his swamp uncomplainingly.*"

Others to lash out, predictably, included friends of the accused business leaders.

Retiring Business Roundtable chairman Doug Myers "strongly criticised NZ First leader Winston Peters and unnamed journalists over the affair," wrote *Dominion* reporter Steve Evans.

Myers blamed the "anti-business mentality of New Zealand's socialist past" for the "McCarthyist" Winebox witchhunt.

"Three years and tens of millions of dollars later, the Inquiry confirmed that the Winebox claims were 'false and completely unjustified', but at a huge cost to individual reputations, business and the political system," railed Myers.

"His grossly overstated campaign damaged the careers of two senior public servants and the standing of several New Zealand businesses and leading business people."

Myers told Peters to drop any idea of appealing the Davison judgment and immediately apologise to the businessmen and civil servants, "and his fellow politicians should insist that he does so."

The retiring Lion Nathan boss reserved some venom for the news media, saying the media were supposed to examine evidence and maintain objectivity and balance.

"Some journalists failed in this regard; they did not do their job of scrutiny and analysis and they joined in the witchhunt. They too should have the

---

20   The response of a senior Labour politician, upon learning of the Court of Appeal verdicts supporting Peters, was "Oh, shit!"

integrity to acknowledge their mistakes."

Well, if Doug can tell me after reading this book where – in the four books I have written on this subject – I have reached a conclusion that isn't capable of being backed up by the Court of Appeal or the Privy Council, then I'll look at it.

The reality, of course, is that the most serious allegations I have raised in my books were not considered by the Winebox Inquiry, have not been proven wrong by one single person, and have been ignored by the Government. In my opinion, there was enough information in *The Paradise Conspiracy* to warrant Charles Sturt's sacking four years ago.

As for journalists not applying scrutiny and analysis, the *Independent* reminded Myers that

> "People are entitled to know that some of our top tax inspectors admitted under oath that they could not understand the winebox documents until reporters [such as the Independent and TVNZ] showed them how.
>
> "After observing former Serious Fraud Office boss Chas Sturt in the witness box, and noting that among other things he appeared unable even to define fraud – the crime he had been charged by statute with investigating and prosecuting – the public will draw its own conclusions.
>
> "Similarly, people will make up their own minds about the apparent reluctance of Sturt and the IRD to mount a proper investigation into the Winebox until the spectre of a public inquiry forced their hand."

Winston Peters, however, had no intention of letting the matter rest. He lodged legal action to get Sir Ronald Davison's verdict overturned on the basis that it was wrong in fact and in law.

Central to the case was his belief that Davison had exceeded his terms of reference by making a definitive finding that the transactions were not criminal.

Secondly, the Peters legal team argued that the finding was based on a flawed interpretation of the criminal law – a pretty serious allegation to make about the legal judgment of a former Chief Justice.

But, said Brian Henry, if Davison had got the law wrong, and then used it as the foundation for his claim that the two departments were competent, it cast doubt over the integrity of the entire Winebox Inquiry report.

In addition, Davison had pilloried Peters without once telling the politician that he was on trial or giving him a chance to respond to the allegations. It was, although they didn't argue the point in court, a breach of natural justice.

In March 1998 Justice Rob Smellie of the High Court threw out Peters' challenge. Smellie called Peters' case "a pointless waste of court and judicial resources" that was so clearly untenable it could not possibly succeed.

Smellie told Peters to give up and stop stringing it out.

Once again the knives came out for Peters, especially when he announced he would take it to the Court of Appeal.

The public, heartily sick of New Zealand First and the Winebox, fell in large measure for the media line that Peters was tilting at windmills and wasting money.

Cynics who suggested it was done only to boost flagging poll ratings couldn't have been further from the truth: the poll ratings sagged because of the blows to Peters' credibility on the Winebox, and also because of New Zealand First's parliamentary dramas.

Sticking with the Winebox during this period was not a vote-grabber by any stretch of the imagination. It only added to the public's mental image of an obssessed, desperate man who refused to admit that he was wrong.

Except, of course, that he wasn't.

Chapter 19

On The Wrong Side Of The Law

"And I know that I'm damned if I never get out, and maybe I'm damned if I do, But with every other beat I've got left in my heart, You know I'd rather be damned with you."
– Jim Steinman, Bat Out Of Hell, 1977

The Court of Appeal was damning of Sir Ronald Davison and his Inquiry. A full five-judge bench heard the legal argument in mid-1998, a year after the Inquiry report had been delivered.

> "The Commissioner initially indicated a proper understanding of the function of a Commission of Inquiry," Justice Ted Thomas' ruling began, ominously.
> "The immediate point I wish to stress, then, is that questions of law were intrinsic to the terms of reference. They were inextricably germane to the conduct of the Inquiry and the completion of the report.
> "Clearly, an incorrect understanding or analysis of the legal effect of the transactions or a misconstruction of the relevant [laws] would be likely to affect the outcome of an inquiry into the conduct of the public servants involved."

Justice Thomas came to the conclusion that the Government must have expected Sir Ronald Davison's Inquiry to proceed on the basis of correctly applying the law.

"Otherwise, why have an inquiry? What would be the value of the resulting report?"

The Court of Appeal then turned to the Magnum transaction, repeating the Privy Council analysis of it mentioned earlier, but adding two important points.

The whole essence of the Magnum deal was that EPFML, a New Zealand company, had taken out an interest-bearing debenture on a Cook Islands company called Harcourt, which was also a European Pacific company.

But Justice Thomas indicated that the debenture, governed by the relevant Cook Islands laws, actually required Harcourt to incur the two million dollar tax liability, not EPFML.

What does this jargon mean?

It means that EPFML never paid tax in the Cook Islands, but nevertheless claimed a credit for doing so.

> *"European Pacific [FML] received the full interest due under the debenture free of Cook Islands income tax. The company itself paid no tax. Harcourt was required to pay the tax on its behalf.*
>
> *"This feature is of particular significance in that it demonstrates the inter-related nature of the arrangement and bears on the question of the nature and extent of European Pacific's obligation of disclosure.*
>
> *"When European Pacific presented the tax credit certificate to the Inland Revenue Department, it did not disclose that it had not, itself, paid the tax allegedly paid in the Cook Islands, nor that the tax had been paid on its behalf in such a manner that it received the interest tax-free, nor that as a result of the sale and purchase of the promissory note, a sum equivalent to the tax of $2 million (less $50,000) had been paid to an associated company.*
>
> *"Unaware of these facts the Commissioner of Inland Revenue issued a certificate pursuant to section 293(3) of the Companies Act 1955 to the effect that there were no outstanding returns or arrears of tax due from European Pacific, and the company was duly struck off the register.*
>
> *"There was no successor company which could be held accountable for European Pacific's tax obligations.*
>
> *"It is not surprising that when the Commissioner of Inland Revenue learned of the full facts he formed a different view. In March 1994 he reported to the Minister of Revenue that ... the claim amounted to tax avoidance.*
>
> *"The Commissioner [Sir Ronald] rejected this conclusion. He held that the Magnum transaction was neither illegal nor fraudulent. Nor had it resulted in either tax evasion or tax avoidance. He viewed the Magnum transaction as a 'smart' transaction designed to take advantage of 'loopholes' in income tax law.*
>
> *"It is difficult to accept that the Commissioner would have reached this conclusion if he had proceeded on a proper appreciation of the law. Most*

people, including many lawyers, would be surprised to learn that, whatever its shortcomings, the law was so deficient.

"At the point European Pacific presented the tax certificate to the Inland Revenue Department, it knew that the tax which it represented had been paid by it to the Cook Islands Government had [in fact] been paid on its behalf by an associated company which had then received the amount of the tax back from the Government (less $50,000).

"Most people would expect such conduct to constitute tax avoidance, if not tax evasion or fraud. At the very least, these possibilities requird serious consideration on the basis of established law."

In the space of just those few paragraphs, Justice Thomas was letting Sir Ron Davison have it, along with European Pacific and the two Government departments. The Court of Appeal was saying the issue of fraud should have been fully investigated.

We know, of course, that it wasn't.

"I agree with the view expressed in the main judgment that the Court is not in a position to state any final conclusions on the alleged errors of law in issue. But as I see it, this inhibition arises because of the way the issues were dealt with at the hearing of this appeal, and not any factor relating to the inherent difficulty in reaching a firm determination.

"Many legal issues are uncertain. Lawyers can reasonably differ as to the content of the law or the meaning of a statute. I do not apprehend, however, that the errors of law which are attributed to the Commission fall into this category.

"The legal effect of the Magnum transaction is capable of being determined and the statutory provisions are capable of a relatively precise interpretation."

What the judge was saying here is that the Court of Appeal could have ruled on the spot that Magnum was a criminal fraud, but he went on to say that for reasons of fairness to the corporates involved who hadn't had the chance to defend their positions, final decisions would be left until a substantive court hearing.

Justice Thomas then laid out what he considers are Sir Ronald Davison's greatest errors:

1) *A misinterpretation of s301 of the Income Tax Act*
"If the Commissioner's interpretation were correct, s301 would be largely

ineffective to achieve its purpose. By focusing on the taxpayer's subjective view of its entitlement it would be open to a taxpayer to legitimately conceal a tax avoidance scheme, or even tax evasion or fraud, at will. The effect of the concluding words of the section, 'necessary for determining the amount of the credit', cannot be ignored."

Then came an extremely important part of his judgment. Justice Thomas suggested Davison "would have been assisted" by a 1997 ruling from the House of Lords, *Commissioner of Inland Revenue* v *McGuckian*. [pron: McGoochian]

The case, said Thomas,

"Had marked the rejection by the House of Lords of pure literalism in the interpretation of tax statutes. The principle enunciated in that case was not based in a linguistic analysis of the meaning of particular words in a statute.

"It was founded on a broad purposive interpretation, giving effect to the intention of Parliament'. While the general liberty of the citizen to arrange his financial affairs as he thinks fit remains a material consideration, it has 'ceased to be canonical as to the consequence of a tax avoidance programme'.

"If it is shown that a scheme was intended to be implemented as a whole,, legal analysis permitted the court in deciding a fiscal question to take into account the composite transaction.

"In asserting the power to examine the substance [author's emphasis] of a composite transaction the House of Lords, it was explained, was simply rejecting formalism in fiscal matters and choosing a more realistic legal analysis."

Justice Thomas believed Davison would have been 'assisted' if he had read *McGuckian*. Well here's another little shock for the reader: Sir Ronald Davison had been given a full copy of *McGuckian*, weeks before his final report came out. It was given to him by renegade IRD solicitor Michael Scott.

Davison should have known that his decision to support European Pacific's "form over substance" claim was a legal dead duck.

Which only makes Davison's ruling even more inexplicable. Justice Thomas was giving the Commissioner the benefit of the doubt. Justice Thomas didn't know that Davison already had the judgment.

2) A misinterpretation of s229A of the Crimes Act
"Again, the Commissioner's misapprehension of the meaning of s229A of the Crimes Act is traversed in the main judgment.

> "The Commissioner held that the Magnum transaction was not fraudulent under either s257 or 229A of the Crimes Act. He based this conclusion on his view that European Pacific was not obliged to disclose to the Inland Revenue Department the repayment of the amount of the tax to Harcourt.
>
> "In the result, he said, there was no fraud in the way that the tax credits were presented to the Department and credits of tax obtained.
>
> "Consequently, because of his analysis of the Magnum transaction, the Commissioner excluded the operation of s229A altogether.
>
> "For myself, I would have thought that s229A was prima facie applicable, necessarily leaving open the question of the element of intent. So much of the section as is pertinent may be repeated:
>
> '... with intent to defraud ... uses ... any such document [a document capable of being used to obtain any ... pecuniary advantage] for the purpose of obtaining, for himself or any other person, any ... pecuniary advantage.'
>
> "It would seem indisputable that the tax credit certificate was a document capable of being used to obtain a pecuniary advantage, that is, a saving in tax. The certificate was 'used' when presented to the Inland Revenue Department.
>
> "The purpose was to obtain a pecuniary advantage, that is, a saving in tax if not for European Pacific [FML], then the associated company or the European Pacific group, which would fall within the phrase 'any other person'.
>
> "For an offence to be committed, of course, the document would have to be used 'with intent to defraud', and it may well be that in the circumstances such intent would never be proved in a criminal prosecution.
>
> "The present point is that, if the alleged errors of law are substantiated, the Commissioner's finding that there was no fraud as there was no breach of s229A cannot be sustained on the basis which he advanced in his report."

So, contrary to the assertions of the SFO that there was no fraud apparent from the Winebox documents, the Court of Appeal has ruled that there is.

Enough, indeed, to warrant a serious investigation with the only missing factor being one of criminal intent. And intent is something that can only be determined *after* conducting a full investigation and speaking to those involved, which the Serious Fraud Office never did.

3) *A misunderstanding of the doctrine of form over substance.*

"To my mind, the most significant of the alleged errors of law relates to the Commissioner's apparent misconception of the doctrine of form over substance.

"The Commissioner appears to have adopted an extreme version of the doctrine which, however prevalent it might be among tax advisers, is not supported by decisions of this Court.

"This perception led the Commission to disregard that part of the prearranged scheme relating to the repayment of the tax in the Cook Islands when determining the effect of the Magnum transaction, and it contributed to the restricted view which he took of European Pacific's disclosure obligations under s301 and ss229A and 257.

"Whatever one's view of the doctrine of form over substance, it does not apply to instances where the transaction is a sham, that is, where the form merely conceals the fraudulent reality.

"There must be a strong argument that this was the case with the Magnum transaction."

Justice Thomas also questioned how Sir Ronald presumed that he had the authority to break Magnum down into smaller portions, take them out of context and then decree that they were legal?

"This Court unequivocally stated [in Mills v Dowdall] that the ascertainment of the true nature of the transaction 'requires consideration of the whole of the contractual arrangements and if the transaction is embodied in a series of interrelated agreements they must be considered together and one may be read to explain the others'.

"The rationale for having regard to the substance of a transaction is simple enough. The objective of the Income Tax Act is to collect tax on income. Income is derived from the substance of a transaction, not its form.

"It is therefore necessary to have regard to the substance of a transaction and not just the form in which it is fabricated to determine the true income and the tax which is payable on that income.

"For either the tax authorities or the Courts to do otherwise is to thwart the objective of the Act."

And yet the tax authorities in New Zealand were doing otherwise.

"We don't tax on substance, or economic substance," John Nash had told the Inquiry, "and the problem is, you must analyse the legal character.

"The interpretation I am restricted to is not one of substance, it is one of form – it is the formality that the Courts do give to these types of arrangements that drives these arrangements. It's the ability to structure that the Court of Appeal and the Privy Council has given to taxpayers that cause these problems.

"I wish I was in the United States, sometimes. They have a far more substance approach to life than Commonwealth countries, and you know, that is a wish. But the reality is something different."

John Nash should be so pleased now that his wish has come true. What the Court of Appeal judgment means is that the way the IRD and SFO approached the Winebox was thoroughly and totally wrong, based on an incorrect interpretation of the law.

How many millions of dollars has the IRD failed to collect from massive companies by failing to correctly interpret and apply the law? *It may well run into billions and billions, of dollars.*

And what credibility can the so-called leading 'tax advisers' who supported European Pacific have left, in the face of the Court of Appeal verdict?

"However prevalent it might be among tax advisers," wrote the judge, their view of form over substance "is not supported by decisions of this Court."

Ultimately, it could be argued that the best legal advice did come from people like Tony Molloy QC, Peter Jenkin QC, Dr John Prebble and Dr Gary Muir. In my opinion, the nickname given to President Clinton – 'Slick Willie' – could equally be applied to a number of corporate QC's and tax lawyers.

Justice Thomas continued his devastating dissection of Davison's Commission verdict.

"The terms of the report are damning of Mr Peters' reputation. His actions both before and during the course of the Inquiry are forthrightly condemned. Some condemnation may or may not be warranted if relevant to the terms of reference but, if his reputation is to be put in issue, Mr Peters, as with any other citizen, has a right to have that condemnation based upon a correct appreciation of the law.

"In this case, the Commissioner's apparent errors of law caused him to take a legally benign view of the Magnum transaction which in turn led to him being severely critical of Mr Peters.

"Secondly, there is in this case a substantial public interest in having any error of law material to the Commission's report publicly declared.

"The opinion of a Commissioner, who as a past Chief Justice enjoys considerable stature, following a hearing of up to two and a half years will almost certainly be given considerable weight.

"For the commercial community, in particular, it must be of considerable importance that any error of law be corrected so that businesses are not under any misapprehension as to the taxpayer's obligation of disclosure and the

scope and limits of the doctrine of form over susbstance.

"A different interpretation of s301 and European Pacific's obligation of disclosure could possibly have led to findings of possible evasion or fraud. Once findings to this effect had been made, or at least recognised as a serious possibility, it would not have been possible for the Commissioner to make the trenchant criticism which he made of Mr Peters.

"Moreover, he would have necessarily approached the question of the competence of the Commissioner of Inland Revenue and the Director of the Serious Fraud Office on a different and possibly more critical basis."

In the main judgment of the Appeal Court, delivered by Justices Richardson, Henry and Keith, they ruled:

"The 'intent to defraud' required under s229A is not materially different from the intention required for false pretences.

"Where a person makes a positive representation of some kind and is silent as to other matters which would qualify or alter the impression made by that positive representation, the combined effect of the representation and the silence may be to mislead."

In regard to the Magnum transaction, the Court stated:

"It may be contended that by telling only half the story EPFML misled the Inland Revenue Department and gained at least the pecuniary advantage of immediate acceptance of the tax credits without the risk of having to withstand a tax avoidance investigation by the Department.

"If there was evidence to support a finding of tax evasion, then the failure of the Inland Revenue Department to identify that and possibly take some consequential action had to impact on a consideration of its competency.

"If there was evidence to support a claim of criminal fraud on the part of those concerned in the implementation of Magnum, then the failure of the Serious Fraud Office to recognise that and further its investigations had to impact on its competency."

The Court of Appeal unanimously quashed Justice Smellie's decision to throw Peters out of Court, and ordered the High Court to re-hear the politician's case.

Waiting at the Court of Appeal for the written verdict were IRD lawyers Grant Pearson and Angela Satterthwaite, and senior IRD executive Tony

Bouzaid. They were still waiting for the verdict when *One Network News* reporter John Stewart approached them.

"Five-zip to Winston," Stewart grinned.

Pearson sprang to his feet. "It can't be! Ted Thomas wouldn't let us down!"

Whatever Pearson's expectations of Justice Thomas, he was one of the toughest on the IRD and SFO.

Stewart later described the faces of the three IRD staff as ashen. Given that the Court of Appeal had just signalled that the way the IRD has applied the law for the past decade is wrong, the stunned-mullet response is not really surprising.

The issue now goes back before the High Court in what is expected to be a three day hearing. Given the strident tone of the Court of Appeal rulings, it would be a good bet that the Winebox Inquiry verdict on the Magnum transaction will be overturned, meaning the IRD and the SFO were almost certainly incompetent. But hey, we already know that, don't we?

Chapter 20

A Finding Of Corruption

"The Revolution was effected before the War commenced. The Revolution was in the minds and hearts of the people; a change in their religious sentiments of their duties and obligations. ...This radical change in the principles, opinions, sentiments, and affections of the people, was the real American Revolution."
– John Adams (1735–1826), US President

So, was a four year inquiry worth it?

Firstly, the Court of Appeal rulings on what constitutes illegal concealment from the revenue mean that a large chunk of the Winebox transactions could have been treated as evasive or fraudulent.

Around $140 million dollars in extra tax was reassessed as a result of the Winebox documents. Much of that is still being disputed by the corporates involved, although should the IRD have the intestinal fortitude, that up until now it has lacked on this front, to apply the law properly, it has the power to charge penalties of 300 percent.

And again, this is just on the Winebox deals. One carton of documents. How many thousands of deals have slipped through the IRD net with no action, because of the Department's fundamental failure to understand the law and its own powers.

While the IRD applies fatal pressure to small businesses and individuals who don't have the resource to fight, large corporates may have been getting away with not just hundreds of millions, but *tens of billions* of dollars in unpaid taxes through what we now know was probably tax evasion.

How many large corporates have used tax havens in the 80's and 90's, and which parts of the deals have stayed hidden from the Revenue illegally?

The $140 million assessed by the IRD on the Winebox came from just six transactions! A drop in the ocean.

New Zealanders in this coming election should demand that there are no tax increases, but that the IRD should be forced to properly apply its powers against large corporates.

Inland Revenue incompetence may have cost ordinary wage and salary earners billions of dollars.

It's your money they've squandered. And that, at the end of the day, is why the Winebox Inquiry was relevant.

It's a shame that it wasn't until Winston Peters finally made it to the Court of Appeal that the truth about our tax laws was revealed.

There's another important point: when I wrote *The Paradise Conspiracy* back in 1995, I considered the allegations it contained – particularly in relation to the conduct of Charles Sturt and the Serious Fraud Office – warranted immediate action.

Here was the head of a Government Department who had deliberately lied to the public and the news media, about his alleged "investigation" into the Paul White affair.

Sturt's book, which recounts what his office did, only raises even more questions about the SFO's competence.

The actions of the SFO in "investigating" the White case wouldn't pass muster in an episode of *The Keystone Cops*. The SFO went to Citibank and asked to see the 88 computer disks that had been in White's possession.

Without intending to cast aspersions on Citibank here, the bank could just as easily have provided the SFO with sanitised disks or even a collection of computer games.

My point is that the SFO never actually looked at Paul White's disks, which is the claim that Sturt made in a press release. Paul White's disks were in police custody at the time, and Citibank didn't have them. The SFO never asked to see the disks held by the police, so the SFO has no way of proving that the information it was shown was genuine.

What was the point of this charade?

In seven years of research, published now in four books, I have been unable to come to any other belief than the possibility that Charles Sturt and the SFO are indeed corrupt. The definitions of corruption I referred to earlier appear to fit snugly.

The question then is: for whose benefit?

Perhaps Sturt's aim, as hinted at in his book, was to retire as a top civil servant, perhaps get a knighthood or some similar honour, and feed from the public trough in a cosy retirement paid for by Government contracts thrown his way for a job well done.

How did he do that job?

He saved the National Government from potential international embarrassment with his statement, to the media and Parliament, that he had looked at Paul White's disks and found nothing. All of a sudden, the wind went out of the story.

What might the story have been? Well, readers of *The Paradise Conspiracy* will know that White told friends before he died of two major discoveries he claimed were on the disks – one being arms dealing involving a New Zealand enterprise, and the other being massive Cook Islands tax deals.

When I wrote *The Paradise Conspiracy* I had strong circumstantial evidence of the involvement of the Security Intelligence Service in surveillance operations against White before he died in a car crash.

We have now discovered that the US$1.2 billion JIF deals went through Citibank during the time period covered by White's disks – were these the Cook Islands tax deals he talked of?

So Sturt killed off any further examination of White's death.

Then he killed off an investigation of the Bank of New Zealand collapse – the biggest corporate collapse in New Zealand history. The bank lost a billion dollars – where did it go?

Sturt allegedly investigated two Government politicians, but cleared both of them. In one case witnesses had filed affidavits which the SFO apparently chose not to give credence to.

Sturt's office investigated a good friend of his, prominent lawyer Derek Firth, after Firth was named in the infamous Cook Islands Letter of Guarantee scandal. Sturt didn't believe Firth had formed the necessary criminal intent.

Sturt was asked to investigate the secret IRD non-prosecution agreement involving the alleged blackmailing of the IRD by lawfirm Russell McVeagh. The National Government was taking a hammering from Winston Peters over this at the time. Sturt issued a statement saying there was no substance to Peters' allegations.

Subsequently, at the Winebox Inquiry, we learned that the Serious Fraud Office had not asked the Inland Revenue Department for a copy of the secret agreement, nor had the SFO questioned IRD boss David Henry about it, prior to clearing Henry and the IRD publicly.

Charles Sturt quashed further investigation into the film and bloodstock frauds involving Russell McVeagh, after a meeting with a Russell McVeagh lawyer, who subsequently was given a contract to act as prosecutor on certain SFO cases.

Again, this was another issue causing the Government some significant political embarrassment.

In the Fortex fraud case, the SFO decides not to charge one man. The judge later expresses surprise, indicating conviction would have been likely. Winston Peters then reveals to the Winebox Inquiry that the SFO's main legal advisor, Willie Young QC, also happened to be representing the man the SFO decided not to prosecute.

Then, of course, there is the Winebox.

The SFO's inaction on all of these matters is, I believe, a matter of the gravest public interest and concern. I am also extremely concerned that Justice Minister Doug Graham, former Attorney-General Paul East and the State Services Commissioner apparently did nothing to investigate the allegations against the SFO and its director.

Finance Minister Ruth Richardson knew of Fay Richwhite's massive borrowing from the BNZ and its taxation implications, but stayed silent while her Government colleagues chided Peters for having no proof.

Sir Ronald Davison heads a probing Winebox Inquiry, telling others that he regards the transactions as fraud, then issues a verdict saying the opposite, taking his own legal team entirely by surprise. He clears the IRD and SFO of every allegation, and drives a wooden stake through the heart of the Peters vampire.

Wake up and smell the coffee, New Zealand. The Emperor has no clothes. I must disagree with the Davison verdict. Prima facie, the evidence contained in this book, and my two previous investigations, reeks of corruption in my opinion. *I can find no other credible explanation.*

A simple case of Sturt misinterpreting the law? I don't think so. The head of the Serious Fraud Office wasn't paid to "misinterpret" the law. And the added dimension of deliberate deception concerning investigations casts a sinister shadow over any innocent mistakes that the SFO might have made.

Don't forget, the Government's first choice to head the Serious Fraud Office, Warwick Reid, turned out to be a major-league criminal involved with organised crime in Asia. Their second choice didn't turn out too well either, in my view.

Here then, is my challenge to the news media:

I can factually prove every one of the above items that leads me to the corruption conclusion. Take those facts, ask me for the documentation, and start joining the dots.

Currently the New Zealand media are the laughing stock of Hollywood. And that's saying something!

Media wisdom in this country would have you believe in "cock-up theory" rather than conspiracy: that two leading Government enforcement agencies were coincidentally headed by "clowns", each with a team of incompetent "clowns" underneath them.

In the IRD's case, these clowns totally misunderstood the tax laws they had been given the duty of enforcing, and failed to ping possibly billions and billions of dollars worth of allegedly criminal schemes.

In the SFO's case, the clowns had absolutely no idea how to investigate serious or complex fraud, nor did they even understand what fraud was. These clowns had also misinterpreted the criminal laws relating to concealment, and intent.

And then, according to cock-up theory, we have a Commission of Inquiry headed by a Chief Justice "clown" who also, totally coincidentally, fails to comprehend the laws relating to concealment and intent.

All of this set against a background of a Government of "clowns" who were *not* "deliberately" trying to stop the Winebox from ever getting into the public's hands. It was all just an unfortunate misunderstanding. Like hell.

As we saw in the recent controversies over National MP Ian Revell who allegedly threatened to interfere in the promotion of a police officer who gave him a parking ticket, or in the allegations surrounding Tourism Minister Murray McCully and the Government's use of Saatchi & Saatchi advertising, there are toadstools sprouting everywhere.

There has been a tradition in New Zealand politics of the party faithful being rewarded by their respective Governments. We saw it in the eighties, in the way new-found business heroes were appointed to review Government departments, then appointed to the boards of newly created SOEs, then bidding to purchase some of those SOEs after their companies acted as advisors to the Government on the sales.

The rest of the New Zealand news media, particularly some craven examples in the business press, may see this as normal business experience but in other parts of the world this kind of behaviour is criminal.

Newstalk ZB radio host Chris Carter recently asked a similar question: at what point does big business support for a political party cross the line from legitimacy to corruption?

The only reason New Zealanders are not up in arms about it, I suspect, is because the public have been told for so long that New Zealand is corruption-free, that all of this is of no consequence and there are bigger issues to worry about.

Richard Prebble, the illustrious leader of the ACT party, tried to deflect attention from Prime Minister Shipley's predicament by describing as "sleazy" the media and political frenzy over her dinner with Saatchi boss Kevin Roberts.

It is not sleazy. It is time New Zealand faced up to its heritage.

Huge sums of money are paid to consultants by Government departments, sometimes as a result of Ministers requesting reviews. It's your money they are spending.

It is interesting that Fay Richwhite obtained so much Government consultancy work from Labour and then National, and then the work dried up once the full truth about the Winebox deals became public.

And yet, as you have seen in this book, Finance Minister Ruth Richardson *knew* about Fay Richwhite's deals – deals which, using the Court of Appeal analysis – could be criminal.

The only way anything is going to change in this country is through the expression of public rage. Public rage forced the Government to set up a Winebox Inquiry in the first place.

If readers make their views known via talkback, letters to the editor and letters to the Prime Minister (they are free of postage), they may start making the Establishment uncomfortable.

The National Party and big business speak of the public derisively as "the chattering classes", and they rely on public apathy to let them get away with it. They think you are idiots.

But knowledge *is* power. Tell your friends about this book. Spread the word.

If someone lights a fire that becomes a public focal point, in an election year, then you would be a foolish leader if you tried to ignore it directly.

And the focal point is this: Demand a public inquiry into corruption, an Inquiry with the power to subpoena politicians and business leaders.

Is this a witch hunt? I don't think so. The public interest in having good and honest and transparent Government must transcend complaints from corporates and politicians.

If corporates were not making political donations of one kind or another, allegedly with strings attached, then there would not be an issue to investigate.

If lucrative contracts were not being doled out by Governments, there would not be an issue.

If senior civil servants did not believe that they had some kind of right to be awarded lucrative Government contracts upon retirement, there would not be an issue.

But there is.

Here, then, is my verdict. For the sake of the news media, my findings are stated as honest opinion, and can be reported as such:

I believe the evidence is sufficient to warrant a criminal investigation of Charles Sturt, under section 104 of the Crimes Act, which states:

> *"104. Corruption and bribery of law enforcement officer – (1) Every law enforcement officer is liable to imprisonment for a term not exceeding 7 years who corruptly accepts or obtains, or agrees or offers to accept or attempts to obtain, any bribe for himself or any other person in respect of any act done or omitted, or to be done or omitted, by him in his official capacity."*

For the purposes of the exercise, a bribe is defined under section 99 of the Act as:

> *"Bribe" means any money, valuable consideration, office, or employment, or any benefit, whether direct or indirect."*

Sturt, by his own admission, expected to get further employment from the Government upon his retirement, presumably in return for doing a good job. His own staff testified to possible corruption. I believe his inaction on the Winebox may have been influenced by the political wind, as well as his own personal malice towards Peters.

I believe further investigation into the former Director of the Serious Fraud Office is warranted based on the prima facie evidence that exists. Which isn't to pre-judge the outcome of any investigation.

I believe that an investigation should be made into whether corporate interests have ever made political donations to the National or Labour parties conditional upon a lack of official investigation into certain issues. This is covered by section 102 of the Crimes Act which states:

> *"102. Corruption and bribery of Minister of the Crown – (1) Every Minister of the Crown or member of the Executive Council is liable to imprisonment for a term not exceeding 14 years who corruptly accepts or obtains, or agrees or offers to accept or attempts to obtain, any bribe for himself or any other person in respect of any act done or omitted, or to be done or omitted, by him in his capacity as a Minister or member of the Executive Council.*

"(2) Every one is liable to imprisonment for a term not exceeding 7 years who corruptly gives or offers or agrees to give any bribe to any person with intent to influence any Minister of the Crown or member of the Executive Council in respect of any act or omission by him in his capacity as a Minister or member of the Executive Council.

"(3) No one shall be prosecuted for an offence against this section without the leave of a Judge of the Supreme Court. Notice of the intention to apply for such leave shall be given to the person whom it is intended to prosecute, and he shall have an opportunity of being heard against the application."

I also believe that sections 229A – using a document for pecuniary advantage – and 257 of the Crimes Act – conspiracy to defraud – have been broken in regard to several of the Winebox transactions.

The evidence clearly shows incredible incompetence by the Serious Fraud Office and the Inland Revenue Department. The leaders of both departments at the time have both resigned, but members of their staff in key positions have – I believe – some very serious questions to answer about their own competence.

In regard to Winston Peters' allegations of a secret, non-prosecution deal that Russell McVeagh allegedly blackmailed the IRD into signing, I believe that the Court of Appeal's re-stating of the law regarding conspiracy to defraud clearly shows the film schemes involved to have been criminally fraudulent.[21]

The decision by the IRD executives to sign the deal effectively made the department, in my view, an accessory to the crime after the fact, and/or a party to an attempt to pervert the course of justice.

Section 71 of the Crimes Act covers "accessory after the fact" and states:

"71. Accessory after the fact – (1) An accessory after the fact to an offence is one who, knowing any person to have been a party to the offence, receives, comforts, or assists that person or tampers with or actively suppresses any evidence against him, in order to enable him to escape after arrest or to avoid arrest or conviction."

There is also the possible application of s309:

---

21 The full story of the film and bloodstock deals and the factual matrix behind this allegation is contained in the books *Lawyers, Guns & Money* and *Thirty Pieces of Silver*. Both published by Howling At The Moon Productions Ltd.

> *"309. Conspiring to prevent collection of rates or taxes – Everyone is liable to imprisonment for a term not exceeding 2 years who conspires with any other person by force or intimidation to prevent the collection of any rates or taxes the levying and collection of which is authorised by law."*

Under s25 of the Crimes Act, ignorance of the law can be no excuse: The IRD clearly knew there was a possibility of fraud being covered up because of the wording of the agreement. The IRD had a statutory duty to act. By failing to take action or seek expert legal advice on criminality, I believe the IRD helped parties to the scheme "avoid arrest or conviction".

In addition, I believe s107 of the Crimes Act may be relevant, which states:

> *"107. Contravention of statute – Everyone is liable to imprisonment for a term not exceeding one year who, without lawful excuse, contravenes any enactment by wilfully doing any act which it forbids, or by wilfully omitting to do any act which it requires to be done."*

Then there's the Inland Revenue Department Act:

> *47. Offences – (1) Every person commits an offence against this Act who –*
> *(a) Acts in contravention of or, without lawful justification or excuse, fails to comply in any respect with any provision of this Act or any requirement imposed under this Act:*
> *(b) Knowingly deceives or attempts to deceive the Commissioner or any officer of the Department in the exercise of any powers or functions under this Act:*
> *(c) With intent to deceive makes any false or misleading statement or any material omission in any information given to the Commissioner or any officer of the Department for the purposes of this Act:*
> *(d) Resists, obstructs, or deceives any person who is exercising or attempting to exercise any power or function under this Act.*

In regard to the Serious Fraud Office claim that it had investigated the non-prosecution deal and found nothing amiss, I believe this also to be an attempt to pervert the course of justice. It appears a crime had taken place. Clearly an agreement had been struck with the Commissioner of Inland Revenue to cover it up, as a result of pressure, and the Serious Fraud Office did NOT investigate the document or the IRD, despite publicly claiming to have done so.

This is not, in my view, the action of an innocent law enforcement agency. It is the action of a corrupt one that cannot be trusted by New Zealanders.

Again, s71 of the Crimes Act would appear to apply. Section 66 of the same Act may also be useful:

> *"66. Parties to offences – (1) Everyone is a party to and guilty of an offence who –*
> *(a) Actually commits the offence; or*
> *(b) Does or omits an act for the purpose of aiding any person to commit the offence; or*
> *(c) Abets any person in the commission of the offence; or*
> *(d) Incites, counsels, or procures any person to commit the offence.*
> *"(2) Where 2 or more persons form a common intention to prosecute any unlawful purpose, and to assist each other therein, each of them is a party to every offence committed by any one of them in the prosecution of the common purpose if the commission of that offence was known to be a probable consequence of the prosecution of the common purpose."*

In regard to Sturt's untrue public statements, delivered via his Minister to Parliament, section 111 makes interesting reading:

> *"111. False statements or declarations—Every one is liable to imprisonment for a term not exceeding 3 years who, on any occasion on which he is required or permitted by law to make any statement or declaration before any officer or person authorised by law to take or receive it, or before any notary public to be certified by him as such notary, makes a statement or declaration that would amount to perjury if made on oath in a judicial proceeding."*

I do not know if the relationship between a Department chief executive and his or her Minister qualifies as one of the above.

Then there is the possible application of section 116 of the Crimes Act:

> *"116. Conspiring to defeat justice – Everyone is liable to imprisonment for a term not exceeding 7 years who conspires to obstruct, prevent, pervert, or defeat the course of justice."*

In this case, it may apply in regard to the bloodstock/film settlement/BNZ investigation issues, if indeed those investigations were not pursued for improper reasons.

All of these possible crimes, it must be remembered, would require criminal intent to be proven beyond reasonable doubt. The reader should take to heart that it is more than likely that the civil servants involved genuinely believed they had the powers to do what they did.

I am merely suggesting, from a legalistic point of view, that I don't believe they did and I believe they broke the law.

In regard to the Serious Fraud Office Act, the SFO has relied on s20 of that Act which states that no decision of the Director to investigate or take proceedings can be quashed or called into question in any Court.

This has been interpreted as meaning that the SFO's failure to investigate or prosecute can't be questioned either. This is not what the Act says.

A later section says that the Director is under no obligation to investigate or prosecute any fraud, but it does not say that his failure to do so cannot be questioned. If the SFO exercises its discretion, it had better be ready to justify and defend it.

In regard to Willie Young QC, now Justice Young of the High Court at Christchurch, I believe it is a matter of grave concern that he appears to have shown negligible understanding of the concept of fraud, and how it is prosecuted.

As one of the SFO's chief legal advisors, it was Young who took the hard line at the Winebox Inquiry about the difficulty of proving fraud or criminal intent. His 'expert' opinions do not meet the measure of the Court of Appeal's view of what constitutes fraud. That Willie Young is now a High Court judge beggars my belief.

You, as the reader, still have some freedoms. You are free to read this book. You are free to form your own opinion based on the facts contained within, and you are free to discuss the issue.

Make good use of your freedom while you still have it.

Chapter 21

Unfinished Business

"An editor is someone who separates the wheat from the chaff and then prints the chaff."
– Adlai Stevenson (1900–1965), US Democratic politician.

The Fourth Estate, as the media sometimes refers to itself, is supposed to be the watchdog of democracy – the last in a series of checks and balances between a Government and its citizens.

The problem the western world, and particularly New Zealand, faces is that democracy now exists in name only. At the instigation of business leaders and multinational corporations, successive Governments have handed the reins of power over to private companies. We have gone from a democracy to a plutocracy in little more than a decade.

What Governments do, voters can control by exercising their right to toss out an offensive administration every three years. But if the politicians dismantle the mechanisms of state, the powers are transferred away from elected officials and into the paws of entities driven by profit or power – often both.

Some in the news media like to describe me as a "conspiracy theorist" – a term of derision. And yet I have never been sued over the contents of my books, and all of them stand capable of being proven in a court of law. I don't subscribe to conspiracy theory, only conspiracy fact, and here's one I can prove:

In October 1995 my first book, *The Paradise Conspiracy*, was published. Journalists from Wilson & Horton's media flagship the *New Zealand Herald* rang me and interviewed me on a couple of occasions for up to an hour a time, but stories about the book never appeared in the newspaper, despite the very serious allegations being made.

When I inquired of the journalists involved I was told, "We're really sorry, but every time we file a story the editors spike it. They're refusing to run them."

This, despite the review that appears on the back cover of this book.

For those who aren't familiar with volume one, the allegations included:

1) That Serious Fraud Office head Charles Sturt had lied about investigating the Paul White affair,

2) That New Zealand SAS soldiers have been involved in covert military operations overseas and have been killed in action, despite Government denials,

3) That the police failed to investigate the death of Paul White properly and missed key clues,

4) And that Paul White may have been murdered by SAS soldiers because he was leaking information to Winston Peters that had national security overtones.

Now, that list is by no means exhaustive, and much of the proof was already contained in *The Paradise Conspiracy* – certainly as to the duplicity of Sturt, the stupidity of police and the role of the SAS overseas.

And yet the substance of these allegations never appeared in the *Herald*. It wasn't until three years later, towards the end of 1998, that the newspaper 'bravely' reported that NZ SAS troops had been killed in secret missions overseas – the report following a TV documentary that claimed to "break" the story.

A pox on both their houses. But it is worse than that.

Aside from the *Herald* effectively covering up, in my view, the scandal involving the Serious Fraud Office director and the police, the newspaper has continued its tradition of not publishing 'the whole truth and nothing but the truth'.

In the first instance, the paper begged for an exclusive on the launch of the book *Lawyers, Guns & Money* which examined the involvement of New Zealand's largest lawfirm, Russell McVeagh McKenzie Bartleet & Co in film and bloodstock fraud, but nothing appeared and to date the number one bestseller has never even been reviewed by the *Herald*.

Certainly one could argue that this is merely sour grapes from a disgruntled author, but that would simply be the icing on the cake. For me the concern lies with delivering major stories and hard evidence to the media, and having it ignored.

The second instance is more sinister, and involves the launch of Dr Tony Molloy's runaway number one bestseller *Thirty Pieces of Silver*.

The *Herald* attempted to pour cold water on the book from day one, even going to the extraordinary extent of interviewing lawyers around town for their opinions on the book and Dr Molloy's extremely serious allegations, and then printing only the opinions of those who were critical of Dr Molloy.

I and my fiancee Heidi, who are the embodiment of Howling At The Moon Publishing Ltd, fired back a news release putting Russell McVeagh and the news media on notice. It was unprecedented – a journalistic gauntlet-throwing of the kind the NZ media appear too timid to do.

I wrote:

"An Auckland publishing company has challenged lawfirm Russell McVeagh McKenzie Bartleet to put up or shut up.

"Howling At The Moon Productions Ltd[22] is the publisher of Thirty Pieces of Silver by Dr Anthony Molloy QC, which alleges that Russell McVeagh has assisted in the commission of money laundering and fraud.

"Managing editor Ian Wishart says it's time for the news media to stop accepting outrageous and inaccurate press statements from Russell McVeagh without checking the facts first.

"In this morning's New Zealand Herald, for example, Russell McVeagh chairman John King claims Thirty Pieces of Silver contains 'many wild and extravagant allegations against the firm.'

"I am stunned that such a sweeping generalisation can be re-published by a major news organisation without anyone asking the basic question: please specify the 'wild and extravagant' allegations.

"The allegations in Thirty Pieces of Silver are the most serious ever published in a New Zealand book. They can all be proven, and a call to the author or publisher would verify this.

"If John King is unable to list in a material way the allegations he takes issue with, then in my opinion the media are misleading the public by simply reprinting such vague assertions under a cloak of credibility.

"It is time for Russell McVeagh to put up or shut up, in my view. The book makes specific allegations about Russell McVeagh's involvement in assisting with money laundering and fraud. The book names names, details the money involved, outlines the dates and provides the documentation needed to prove it.

"I challenge John King to specifically address these allegations, without resorting to obfuscation."

---

22 Our old company, placed in voluntary liquidation in 1998. Apart from passing on its brand, it is not connected to Howling At The Moon Publishing Ltd.

The news release then took the media to task, asking them to "keep the ball in sight".

> "We are journalists, not stenographers. I appreciate that allegations of international money laundering and multi-million dollar fraud are not easy concepts for newsrooms to address in a hurry, but we stand ready and capable of proving all of these allegations, and they cannot be dismissed just because of vague denials of wrongdoing by the lawfirm involved.
>
> "Finally, Mr Wishart took issue with other points in John King's statement. He pointed out that the book contains never before published material, and Russell McVeagh's claim to the contrary was merely an attempt to pull the wool over the eyes of the public and the media.
>
> "He also denied that the allegations in Molloy's book had been found to be 'false and completely unjustified' at the Winebox Inquiry.
>
> "That statement is wrong in fact. The allegations about the film and bloodstock deals were never ruled on by Sir Ronald Davison, and certainly never described as false and unjustified. If Russell McVeagh can find evidence to prove that these deals were rejected by the Winebox Inquiry, then I challenge the lawfirm to provide it."

Now, you would think that after running a story where Russell McVeagh rubbished the Molloy book, that journalists with integrity would balance that out by printing the response of the publisher. Fat chance.

The news release you've just read never saw the light of day, in the *Herald* or any other media outlet that ran the lawfirm's scathing comments.

On the day of launch, the NBR gave Molloy's book front page coverage in a fair report.

By the following week, however, it was suddenly under attack in a sustained fashion by the NBR.

Russell McVeagh's John King had told the newspaper that "anyone with half a brain will not take any notice" of *Thirty Pieces of Silver*.

"People with half a brain may side with John King," I fired back in a news release. "The rest of us with entirely full cranial cavities realise that Dr Molloy has gathered major new evidence that cannot be dismissed by a few cheap shots and a PR campaign."

King also described Dr Molloy as "a discredited fellow", which was laughable given that senior Russell McVeagh litigation partner, Robert Fardell, had reviewed an earlier Molloy book praising his acumen:

"... has an established reputation as an author of legal texts and publications. He writes with panache and clarity, making his style truly distinctive ... these qualities and Mr Molloy's wide experience in the taxation area are evident in this, his latest publication."

The review went on to describe Dr Molloy as "even-handed, consistently balanced ... the final result is a pragmatic but illuminating analysis ... attention to detail is impressive."

How could the news media print Russell McVeagh's baseless claims without checking the truth of them? Well, in my view there are only two options: either the journalists who wrote the stories and the sub-editors who approved them are incompetent, or it was a deliberate attempt by elements in the media to help Russell McVeagh attempt to discredit the book.

Not content, however, the NBR then arranged for Molloy's book to be reviewed *twice* – on both occasions by reviewers inimical to Molloy and myself.

One of those reviews was particularly galling, as the person responsible was none other than Bernard Robertson, the editor of the New Zealand Law Journal. He'd already had a negative crack at the book in the journal, and was invited by NBR to have another in the business paper.

I did not know at the time that Robertson was not a journalist or an unbiased reviewer, but instead was a former British bobby turned right-wing lobbyist, associated with the New Zealand Business Roundtable.

In their book *First Knights: an investigation of the New Zealand Business Roundtable*[23] the authors write of Robertson thus:

> "Robertson's New Right allegiances proved a blessing when the National Business Review newspaper provided him with a forum to try and do a hatchet job on Dr Anthony Molloy QC's *Thirty Pieces of Silver (NBR, 17/4/98)*, and Robertson showed he wasn't above being a paranoid conspiracy theorist.
>
> "In a review peppered with factual errors, Robertson made the assertion 'It is also interesting to consider how much of publisher Ian Wishart there is in the book. Dr Molloy is concerned to attack the firm of Russell McVeagh as a whole.
>
> " 'Sometimes the evidence enabling this to be done is a bit thin. So one can imagine Wishart and Molloy in conversation, Wishart urging a bit of

---

23 Paul Harris & Linda Twiname, Howling At The Moon Publishing Ltd, 1998.

speculation and innuendo and Molloy insisting on the facts as he sees them.'

"It subsequently transpired that Ian Wishart's only editorial contribution to *Thirty Pieces of Silver* was the correction of some minor typographical errors. Wishart's response to Robertson's efforts?

"'There's a big difference between a good investigative journalist and a poor Law Journal editor and book reviewer, and in my opinion if that article is indicative of Robertson's journalistic abilities, then he should give up his day job and try moonlighting as PR man for Russell McVeagh.'"

It was as if we were attacking some giant beast. With every book that Howling At The Moon published, more grievous wounds were inflicted. But at the same time, the beast and those who protected it were gathering ever more tightly to ensure we could not harm it further.

In a sense, this is exactly what the Establishment was doing and is still doing. It had tried to ignore our allegations when the first book was published in 1995, but that book reached out to the hearts and minds of New Zealanders and became a bestseller.

Now the Establishment was attempting to marginalise us, and instead of dealing with a news media that simply wouldn't cover the story, we now dealt with a media who would cover only one side of the story, and that was generally the side favourable to the beast.

As I mentioned earlier, the final straw for me came when I discovered that the *Herald* had not printed supportive comments about Tony Molloy or his book made by other lawyers, but only printed the derogatory comments.

On April 3 1998, after *Thirty Pieces of Silver* had enjoyed its sixth straight week at number one on the bestseller list, I fired off another news release, this time expressing extreme concern about my discovery that "some elements in the news media may be trying to help 'cover up' the fraud and money laundering, by downplaying the book and refusing to print comments from other senior lawyers critical of Russell McVeagh.

> "Howling At The Moon Productions Ltd now has direct evidence that at least one media company interviewed many lawyers who supported Molloy, and who could back up his allegations with their own first hand experience ... and none of those comments were printed.
>
> "Instead, commentators ridiculing Molloy were given prominence.
>
> "Let me say directly to the editors involved in this now: you are treading on dangerous ground. The lawyers who you misquoted or failed to quote are known to us, and we are now seriously considering publishing in book form

examples of what appears to be a media conspiracy to suppress the truth.

"I will comfortably predict that such a book will be a number one bestseller on a scale never before seen in this country, and Howling At the Moon Productions Ltd will have no hesitation in naming the media companies and journalists involved.

"I am sickened to see stories surfacing that continue to ridicule both Thirty Pieces of Silver and its author, without any attempt made to establish a factual basis for such opinions.

"If an editor wishes to run a comment from a lawyer friendly to Russell McVeagh stating that Molloy is discredited and the book is wrong, then that editor must now be ready to defend that stance in court, because we are going to want to see proof of such discreditation, and hard examples of where Molloy's book is wrong.

"Howling At The Moon Productions Ltd put news organisations on notice a month ago when we called on Russell McVeagh to put up or shut up.

"This time the gloves are off. I expected it of Russell McVeagh, I don't expect it of people who claim to be journalists. In plain language, we are now reserving our right to sue for defamation and slander of goods in any case where we see biased reporting and unfounded criticism of Molloy's book."

It couldn't get plainer than that. In all, eight separate news releases were published to the media about Tony Molloy's book and the issues surrounding it. Apart from the *Dominion* in Wellington and the *Sunday Star-Times*, the major dailies tended to run only the Russell McVeagh line.

Which brings me back to the point raised at the start of this chapter. We have moved as a society away from democracy – Government by the people and for the people – towards a plutocracy, which is Government by the rich and powerful.

To see just how entrenched and dangerous this has become, one has only to read the book *First Knights*, mentioned earlier, which concludes that the Business Roundtable has become a serious threat to democracy in New Zealand.

The authors quote Roundtable spokesman Roger Kerr, who maintains that "counting heads is no substitute for pursuing scientific truth and sound policies."

Which is Big Brother-speak for "we know best what's good for the peasants."

Kerr's comments echo those of Hayek, an intellectual upon whose theories much of the New Right economic agenda is based, who believes it may be "appropriate to discard democracy".

American political analyst Noam Chomsky hit it on the button in one of his observations:

> "The basic idea which runs right through modern history and modern liberalism is that the public has got to be marginalized.
> "The general public are viewed as no more than ignorant and meddlesome outsiders, a bewildered herd."

So who do the news media serve in New Zealand? Do they serve the public interest, or the corporate interest? If a threat to democracy were to emerge in this country, dressed in a pin-striped suit, wearing a suave smile, oozing charm and wealth and preceded by equally charming PR people who could "explain" to the media what really needed to happen – if such an event transpired does any sane and intelligent New Zealander actually believe the news media in this country would:
a) recognise it, and
b) do anything about it?

A lot of the time the media do a reasonable job. Usually on the little issues or the mundane and non-threatening. But try and get the media to tackle something that goes to the heart of the power struggle for control of the nation and the journalists scatter like fieldmice in a shower of cats and dogs.

Contrast the NZ media with the US media. Look at, rightly or wrongly, the way the US media continued devoting serious coverage to the Clinton issue even though the poll ratings indicated the public were not interested. The media saw it as their responsibility to report, regardless.

The danger of paying too much attention to public opinion polls is that you have to rely on the integrity of the polling system being used and the objectivitity of the questions. There is also a danger that the public may be bored by something because it has not been properly explained to them, or they haven't been told the truth about it. Does that mean that the truth should be tossed aside because somebody successfully fooled the public?

The same point was made by German philosopher Walter Benjamin earlier this century.

> "It is precisely the purpose of the public opinion generated by the press to make the public incapable of judging, to insinuate into it the attitude of someone irresponsible, uninformed."

The difference between the professionalism of American media outlets and their NZ counterparts was highlighted during negotiations to sell a fictional screenplay – loosely based on *The Paradise Conspiracy* but adapted to the international market – to Hollywood.

"Be sure to observe the rules of the news game," the US script analyst wrote. "Once the story breaks about murder and corruption, the other stations, newspapers and tabloids would be all over it. That's the way it happens, especially here in the US."

Well, as anyone who read *The Paradise Conspiracy* knows, the daily press and television did not pursue either Charles Sturt or the Government over the revelations in that book.

As anyone who read *Lawyers, Guns & Money* or Anthony Molloy's *Thirty Pieces of Silver* knows, the media have not hounded the Government agencies, nor have they called for the investigation of certain judges or lawyers named in those books in regard to alleged improper or in cases illegal behaviour.

There have been exceptions. *The Paradise Conspiracy* was the subject of articles in the *Listener* upon its release, and National Radio and IRN covered it. The *National Business Review* serialised the Paul White section. *20/20* looked at *Lawyers, Guns & Money* and *One Network News* covered Tony Molloy's book. But no one kept the pressure on. No daily media outlet picked up the ball and ran with it.

The New Zealand news media barely deserve the collective title of "journalists". I'm not blaming the reporters on the ground floor – I'm targeting their bosses, the people who make the decisions about what stories will be investigated, printed or broadcast.

It's a bit bloody rough when Hollywood doesn't believe the NZ media could be like that!

I hope that the media coverage of Jenny Shipley's Saatchi dinner is a sign of a brighter future. If the media would only apply that kind of blowtorch to the kind of issues raised in these books they might be surprised at what catches fire.

See Amazon.com or www.howlingatthemoon.com for more Ian Wishart books

THE CRITICS ON *BREAKING SILENCE*:

"*Breaking Silence* is not on my recommended read list. I firmly believe it is *compulsory* reading for anyone over 18." – Andrew Stone, *Albany Buzz* business magazine

"The book has real value" – Larry Williams, Newstalk ZB

"I found it an incredibly surprising book, and a very relevant book, and a very important book". – Anna Smart, Newstalk ZB

"I had no particular views on the case before this book came out but I have to say it's a powerful read. An influential read, one might say...All those people who poured out their invective when it became known the book was about to hit the book shops really should just read it for themselves. It may not be quite what they think." – Helen Hill, *The Marlborough Express*

"*Breaking Silence* is a chilling narrative and the most important I have read. Adults may need to read the story to gain any understanding. Younger people should read in it a warning: that it is the way we make decisions early on that may determine the course of our life and the lives of those entrusted to our care." – Pat Veltkamp Smith, *Southland Times*

"The book so many maligned before it came out reveals a mother we haven't met. When I last wrote about Macsyna King, I said I didn't think I'd like her. I've changed my mind. I certainly think she outclasses the Wellington radio announcer who posted on Facebook that after receiving her advance copy of *Breaking Silence*, she had "spat on it, wiped my ass on it, and ripped it up". – Tapu Misa, *NZ Herald*

"Actually, the rumours of Wishart's death as an investigative journalist turn out to be greatly exaggerated. *Breaking Silence* will likely enhance his reputation considerably. As we said at the outset – we are very, very glad to have read the book." – John Tertullian, *Contra Celsum*

BREAKING SILENCE

THE KAHUI CASE

MACSYNA KING AND
THE REAL STORY OF THE
MURDER OF HER TWINS

IAN WISHART
#1 bestselling author

THE CRITICS ON *THE INSIDE STORY*:

"Undeniably...when Wishart hits he hits big. *Arthur Allan Thomas: The Inside Story* is a book two generations of New Zealanders have waited for... Wishart...offers an explosive new theory about who pulled the trigger of the gun that killed the Crewes in their Pukekawa farmhouse and theorises about the mystery woman who fed their infant daughter, Rochelle, for days after the murders.

"...With his thorough analysis of the evidence and his generous use of first-person accounts it's a stellar piece of journalism..." – *Southland Times*

"Wishart has a brand new prime suspect and he lays out his case in this fascinating and highly readable book. Wishart is painstaking in his investigation, and his interviews with the man at the centre of the case, Arthur Thomas, offer a remarkable insight into one of New Zealand's most memorable characters. " – Kerre Woodham, Newstalk ZB

"Wishart's report of Detective Sergeant Len Johnston's brazen arrogance collecting items for later use as evidence from Thomas's farm – pieces of wire, .22 shells and axle stubs - exposes a dark and scary side to our guardians.

"Through the book Wishart lays the ground for his claim that Johnston was actually the murderer and by his position on the inquiry team and proximity to Hutton, was able to influence an outcome which saw Thomas convicted twice of a double murder. Wishart's conclusions are disturbingly possible in my view.

"The question of to what extent Hutton had the wool pulled over his eyes by Johnston is moot. Based on Wishart's debunking of transcripts and evidence previously recorded, I think Hutton could well have been fooled by his best mate. Which means so too were the rest of the team deluded."
– former Det. Insp. Ross Meurant, *NZ Herald*

Arthur Allan Thomas:
THE INSIDE STORY
CREWE MURDERS: NEW EVIDENCE

Jailed for a crime he didn't commit, now for the first time in 40 years, he tells his incredible story as we name a new prime suspect

Ian Wishart
#1 bestselling author

THE CRITICS ON *AIR CON*:

"*Air Con* is a thorough summary of the current state of the debate, the science and the politics; it will be an important reference in any AGW skeptic's arsenal." – Vox Day, *WorldNetDaily*

"I started reading this book with an intensely critical eye, expecting that a mere journalist could not possibly cope with the complexities of climate science...[But] The book is brilliant. The best I have seen which deals with the news item side of it as well as the science. He has done a very thorough job and I have no hesitation in unreserved commendation." – Dr Vincent Gray, *UN IPCC expert reviewer*

"Ian Wishart's *Air Con* is another masterpiece of scientific reason, letting the thinking world know that so-called man-made global warming is the greatest scam ever aimed at humanity. Please read this book." – Professor David Bellamy, England

"This book by New Zealand journalist Ian Wishart – a #1 bestselling author four times – surprised me by the completeness with which he reviewed and presents alternatives to the plethora of IPCC inspired spin and publicity which floods our media today.

"His sixteen chapters examining aspects of the debate are meticulously footnoted and thus are a valuable reference resource for those wishing to dig deeper or keep up to speed with the unfolding global warming / carbon reduction political drama in years to come." – Dr Warwick Hughes, climate scientist

"Ian Wishart carefully and painstakingly looks at the topic, examining the evidence and weighing up the pros and cons. He not only finds the science to be unconvincing, but believes that following the proposed remedies will well-nigh bankrupt the West and in fact compound problems. An eye-opening treatment of a controversial issue. – *Quadrant* magazine, Australia

AIR CON
THE ~~IN~~*seriously* CONVENIENT TRUTH ABOUT GLOBAL WARMING

IAN WISHART   #1 BESTSELLING AUTHOR

THE CRITICS ON *LAWYERS, GUNS & MONEY*:

"Wishart has grown as an author" – *Otago Daily Times*

"He's onto another winner. Wishart is...exceptionally thorough. He skilfully blends official documents with his own observations and material from his own inquiries, giving a more informative picture than could ever have been possible in the daily media." – *Manawatu Evening Standard*

"If you like to mix business with pleasure, take *Lawyers, Guns & Money* to your beachside accomodation with you" – *North & South*

The #1 bestseller

Lawyers, Guns & Money
Ian Wishart

A true story of horses & fairies, bankers & thieves...

THE CRITICS ON *THE PARADISE CONSPIRACY*:

"*The Paradise Conspiracy* is required reading...pacey, penetrating scrutiny" – *New Zealand Herald*

"It is the closest thing to a John Grisham novel, but it is the real thing...among the best investigative stories about New Zealand business for many years" – *Waikato Times*

"...a compelling book...a Watergate-type tale" – *NZ Listener*

"Sensational stuff and hard to fault. Wishart is a professional...it is the most controversial New Zealand book that I can remember" – Bruce Jesson, *The Republican*

"Wishart presents facts he can totally substantiate, and leaves readers to draw some obvious conclusions...compelling, revealing and worrying reading" – *BOP Times*

"It's the closest thing to a John Grisham novel, but it's the real thing"

The Paradise CONSPIRACY

Ian Wishart

From the shady cover of a tropical tax haven, they hatched a billion dollar plan to raid the treasuries of the world, robbing the poor to give to the rich

www.ingramcontent.com/pod-product-compliance
Lightning Source LLC
Chambersburg PA
CBHW050555170426
43201CB00011B/1703